The Quest for the Cuban Christ

The History of African-American Religions

Florida A&M University, Tallahassee
Florida Atlantic University, Boca Raton
Florida Gulf Coast University, Ft. Myers
Florida International University, Miami
Florida State University, Tallahassee
University of Central Florida, Orlando
University of Florida, Gainesville
University of North Florida, Jacksonville
University of South Florida, Tampa
University of West Florida, Pensacola

The History of African-American Religions
Edited by Stephen W. Angell and Anthony B. Pinn

This series will further historical investigations into African religions in the Americas, encourage the development of new paradigms and methodologies, and explore cultural influences upon African-American religious institutions, including the roles of gender, race, leadership, regionalism, and folkways.

Laborers in the Vineyard of the Lord: The Beginnings of the AME Church in Florida, by Larry Eugene Rivers and Canter Brown, Jr. (2001)

Between the Cross and the Crescent: Christian and Muslim Perspectives On Malcolm and Martin, by Lewis V. Baldwin and Amiri YaSin Al-Hadid (2002)

The Quest for the Cuban Christ: A Historical Search, by Miguel A. De La Torre (2002)

The Quest for the Cuban Christ

A Historical Search

Miguel A. De La Torre

Foreword by Stephen W. Angell and Anthony B. Pinn, Series Editors

University Press of Florida

Gainesville · Tallahassee · Tampa · Boca Raton
Pensacola · Orlando · Miami · Jacksonville · Ft. Myers

Copyright 2002 by Miguel A. De La Torre
Printed in the United States of America on acid-free, TCF (totally chlorine-free) paper
All rights reserved

07 06 05 04 03 02   6 5 4 3 2 1

Library of Congress Cataloging-in-Publication Data
De La Torre, Miguel A.
The quest for the Cuban Christ : a historical search / Miguel A. De La Torre
p. cm. — (The history of African-American religions)
Includes bibliographic references and index.
ISBN 0-8130-2547-8 (alk. paper)
1. Jesus Christ—History of doctrines. 2. Theology, Doctrinal—Cuba—History.
I. Title. II. Series.
BT198 .D35 2002
232'.097291—dc21   2002024368

The University Press of Florida is the scholarly publishing agency for the State
University System of Florida, comprising Florida A&M University, Florida Atlantic
University, Florida Gulf Coast University, Florida International University, Florida
State University, University of Central Florida, University of Florida, University
of North Florida, University of South Florida, and University of West Florida.

University Press of Florida
15 Northwest 15th Street
Gainesville, FL 32611–2079
http://www.upf.com

To

... my parents, Mirta and Miguel, from allá, who love and support me even though I'm too Americanized to be understood

... my children, Vincent and Victoria, and brother, Ricky, from aquí, who love and support me even though I'm too Cubanized to be understood

... and my wife, Deborah, who does understand my pain and willingly served as midwife to birth this project.

Contents

Figures

Foreword

The History of African-American Religions series seeks to further historical investigations into the varieties of African-American religions and to
encourage the development of new and expanded paradigms, methodologies, and themes for the study of these religions. The editors see this series
as an opportunity to expand the knowledge of African-American religious
expression and institutional developments to include underappreciated re-
gions and forms. This fine volume by Miguel A. De La Torre, the third in
our series, concretely demonstrates that by the word *American* we include
the whole of the Americas, including the Afro-Latin diaspora of the Caribbean and of Central and South America.

The story of religion in Cuba, an island only ninety miles from U.S.
shores, uniquely brings together North American and Latin American realities that mutually and unexpectedly illuminate each other. Even the
most cursory consumers of headline news found their minds and emotions engaged by the controversy over a six-year-old Cuban boy, Elián
González, which preoccupied Cuban and American officials and their re-
spective publics from November 1999 to April 2000. De La Torre, in his
brief comment on this matter, throws new light on the religious significance of the Elián story, so he does not ignore the topical.

But he goes much further, illuminating the current reality of Resident
and Exilic Cubans by making profound use of long-ago manifestations of
this bifurcation of Cuban existence. He highlights the ambiguity of usable
memories by showing how the present exiles and Cuban residents both
misappropriate and justifiably appropriate the figure of José Martí, a
North American exile for fourteen years before his martyrdom for the
cause of Cuban independence. At times, De La Torre's quest for the historical Martí seems to be as intricate as the quest by Albert Schweitzer and
others for the historical Jesus. And De La Torre shows that even Fidel

Castro himself found the North American exile community useful in 1955, as he raised funds for his coming campaign against the regime of Fulgencio Batista.

Inevitably, the race question in Cuba looks somewhat different from the way it appears on the other side of the Florida Straits. "Blackness" is not always as obvious a theme in De La Torre's work as it will be in many other volumes in this series, but it remains a very important factor in the background and sometimes in the foreground. De La Torre provides a forcible rejoinder to those (including, at times, Castro) who have insisted that Cuba does not have a problem with racial discrimination. Neither does De La Torre portray Cuba as employing the mestizo racial category as easily as most other Latin American nations. But, quite appropriately, not all matters of oppression and injustice in Cuba are rendered in black-and-white dimensions. In fact, the opening of his book gives a penetrating look at the original sin of Cuban existence, what he calls the Spanish "ethnocide" of the island's aboriginal inhabitants, the Taíno. De La Torre commendably resists efforts to reduce Cuban complexities to patterns more familiar to its North American neighbors.

De La Torre's study gains great strength from its fascinating blending of methodologies, including ethnohistory, historical theology, and art history. Just as the Cuban and American historical relationship plays on minds and hearts at many levels, so does this work. As De La Torre methodically searches the Cuban cultural inventory for a vision of Christ that will speak to all of the varying needs of Cuba's *humildes* (the poor), he will bring all of his readers to new levels of appreciation of the richness and poignancy of Cuban religion and history. Readers are urged not to overlook the beauty and provocativeness of the images that he has employed to illustrate his concept of the "*ajiaco* Christ." These he hopes will truly pull together the significant themes from the essence of Christ's nature to speak to the spiritual needs of the *humildes.* Anyone interested in liberation theology will find important insights in De La Torre's book.

For all of these reasons, we strongly commend this illuminating book to the widest possible readership.

Stephen W. Angell and Anthony B. Pinn
Series Editors

Preface

When Pope John Paul II visited Cuba in 1998, he began his pontificate with these challenging words: "Do not be afraid to open your hearts to Christ." The question, though, is "Whose Christ?" Anyone who reads the biblical story of Christ does so from a particular social location. We are all born into a culture that shapes and forms us. When we turn our attention to the biblical text as the source for understanding who Christ was, we participate in a dialogue between the written word and the meanings our community taught us to give to these words. Cubans, especially those living in the diaspora, have been taught to read the Bible through the eyes of white, middle-class Euroamerican males. Yet, can the text speak to Cubans through their own culture? To do so, it must be read with Cuban eyes.

But how do we learn to read the biblical story of Jesus with Cuban eyes? After all, Cuba appears to have always been the fantasy island of dreams, an illusion of outsiders' imaginations. As a people, Cubans have existed on the periphery of the colonial venture, first as a colony of Spain, then as a neoimperial satellite of the United States. Yet these fantasies have nothing to do with Cuba's reality when ascertained from the Cuban center. If history is kept in the memory of a people, a memory at times intoxicated with false memories, how then do Cubans recall their history apart from the imagery imposed upon them by the colonial gaze? And how does this history contribute to the creation of a Christ who is Cuban? Any religious reflection or speculation on the divine requires an understanding of the historico-ideological genesis of its principles, especially its spatial, worldly setting. Hence the development of a Cuban perspective on Christ is frustrated by the imposing dominance of Eurocentric thought.

In 1910 Albert Schweitzer published the English version of his book *The Quest of the Historical Jesus.* His groundbreaking work revolutionized both biblical studies and christological scholarship while creating tremendous controversy. He presented the notion that Jesus of Nazareth could not be apprehended except in the historical particularity and social circumstances of Jesus' own time. All attempts since the so-called Age of Enlightenment to write the life of Jesus were futile, he believed, because scholars read their own ideals into the sources. Schweitzer's pronouncements proved unwelcome news to those who wanted to see Jesus as the product of the age of modernity, a prophet of reason and progress. Without a doubt Schweitzer's work changed the course of Christian scholarship.

Almost a century later, my own endeavor at Christology is more modest. While the Eurocentric search for Jesus created a schism between the historical person named Jesus and the Christ of faith constructed by the church, I attempt to affirm simply that whatever Christ means for a people (in the case of this book, Cubans), he must be understood within the socio-historical and the ecocultural context of those responding to the biblical text. Why should we even bother searching for the religious symbol of Christ in order to better understand the Cuban culture? For us to comprehend the diverse elements of any culture, careful attention must be given to its implicit connection to religious traditions and heritages, for the so-called secular space is at times an amalgam of the sacred customs and convictions of previous generations. Hence, the Cuban search for Christ raises more questions and concerns about those doing the searching than about the figure of Christ. Who are these readers whom we call Cubans? How do they apprehend this text about Jesus? How is this comprehension developed when the search originates and occurs from the underside of Cuban history?

This book argues that for Cubans, Christ must be understood through the historical development of Cuban culture. Clement of Alexandria once said, "God saved the Jews in a Jewish way, the barbarians in a barbarian way." The Brazilian liberation theologian Carlos Mesters continued this trend of thought by stating, "God saves Brazilians in a Brazilian way, blacks in a black way, Indians in an Indian way, Nicaraguans in a Nicaraguan way, and so on." I would add, God saves Cubans in a Cuban way. What then is the Cuban way of being saved? As I shall argue, God's movement in Cuban history translates both Christian principles and an understanding of Christ into cultural symbols understood by all Cubans, Resident and Exilic. Theological reflections become incarnated through the historical social location of Cubans. The Christ of the conquistadors, the apotheosis of Martí as the ideal Cuban Christ, the Black Christ of the African slaves, the understanding of Christ through Marianism, the Euroamerican Christ, the Christ of the Revolution, and the Exilic Christ are all a part of, if not central to, Cuban identity. As such, this book attempts to come to terms with these sociohistorical dimensions formulated within the depths of Cuban culture. By seriously reevaluating these cultural symbols, we can find rich resources for understanding Cubans and their God. Additionally, this quest can serve as a paradigm for non-Cuban groups wishing to search within their own culture for the presence of the divine.

Until now, few scholars of the Cuban experience approached their studies from a sophisticated religious scholarly perspective. The religiosity of Cubans is seldom taken into consideration when attempting to understand the Cuban ethos, with the possible exception of inquiries into Santería. Likewise, few Exilic Cuban religious scholars address their social location from within the context of the sociopolitical power achieved by the Cuban community in the United States. Ironically, while many of these scholars may claim to do "grass-roots theology," the Cuban experience, specifically as manifested in Miami, is seldom consulted. Why? Most Exilic Cuban religious scholars are highly influenced by the liberationist tendency of Latino theology. Rooted in the theological movement of Latin America known as "liberation theology," this liberationist tendency is not adverse to using Marxist economic analysis to elucidate the religious impetus of those who are most economically oppressed. Because liberation theology has been portrayed as a communist movement by those in power, and because of the overall abhorrence Exilic Cubans have toward communism, is it any wonder that Exilic Cuban scholars have found little, if any, reception among the Exilic Cuban audience? Regardless, this book will investigate how Cubans perceived Christ so as to better understand the identity of the Cubans who are doing the perceiving.

Our quest begins with an understanding of the Christ brought to the island by the conquistadors and the tension created with the Christ of those who suffered by the conquistadors' swords. The quest continues with the nationalistic Christ of Varela and the postnationalistic Christ of Martí. After Cuba gained independence from Spain, the Cuban understanding of Christ further developed through the influence of Cuban slaves, Santería, and the early twentieth-century Cuban feminist movement. More recently, liberation theology and revolution theology contributed to the development of the Cuban Christ. The final section of this work will tie together all of these diverse trends by turning our attention to art. The works of Cuban artists, both on the island and in the States, depicting the image of Christ will be closely examined. These paintings provide the observer with insight about, and an entry into, reality. Several works by

Cuban artists will be reviewed for the purpose of depicting the mysteries of God, the construction of a Cuban Christ, and the search for a common intra-Cuban identity.

Although this book is written by one author, it would be erroneous to assume that one person was solely responsible for its contents. I will always remain indebted to my original dissertation committee. Its members willingly served as intellectual mentors by first hearing and contesting, and then helping me to develop, the ideas and concepts expressed in this book. The insight, challenges, encouragement, and critiques given by Dr. John C. Raines, Dr. Katie Cannon, Dr. Justo González, and Professor Phillip Berryman will be eternally appreciated. I am especially indebted to Dr. Fernando Segovia, Dr. Manuel Vasquez, Dr. Edwin Aponte, and Dr. Nelson Rivera, who saw the worth of my work when others didn't, and who were quick to support and encourage me. I am also grateful to my colleagues at Hope College's religion department who debated my presuppositions and provided constructive criticism, specifically Dr. Allen Verhey, who read portions of this work while it was in its infancy. Jeremy M. Latchaw, my research assistant, and Jonathan Schakel, who proofread the manuscript submitted for publication, deserve my appreciation for their faithfulness to the goals of this project. During the Cuban art research stage, many individuals gave of their time and resources. I would be remiss if I did not specifically thank Alejandro Anreus, Ray Blanco, Pablo D. Cano, Ramón Cernuda, Juan Espinosa, Bunny Heller-Greenman, and José Navarro. Finally, a special thanks is due the Hispanic Theological Initiative, whose generous summer grant made the editorial advice of Patrick Alexander possible and freed me from other responsibilities, allowing me to concentrate on writing.

Of all the people needing to be acknowledged publicly, the most important is my soulmate and wife, Deborah De La Torre. She was the first to see my potential; she believed in me, encouraged me, plagued me, and questioned me, but above all, she loved me into realizing my dreams.

I

A Historical Quest

The Conquistador Christ

Women were raped. Children were disemboweled. Men fell prey to the invaders' swords. Within a generation, the lives and culture of the indigenous people of an island that would eventually bear the name "Cuba" came to a bloody end. Avarice for gold and glory took its course and decimated the population. The original inhabitants of this Caribbean island suffered cruelly at the hands of their conquerors. Yet, wherever there is oppression, resistance exists. In eastern Cuba, a *cacique* (a chieftain) named Hatuey created a loose confederation of Amerindians to resist the invading colonizers. For three months he carried out a style of guerrilla warfare against the Spaniards. Diego Velázquez, Cuba's first Spanish governor, led an expedition in 1511 to capture the renegade chieftain and pacify the island. Once apprehended, Hatuey was condemned to death as an example for others. As Hatuey was about to be burned at the stake, a Franciscan friar attempted to convert him to the Christian faith with the promise of heaven and the threat of hell. Hatuey is reported to have asked if Christians went to heaven. The friar answered in the affirmative, to which the condemned Hatuey retorted that he did not want to go to heaven where he would see such cruel people.

Today, Hatuey is a modern symbol of Cuban resistance, specifically against foreign powers such as Spain and later the United States. More importantly, Hatuey can also function as a religious symbol, a proto-Christ, and as an example of Christ's mission for those residing on the underside of Cuban history, those we call *los humildes* (the humble). Those supposed Christian invaders who claimed allegiance to the "true" God of the Bible while ignoring the Bible's basic call for justice were not the true representatives of Christ. The violence they unleashed witnessed their disregard for the very mission of Christ that they claimed to represent. Ironically Hatuey, the so-called heathen, best depicted Christ. Like Christ, Hatuey cast his lot with the persecuted and suffered death for the cause of justice at the hands of those desiring to enslave him and his people.

Hatuey reminds us that what Christians call "sin" is best expressed in the relationships established between humans, specifically the oppressor-oppressed relationships of exploitation. This relationship is manifested in Cuban history through the domination of European over Amerindian, white over black, male over female, rich over poor—in short, "civilization" over "barbarism." The history of Cuba can be understood as a history of domination in which the elite created social structures to safeguard their privileged space, allowing them to assert their "rights" in claiming power and benefits over those they considered to be their inferiors. Benefiting from social structures that bring death to large portions of the population requires some form of justification for the structure's implementers. Religious justification, along with scientific and political justification, masks the reality of the horrors committed and affords a thin facade of spirituality.

To a certain extent, religion provides the psychological reassurance of legitimacy. When Cubans with power compare their own position with the less privileged space of those they oppress, they fail to be content with their success. They desire "the right to their happiness" (Weber 1963, 107). They need to believe that their present wealth and privilege were earned. Similarly they reason that the misfortune of their inferiors is the direct consequence of their own laziness or incompetence, or the cause of divine retribution. They believe that the marginalized space of their inferiors proves their illegitimacy as Cubans in that it makes the less privileged envious of the success of their supposed superiors. Hence the disenfranchised become potentially dangerous objects. Yet, if religion is used to justify oppression, how then can it be used as a source for liberation? Christ, whatever else he may be, is foremost a liberator, not just from the narrow constricts of "personal sins," but also from the sins of the whole community, which wreaks havoc on peoples' lives when it attempts to protect the privileged space of the few at the expense of the many. From the underside of history, where multitudes are forced to suffer under the yoke of domination, a quest for Christ becomes a quest for liberation, liberation from racism, classism, and sexism.

Have Cubans seriously considered on which foundation they should base their understandings of the deity? In this chapter we begin a quest for a Christ attainable by Cubans. For Christ to be accessible to Cubans, we must first de-center the myriad influences of colonialism, both Spanish and Euroamerican. This task can be accomplished by looking toward Cuba's cultural legacy in order to understand who this Cuban Christ is. Although the versions of Christ presented by Spain and the United States are and remain major aspects of Cuban identity, they are not the only intellectual or spiritual saviors for Cubans. Yet Cubans look toward Europe and the United States in order to revitalize their study of Christ. Doing so causes Cubans to envision Christ as a cultural extension of the Eurocentric mission. The necessary process of formulating their own Cuban space from which Cubans can commune with Christ begins with the realization that Europe and the United States, since Cuba's inception, have been hostile to their existential being, specifically to their Amerindian and African roots.

In this chapter, we will begin our quest for the historical Cuban Christ by examining Cuba's first inhabitants, the Taínos. These were the first to suffer under the imported Christ of the conquistadors. Afterward, we will explore the historical milieu of Spain that gave rise to a militant conquering Christ who merged the Cross with the Crown. Then we will examine the church and the Christ that were constructed on the island by the invading Spaniards to justify their colonial venture. Finally, the chapter will explore how, amidst the brutality done in the name of the conquistadors' Christ, the subversive voices of los humildes, through individuals like Las Casas, gave rise to the first expression of an indigenous Cuban Christ.

The Taínos

The tropical forest peoples of Central and South America first settled Cuba around 4190 B.C. By the time of Columbus's arrival scholars estimate that Cuba had about fifty thousand inhabitants. Prior to Columbus, Cuba was occupied by three groups of peoples, the Classic Taínos, the Western Taínos, and the Guanahatabeys (not to be confused with the Ciboneys, a local Western Taíno subgroup). Both the Classic Taínos and the Western Taínos were subgroups of the overall Arawakan society. Normally a peaceful culture, by 1492 Arawakans were making weapons and establishing lines of defense in response to the threatening Carib people, who were hopscotching through the Lesser Antilles toward the Greater Antilles.

The Guanahatabeys, not ethnically a part of Arawakan society, occupied the western portion of the island. At one time they may have occupied all of Cuba, but by 1492 their lack of advanced technology had reduced them to servitude to the rest of the island's inhabitants. The vast middle of the island consisted of the older subgroup of Taínos known as Western Taínos, who are believed to have been the most peaceful and less developed Arawakan subgroup. They appeared during the ninth century. The Classic Taínos occupied the eastern point of the island and represented the western migration of Hispaniola's more advanced Arawak subgroup. They arose during the mid-fifteenth century, not long before the Spanish arrival. By European standards they were deemed to be on the verge of civilization.

Arawakan society consisted of theocratic chiefdoms led by either men or women. Taínos developed a two-class system: *nitaíno* (nobility) and *naboria* (commoners). Their cosmology consisted of deities known as *zemis*, spirits of nature, and ancestral spirits. They were non-militaristic (considered the least aggressive people of the Americas), organized as manioc-producing agriculturists who also engaged in fishing and rearing livestock (Alegría 1978; Lovén 1935). Their way of life was eternally changed when the Spaniards let loose upon the island vast droves of their livestock. Free from European diseases and local predators, these animals multiplied at an astonishing rate. Unfenced ranges led to freely roaming wildlife. Goats, horses, mules, donkeys, sheep, pigs, and domestic fowl thrived at Amerindian expense as they caused havoc on Taíno agriculture. As these vast grazing herds destroyed crops, food supply dwindled. Famine soon followed. As Exilic Cuban historian Louis Pérez explained, "This was nothing less than the wholesale substitution of an animal population for a human one. The pre-Columbian ecological equilibrium was shattered irrevocably" (1988, 29).

It would be misleading to assume Taíno docility. In spite of the name *Taíno*, their word for noble, and their lack of expertise in warfare, they fought against incredible odds rather than submit to the Spaniards, and bravely battled against a technologically superior invader. Forms of resistance employed by the Taínos included reducing the cultivation of food (which the Spaniards mistook for laziness) as a way of starving out the Spaniards; instead, it contributed to their own decimation. An ultimate act of resistance was mass suicide. Entire villages would choose death rather than serve the conquering Spaniards. In spite of resistance, by 1514 the colonization of Cuba was complete; however, this colonization did not mean the eradication of the Amerindians. By 1570, despite the massive destruction of Amerindian life, three towns (Los Caneyas, Trinidad, and Guanabacoa) were entirely inhabited by Amerindians; two towns (Sabana de Vasco Porcallo and Sancti Spíritus) had Amerindians representing over half the population, and only two towns (Santiago and La Habana) were entirely Spanish. Spanish control of the land was restricted to small, scattered settlements of largely non-Spanish populations. Rather than being completely eradicated, a large portion of Taínos was assimilated into the dominant Spanish culture. Instead of using *genocide* to describe the final solution of the Taíno people, it is more accurate to use the word *ethnocide*. Although the indigenous ethos basically became extinct, still Taíno ancestry survived, transmitting biological, cultural, and linguistic traits toward Cubanness and contributing to the development of the Cuban Christ: specifically, a Christ who, like Hatuey, teaches that salvation entails joining los humildes in their struggle to be free from the tyranny and oppression of the dominant culture.

Los Humildes

If the Cuban Christ can best be understood from the underside of Cuban history, then the perspective of los humildes (like the Taíno) becomes crucial in any quest for the Cuban Christ. To reflect on the Deity from the perspective of los humildes is to discover a biblical narrative that proclaims a God who reveals Godself from within disenfranchised communities. Theologians of liberation are quick to claim that God has historically chosen los humildes of the world as agents of God's new creation. It is the stone rejected by the builders that becomes the keystone of God's created order (Matt. 21:42). It was not Rome, the most powerful city of the known world, where God chose to perform the miracle of the incarnation, nor was it Jerusalem, the center of Yahweh worship; rather, it was impoverished Galilee where God chose to first proclaim the message of the gospels. Theological reflections from the perspective of los humildes identify with a God that chooses a stone from the margins, rejected by the dominant culture, to carry out God's salvific plan.

The Gospel message of liberation from oppressive societal structures resonates with los humildes who discover that those marginalized in Jesus' time occupied the privileged position of being the first to hear the Good News. Not because they were holier, nor better Christians, but because God chooses sides. God makes an option for those who exist under the weight of oppression. The radical nature of the incarnation is not that God became human, but that God assumed the condition of los humildes. Why is it important to understand who Christ is through the lens of the los humildes? By making the disenfranchised recipients of the Good News,

Jesus emphasized the political edge of his message (De La Torre and Aponte 2001, 82–85). Any quest for the Cuban Christ requires making los humildes the starting point of all inquiries. This is not an attempt to romanticize los humildes' marginalization, for there is no glorification in being oppressed; rather it is an attempt to understand the Cuban Christ as a unifying symbol for all Cubans.

La Reconquista

While Hatuey is the first "Cuban" to model Christ on the island, it is not to him that the dominant Cuban culture looks to define their understanding of Christ. Cubans look to Spain as the usual starting point in the quest for Christ. Who is this Christ of the conquistadors that was brought to the Caribbean? In order to understand the Christ in whose name the Antilles were conquered, we must continue our search in Spain. The essence of a Spaniard Christ, forged during the centuries of the long campaign against the Muslim enemies of the "true" faith, was transplanted to the islands of the Caribbean during the foundation of New Spain. This was a Christ under whom avarice and evangelism merged. The quest for gold converged with a crusading fervor to rid Spain's dominions of "infidels," whether they were Jews and Muslims on the (main)land or Amerindians on the margins of the emerging empire. The Great Commission to baptize all nations was taken literally by the Spanish monarchs, legitimizing Spaniard sovereignty. Aggravating this crusade was the rise of mercantile capitalism, which upset the entire socioeconomic equilibrium of Spain's medieval society.

Spain had always been the crossroads of cultures and people, a land where the Islamic, Jewish, and Christian worlds collided, cohabitated, commingled, and communed. It was a time prior to the Protestant Reformation of Martin Luther, when the Catholic Church enjoyed the power and privilege of being the sole interpreter of reality, coexisting with a tradition of Spanish folklore and mythology shaped to accompany Christianity. Furthermore, it was a Catholicism undergoing its own reformation. Long before Luther nailed his theses on the church doors of Wittenberg, beginning what has become known as the Protestant Reformation, Isabella, "the Last Crusader," queen of Castile, championed the reformation of the Catholic Church. Upon inheriting the crown in 1474, she secured from the papacy the right to fill high ecclesiastical posts within her domain, a right her husband Ferdinand would later misuse during the conquest of the Americas. Isabella named Francisco Jiménez de Cisneros to the most important post in her realm: archbishop of Toledo. Previously, Jiménez had served ten years in prison for his refusal to participate in the corrupt ecclesiastical practices of his time. Together, the queen and archbishop introduced sweeping reforms to Spain's monasteries and convents. Specifically, they visited monastic houses throughout the country, calling for a renewed obedience to monastic vows and demanding scholarship from within the clergy. They strove to enhance theological scholarship by encouraging the printing of books in all the major cities, through a recent revolutionary invention called the printing press. They founded the University of Alcala and published the Complutensian Polyglot, the multilingual edition of the Bible.

Although Isabella and her court advanced Christianity through reform and scholarship, they showed no tolerance for doctrinal diversity. They secured from the pope the authority to implement the Inquisition as a tool of protecting the faith from heretics. Persecution of Jews and "Judaizing" Christians (Jews who converted under threat of duress) was instituted, eventually leading to the expulsion of all Jews in 1492, the same year Spain became aware of the existence of the Western Hemisphere. Concurrently Granada, the last Moorish stronghold, fell to Christian hands a few months prior to the royal decree against the Jews. After seven hundred years of Muslim rule, Spain had reconquered the land from the hands of the "infidels," creating a Spain that was once again "Christian." Consequently, like the Jews, Muslims faced a choice: convert, die, or leave.

The seven-hundred-year-old struggle to reclaim the land and vanquish the crescent by way of the cross fused and confused nationalism with Catholicism. In fact, to say, *"hablo cristiano"* ("I speak Christian") was a common way of saying, "I speak Spanish." To be a disciple of Christ obliged one to fight the enemies of the faith. Based on the proof-texting of the biblical narrative of Joshua 6, the doctrine of holy war became a duty to Christ. Within this story, divine sanction is given to destroy the city of Jericho and to slaughter its inhabitants because they are heathens. Like the chosen people, Spaniards believed they held a mandate from God to purify the land of all abominations (read non-Spaniards).

As the last crusade ended in Spain, a new, vaster campaign became available. This spirit of reconquest, in which Catholic orthodoxy and Spanish identity became synonymous, did not stop with the vanquishing of Jews and Moors in Spain's domain, but journeyed with Columbus on his voyage to what later was to be called Cuba. He believed that his "discovery" of a new world fulfilled the biblical prophecy of Isaiah 60:9, "The coasts shall await for me, vessels of Tarshish [understood as Spain] in front, to bring your sons from far away, and their silver and gold with them, to the name of Yahweh your God, and to the Holy One of Israel for he has made you glorious."[1] The conquest of the Western Hemisphere acquired apocalyptic proportions for the Spaniards, who saw an opportunity to usher in the second coming of Christ by fulfilling the great commission of Matthew 28:19: "In your goings, then, disciple all the nations, baptizing them in the name of the Father and of the Son and of the Holy Spirit." The evangelization and domestication of the Amerindian "heathens" became a sign that Spaniards stood on the threshold of the eschatological consummation of human history. By subduing the promised land by the sword and cross, Christ's messianic kingdom would be installed on earth.

Contact between Europeans and Amerindians occurred when Spain's feudal age had given way to the rise of a modern centralized monarchical state. Spain's emergence as a nation-state, coinciding with the demise of feudalism, resulted from four factors: (1) the death of feudal barons in battles against the Muslims during *la reconquista*; (2) the rise of a central authority due to the alliance, through marriage, between the house of Castile (Isabella) and the house of Aragon (Ferdinand); (3) the subsequent rise of a nationalist psyche as Spanish patriotism took shape; and (4) the development of mercantilism, which led bourgeois leaders to challenge the powers of the feudal lords. An alliance between the rising mercantile class and the absolute monarch established a strong officialdom. Consistently the Americas were fashioned along the lines of a modern centralized monarchy instead of the outdated medieval feudal order. The uprooting of Spain's feudal order with its manorial system of enclosed lands for pasture and industry left the peasantry landless. A lumpenproletariat, existing on the margins of society because they failed to be integrated into the emerging division of labor, streamed into towns looking for opportunities. Those opportunities, however, existed mostly in the new colonial spaces constructed in the Americas (Zavala 1968, 72–73).

Spain's need for capital to finance its growing ambitions meant that colonies like Cuba (and the rest of New Spain) had to support the Spanish center. Europeans, prior to the consolidation of power (1500), were politically insignificant when compared to the Ottoman Empire, China under the Ming dynasty, or northern India under the Mongol. But the so-called New World, with its enormous human and natural resources, provided the basis for transforming the marginalized Christian European nations encircled by Islamic "infidels" into a world hegemonic power whose dominance continues to be felt today. From the first day of the European conquest, Cuba became a part of the development of Spain, resulting in its own underdevelopment.

Cuba's new purpose was thus to enrich Europe via Spain. This economic relationship, based on exploitation, strengthened mercantile capitalism in Cuba. Mercantilism links the prosperity of a nation to the accumulation of precious metals. Because Spain lacked gold and silver mines, precious metals had to be accrued through trade. Hence, all of Cuba's imports and exports had to be purchased from and sold to Spain. The result was a trade deficit financed by transferring gold and silver to Iberia. While trade with other countries might reduce this deficit, Spain would then lose its hegemonic position as the center of the empire. So, liberalizing trade had to be suppressed.

Cuba's structural underdevelopment became a necessary outgrowth of having its economic surplus expropriated so as to generate economic development in Spain and later in the United States.[2] Cuba's settlement by Spaniards occurred during an intra-European competition to become metropolitan capitals by pillaging gold. The plight of the Amerindians was subordinated to Spain's interest in gold, needed to establish its dominance on the European continent. Although the island originally was considered to be peripheral to Hispaniola (explaining the eastern location of Santiago as capital), it later emerged as the hub of the Spanish colonial venture. But the gold the Spaniards hoped to find could not be found. The search for wealth and status moved on to the newly conquered lands of Mexico and Peru, and by the 1520s Cuba, along with the rest of the Antilles, ceased being the center of the search.

When the dream of perpetual gold dissipated on the island, Cuba was reconstructed as an economic service colony for the lucrative mainlands of North and South America. Between 1502 and 1600 Cuba lost about sixty percent of its Spanish population to the mainland. As the sixteenth and seventeenth centuries progressed, the fortunes of the Cuban church also dropped as opportunities to make greater riches on the mainland increased. With time, Cuba therefore developed an export economy not associated with mining.

Cuba might have been forgotten entirely if not for its fine harbors. Strategically located on the Gulf Stream, La Habana became the ideal port of call for departing bullion-laden galleons and arriving Spaniards searching for fame and fortune on the mainland. Cuba's early value to the Span-

ish empire was therefore her port in La Habana, which served as an inter-
mediate station between Mother Spain and her ever-growing colonies;
hence the port city, in comparison to the rest of the island, prospered.
Within this socioeconomic environment, a church was established and a
Christ created to provide spiritual justification for Spain's attempt to establish itself as a dominant European power.

The Constructed Colonial Church and Christ

The first European to gaze upon the island of Cuba was Christopher
Columbus. Being told of an island called *Cubanacan* in a region called
Cibao, and following the local natives' directions, Columbus discovered
Cuba on October 28, 1492, by simply seeing it! Interestingly enough,
Columbus's name signifies his dialectic purpose. "Cristobal" means the
"bearer of Christ," while "Colón" means "repopulate." Hence, Columbus's
very name represents the image of his being and the fate awaiting the
island's original inhabitants.

Two years after Cuba's "discovery," Pope Alexander VI (of Spanish origin) negotiated the Treaty of Tordesilles, dividing the so-called New World
between Spain and Portugal. All ecclesiastic powers operating in what was
called New Spain became subservient to the Crown. For example, through
patronato real, the king was given the right to appoint the high ecclesiastical offices (including bishops) of the churches in the Americas. The king
also took the responsibility of administering the *diezmo* (tithes) and
church expenses. In effect, the king of Spain became a vice-pope.

The dependence of the church—the earthly representative of Christ—
upon the Crown, bent on enriching Spain at the expense of the so-called
New World, led to a merging of religious and political goals. The colonial
Spanish church on Cuban soil could be characterized as: (1) synonymous
with the conquest enterprise; (2) lacking any solid ecclesiastical organization; (3) unable to minister to or help the Amerindians who were integrated into the Spaniards' economic project; (4) dependent on the Crown
for funding to carry out its apostolic endeavors; (5) riddled with continual
tension and conflict with the island's royal administrators; (6) supporting
the eastern expedition base rather than serving the new needs rising in the
new settlements of the west (explaining why Santiago continued to be the
see of Cuba's only diocese until 1787); and (7) creators of the religious
justification for condemning Protestant heretics who coveted Spain's
riches in the newly conquered lands (Maza 1982, 6–7, 13).

Likewise colonial administrative positions were established to serve the Spanish center. These posts were purchased in Spain. Purchasers intended to recoup their initial "investment" along with a substantial return, always dreaming of returning to Spain to retire in style. Political graft and corruption thus became institutionalized. Because of the weakness of the colonial churches, which were servants of the Crown instead of the church, abuses were numerous as funds intended for hospitals, schools, and houses of worship were expropriated. Hence, both the church and the government established in the Americas were foremost Spanish, while the Amerindians' subservient role excluded them from positions of leadership in both church and state.

A colonial, rather than a national, church served the spiritual needs of the settlers and opened a path to heaven for the Amerindians, but only through their conformity to Spanish rule. Church and state worked hand in hand to preserve and expand Spain's presence in Latin America. Because the church in Cuba (as well as in all of Latin America) was intertwined with the colonial system, it bore the stamps of slavery, underdevelopment, and dependency. The church safeguarded its presence and expanded its power through the use and manipulation of the state's power. In return, the church promoted the colonial venture. With the exception of a few outstanding clerics, the mission of the Spanish church in Cuba was to maintain the status quo and defend the interests of *la madre patria*, Spain. This alliance created a church responsive to the needs of the elite while ignoring the spiritual needs of los humildes. For example, when King Carlos V in 1542 revoked settlers' "rights" to Amerindians' slave labor, it led to rebellion in the colonies, including the murder of the Peruvian viceroy. While the conquistadors revolted, the church remained silent, losing an ideal opportunity to provide moral guidance.

Hence, it is not surprising that like other Latin American countries, Cuba's Christian heritage is minimal. This does not mean Cubans are nonreligious, however, quite the contrary. As we shall see throughout the rest of this book, Cubans, specifically those residing on the underside of Cuban history, were and are spiritual, concerned with the redemptive nature of the Deity. What was lacking was an interest in participating in the official Christian church, designed as it was to protect the power and privilege of the elite.

On the surface it did appear as if the Crown were concerned with the welfare and protection of the Amerindian. Its letters and laws (specifically Isabella's) reveal a pious appreciation for the Amerindians' salvation. For example, the 1512 Laws of Burgos called for good treatment and respect for the Amerindians, along with housing and religious instruction. In reality, the Crown feared that the conquistadors would become new and powerful feudal lords. To prevent the accumulation of power by the conquistadors, Isabella and Ferdinand passed laws forbidding the enslavement of the indigenous population, laws that were regularly ignored. The political maneuvering of the monarchs to preserve their political space and avoid an emergence of feudalism in the new colonies was cloaked in piety. Yet royal "sympathy" for the Amerindian plight could not overcome the demographic reality that Spain's population at the start of the sixteenth century was insufficient for large-scale mining and crop cultivation in the Americas.

Still, someone was needed to cultivate the land and mine the minerals. As early as 1503, Queen Isabella had written to her governor on Hispaniola demanding that the desire to evangelize the Amerindians and the need for massive Amerindian labor be met. The queen's will was satisfied through the *encomiendas*, established in 1509 when Diego Columbus, governor of the Indies, was given royal authority to implement this economic system. The word "encomienda" connotes an entrusting of a person or thing into the care of someone or something else. Amerindians were entrusted by the Crown to the conquistadors for the purpose of religious and cultural evangelization. This arrangement, which provided both free laborers and fertile soil, was more insidious than slavery, since the settler invested nothing in the worker. The conquistadors had no obligation or incentive to ensure their well-being.

The dogma *"extra ecclesiam nulla salus"* ("outside the church there is no salvation") interpreted the encomiendas positively. Since civilization required instruction, converting the Amerindians justified appropriating their labor. In a refreshing outburst of honesty, Francisco Pizarro, who served in Cuba and went on to conquer the Incas, when admonished by a cleric for not living up to the responsibility of Christian tutelage due the indigenous people under the encomienda structure, retorted, "I have not come for any such reasons; I have come to take away from them their gold" (Neill 1990, 145). Likewise, Hernán Cortés, the eventual conqueror of the Aztec Empire, who first participated in the 1511 conquest of Cuba and subsequently became *alcalde* (mayor) of Santiago de Cuba, articulated his mission when he said, "We came here to serve God and the King, and also to get gold" (Skidmore and Smith 1984, 18). In short, conversion to Christ became a pretext for wielding Spanish power and privilege.

Enslaving the Amerindians required philosophical and scientific justification. Aristotle's theory of "natural slaves" was one such rationalization. Aristotle maintained that slavery is not an institution, but a category of humans. Hence, the Amerindians are not slaves because of the actions of the conquering Spaniards, nor because of divine will. Rather, Amerindians are slaves because the construction of the universe relegates some humans to the level of unthinking beasts, in need of domestication in order to fulfill their natural calling for perpetual servitude. Bernardo de Mesa, a member of the royal household and Cuba's first bishop (1516), completely subscribed to the natural slave doctrine, along with a peculiar twist based on the island's geographical location and the configuration of the stars.

Juan Gines de Sepúlveda, the main defender of cultural evolution at the time, saw the difference between the indigenous people and the Europeans as a sociological example of the distinction between barbarism and civilization. The Amerindians' sturdy bodies and "weak" brains displayed nature's intent for them to labor for the superiorly refined Europeans. However, this natural servitude would lead eventually to their cultural elevation as they learned religion, civilization, and moral reason, even if it took the sword to teach them.

The conquistadors' Christ, supported by Spaniard philosophy and science, became the official ideological symbol justifying imperial expansion. In the name of this Christ, the Amerindians were not only reduced to servitude, but also faced sadism. For example, Columbus would order the noses cut off of Amerindians unwilling to submit to his authority. In other instances, the indigenous people were castrated and forced to eat their own dirt-encrusted testicles. Or, they were simply thrown to the dogs. Las Casas writes, "[The Spanish soldiers] would test their swords and their macho strength on captured Indians and place bets on slicing off heads or cutting of bodies in half with one blow." While in Cuba, he recorded the death of seven thousand children within three months because their overworked mothers were so famished they were unable to produce any milk to nurse them. Rather than seeing their babies suffer, they resorted to drowning them out of sheer desperation (1971, 94, 109–15).[3] In Cuba the the Amerindians became the earthly representations of Christ, serving as the nexus for the birth of a Cuban indigenous Christ.

Las Casas Reveals the Indigenous Christ

A dichotomy did not exist between "God and mammon" in colonial Cuba. Unfortunately, the former became subordinate to the latter. Yet, as already mentioned, when power oppresses, resistance exists. When symbols are used to justify the dominance of one culture, these same symbols become subversive in the hands of those being subjugated. The conquistadors' faith constructed a Christ so that "inferior" people could be subdued; yet, from the underside of Cuban history, where these "inferior" people dwelled, voices were raised pointing toward a Christ who liberates, a Cuban Christ. While the church complied with Spain's power structures, ignoring the immorality of the encomienda by becoming the Crown's faithful servant, a few friars of religious orders like Franciscans, Dominicans, and Jesuits became defenders of los humildes. Their vows of poverty led them to live and struggle with the Taínos. A two-tiered, informal ecclesiastical structure evolved consisting of those who represented Christendom, agents for the Spanish church on Cuban territory, and those who represented the church, the body of believers composed of los humildes; hence the popular Cuban idiom *"es un cura de verdad"* ("he is a true priest"). The former is held in disdain, an example of an anti-Christ, the latter honored and respected, a model of the Cuban Christ. Un cura de verda was Bartolomé de Las Casas.

On Christmas Day 1511, Dominican Antonio Montesinos preached in Santo Domingo on the text "I am a voice crying in the wilderness." His sermon caused a sensation because he accused the Christian colonizers of being "no more saved than the Moors or Turks." It is important to note that Montesinos's sermon did not challenge the legitimacy of Spain's colonial venture; rather, he attacked the abusive treatment of the Amerindians at the hands of the Spanish colonizers. "Friends" of the Amerindians still had conquest on their minds, even though they hoped to accomplish their task without bloodshed.

Seated in the audience during Montesinos's homily was a young ordained priest named Bartolomé de Las Casas, and a seed was planted that would bear fruit several years later. Las Casas lived as a gentleman cleric, holding several Taínos in encomienda. Born in Seville in 1484, he first arrived in Hispaniola in 1502, along with Governor Fernández de Ovando. A teenager, he came to the New World to help in the family farming and trading business. The governor saw in the young lad future political competition, describing Las Casas as ambitious with a "wish to rule" (Fernán-

dez de Ovando 1959, 2:199). He was ordained a priest in 1507 and celebrated the first New Mass in the Western Hemisphere in 1510.

Although he did some parish work, he spent the majority of his first ten
years as a priest amassing wealth as owner of a plantation stocked with
Taínos at an encomienda near La Concepción, given to him, most likely, for
his family's loyalty to Columbus. In 1513 he served as a chaplain during
the conquest of Cuba, where he obtained an encomienda on the island for
his role in Cuba's pacification. There he remained, farming and prospering
greatly. Although deeply disturbed and profoundly affected by the massacre of the Cuban Taínos, he remained a benefactor of the encomienda system that allowed him to accumulate more wealth. Yet, one year later, in
1514, while preparing a sermon on his estate near the Arimao River in
Cuba at the newly established settlement of Sancti Expiritus, he came
upon Ecclesiasticus 34 and was forever and profoundly changed:

> The sacrifice of an offering unjustly acquired is a mockery; the gifts
> of impious men are unacceptable. The Most High takes no pleasure in
> offerings from the godless, multiplying sacrifices will not gain his
> pardon for sin. Offering sacrifice from the property of the poor is as
> bad as slaughtering a son before his father's very eyes. A meager diet
> is the very life of the poor, he who withholds it is a man of blood. A
> man murders his neighbor if he robs him of his livelihood, sheds
> blood if he withholds an employee's wages.

Called to be a witness of Christ to the godless Amerindians, Las Casas
realized that it was he, the priest and missionary, who was living without
God. Conversion could no longer mean accepting a theological proposition;
rather, conversion had to be based on action. Conversion to Christ meant
conversion toward Christ-like liberating actions. The actions of his life,
specifically those geared toward the Amerindians, bore witness to his rejection of the idea that the Gospel would deliver the Amerindians. It was he
who was in need of conversion.

So moved was Las Casas by Ecclesiasticus 34 that he renounced his
wealth, joined the Dominican order, and dedicated his life to seeking justice
for the Amerindians. For the remaining fifty years of his life, Las Casas
devoted himself to the Amerindian plight, earning the title "Protector of
the Indians." His conversion is considered a predecessor to the liberation
theology movement in Latin America. According to theologian Gustavo
Gutiérrez, "Among those with the keenest interest in Bartolomé de Las
Casas today are Latin American's liberation theologians, who have recog-

nized in the Dominican friar a prophetic forerunner of the church's radical 'option for the poor'" (1993b, xi, 46–48).[4]

Las Casas equated salvation with the establishment of social justice, thereby inverting the relationship between the "Christ-bearing" Spaniards and the "demonic" savages. The Spaniards risked losing their salvation because of their unjust treatment of the Amerindians. Las Casas warned, "Since the Spaniards have the Indians unjustly as slaves and against their conscience, they are always in mortal sin, and therefore do not live the Christian life and are impeded from their salvation" (Pagán 1992, 144). Conversion for Las Casas was not a profession of faith, for he had lived his life professing Christian beliefs. Rather, what changed for Las Casas was his comprehension of Jesus Christ. Jesus Christ was the Other, and conversion became an act or process by which one came to know Christ as Other through a changed lifestyle seeking solidarity with the Other. Las Casas's starting point was his conviction that Christ could be found among the Taínos because of their oppression, that Jesus Christ exists among scourged indigenous people. If the Spaniards wanted to find Christ, they needed to look at the Taínos. He once wrote, "I leave in the Indies Jesus Christ, our God, scourged and afflicted and beaten and crucified not once, but thousands of times, when the Spaniards devastated and destroyed its people." Gutiérrez's interpretation of Las Casas's theological views leads him to conclude that Christ is the Indian (1993c, 62, 96).

Amerindians are not to be explained by the dominant European culture as pagans, natural slaves, or wild children of nature. They are humans. Their humanity has the capacity for salvation, regardless of the conquistadors' assertion that Amerindians were soulless humans and talking animals. Even though the Taínos may be unbelievers as defined by the dominant Spanish culture, their humanity makes them a member of the body of Christ. They represent the poor of the Gospel, and as such, any gesture made to these, "the least" (as per Matthew 7:21–27) is a gesture made toward Christ. To mistreat the Amerindians, who are part of Christ's body, is to mistreat Jesus. In fact, to look into the faces of these poor, marginalized, and suffering faces is to recognize the suffering of Christ. To establish power and privilege at the expense of the indigenous people is to make a mockery of Christ's blood that was shed for them. Hence, salvation for Las Casas meant crucifying the power and privilege derived from owning an ecomienda so that he could authentically accompany Christ in the struggle to liberate the Amerindians. The encomienda system finally ended in the eighteenth century, not due to any theological considerations, but because the economic need of Spain to strengthen its military meant that less of the tributes from the work of the Amerindians were left for the *criollos* (children of the conquistadors born in the Americas).

Although we look toward Las Casas as demonstrating the task of Christians to accompany los humildes in their struggle for life and liberation, we cannot ignore his complicity in the missionary zeal of evangelical conquest. While he deserves applause for being among the first European voices to criticize the moral stance of the conquistadors' Christ, he also deserves criticism for his tacit assumption that Spanish society was superior to that of the indigenous people. For example, he authored the *reduccion* (reduction) paradigm for missionary conquest, which physically separated Amerindians from their families and communities. They were forced to live on the mission compound under the spiritual (and political) tutelage of the civilized Europeans. This separation insured their inculturation into the value system of the dominant Spanish culture.

Las Casas was motivated by a heartfelt Christian duty to defend the Amerindians from the atrocities of the encomienda system. He even suggested that it would be better if Carlos V ceased being their lord if that would protect human life. An "infidel, but living, Indian" was preferable to a "Christian, but dead, Indian." Ironically, in Las Casas's eyes, the monarchs were blameless of the abuses occurring because of their supposed ignorance of the situation. For Las Casas, guilt rested upon the conquistadors and the members of the Royal Council, who kept the royal family insulated. Salvation for the indigenous population rested on the forging of an alliance between the monarchs and the church against the conquistadors. Las Casas attempted to protect the Amerindians from the abuses of the encomienda while maintaining the authority of the Spanish monarchy, both of which he felt were required for Christianizing the indigenous population.

He designed a system that he believed would be acceptable to the Crown. The sovereigns were to continue receiving the royal income generated by the encomienda while changing the ownership of the indigenous people from the Spanish settlers (whose increase in wealth could become a threat to the Crown) to the ecclesiastical hierarchy. Hence the Crown would continue to receive its revenue, the rising power of the conquistadors would be checked, the church would obtain an opportunity to convert the "savages," and the Amerindian would benefit from hearing the Gospel and from a set of rules designed to limit the degree of their exploitation for labor. Although "saving" the Amerindian from bloodshed by the conquistador, Las Casas nonetheless contributed to their ethnocide, facilitating the task of the conquistadors in their colonial venture even though he wrote volumes against their brutality. In spite of his good intentions, he ulti- mately complied with the conquistadors in destroying the Taínos. While learning from Las Casas about the Cuban Christ, specifically about Christ's identification with the oppressed, we must also recognize the dangers of refusing to be suspicious of the power and privilege derived from one's social position.

By all accounts, the introduction of the conquistadors' Christ on Cuban soil devastated the original inhabitants of the island. The conquistadors' Christ was an anti-Christ of death. Yet, from the destruction and oppres- sion caused by such a Christ, a different understanding of Christ emerged, a Christ of los humildes. This new recognition of the Deity began to in- form the construction of a Cuban Christ, a Christ derived from the tension created by opposing aspects of Cuban identity. Spain is but one aspect of that identity; the theological history of Cuba also reveals an understanding of Christ that resonates within the Cuban ethos.

Varela Reveals a Consciousness-Raising Christ

Although the influence of the Spanish Christ on Cubans because of four centuries of colonialism is undeniable, Cuban consciousness was raised through nationalism, contributing to a new understanding of Christ. In order to comprehend the rise of nationalism and its effects on how Cubans see Christ, we must continue our exploration of the Spanish church on Cuban soil. Since its inception, the church remained politically, socially, and economically weak, especially until the mid-1700s. Spain's lack of re- spect for the Cuban church is illustrated by Spain's delay in appointing bishops to Cuba. For example, in the late 1500s Cubans had to wait thir- teen years for a successor to be appointed after Bishop Juan de Castillo resigned. Governors whose will was ignored when dealing with the church would not hesitate to suspend payments due the bishopric, as was the case with Governor Gaspar Ruiz de Pereda in the 1610s. Clergy, dependent on the government for their salaries, became captives of the political estab- lishment. This political arrangement led to a church that failed to become the voice of los humildes.

The church progressed or regressed according to who was serving as bishop. Bishops who built close relationships with civil society safeguarded their position and expanded their authority by manipulating the state's power. In return the church served as an agent of the colonial venture, gaining minimal relevance in Cuba's colonial life.

One remarkable bishop who expanded the role and power of the church by concentrating on welfare, education, and the formation of a native clergy was Diego Evelino Hurtado de Compostela (1685–1704). The colonial government's lack of interest in social services had left a hole that Bishop Compostela undertook to fill, providing education for the children of the Spanish settlers and governmental bureaucrats and creating orphanages. While past efforts had generally failed, Bishop Compostela was able to succeed by responding to needs of the Cuban situation. But also as important, his missionary ventures secured a niche for the church within the colonial structure.

While the church maintained its support for the monarch, a stirring of nationalism began during the second half of the eighteenth century as clerics began to define their Christianity apart from the Spaniards' perception. The Catholic Church in Cuba entered a "Golden Age" shortly after 1750, as half of the ninety churches were led by native Cuban priests, and after three centuries of Spanish rule, a Cuban native, Santiago José de Hechavarría (1770–88), was appointed bishop. This era was characterized by economic growth and progressive governors. Among the important achievements of this period, specifically important in the quest for the Cuban Christ, was the 1774 inauguration of El Colegio Seminario San Carlos y San Ambrosio, a college and seminary that would soon gain the reputation of being the best school Cuba had to offer.

The school catered to the children of Cuba's elite, who were obsessed with wealth and exposed to liberalism. The elite favored a scientific economic development and were committed to the new techniques of increasing productivity. At the same time, Cuba experienced the same ideological trends that spurred independence movements throughout the Latin American mainland. But it was to Cuba that the clerics who had supported Spanish dominion went after losing their influence in the newly created Spanish American republics. This influx of clergy contributed to a Cuban church hostile to liberalism while friendly to Spanish rule, as well as to a populace who maintained superficial piety while ignoring private or public morality (Maza 1982, 25–26, 33, 35). The majority of native Cubans perceived the church as an obstacle to national liberation precisely because the vast majority of the clergy identified with the aims of colonialism. The church's inability to voice the concerns of los humildes created a version of Christianity that justified the status quo. Nonetheless, even though the Cuban Catholic Church became identified with pro-Spanish forces, from within the walls of the new San Carlos Seminary an awareness of Cuba's dignity apart from Spain and a cultivation of nationalism developed.

Among the faculty of San Carlos y San Ambrosio was a young priest named Félix Varela y Morales. During his 1998 speech at the University of Havana, Pope John Paul II referred to Varela as "a pre-eminent son of [Cuba], considered by some to be the foundation-stone of the Cuban national identity. He is the best synthesis one could find of Christian faith and Cuban culture" (Vatican web site). Varela, who was born in La Habana in 1788, was ordained a priest by his twenty-third birthday. In 1822 he was elected as delegate to the Cortes de España (Spanish parliament), where he distinguished himself by opposing colonialism. He earned a death sentence for proposing two bills, the first abolishing slavery and the second calling for an autonomous Cuba. His views of independence could not be tolerated on a financially lucrative island desperately needed by Spain to pay its public officials and the interest on loans taken from British banks. Varela's views were seen by Spanish eyes as being anti-Spanish and anti-Catholic. Persecution forced him to seek political exile in the United States in 1823, where he worked with the poor and published *El Habanero,* a paper dedicated to science, literature, politics, and faith. He spent the majority of his life as an Exilic Cuban, dying in St. Augustine, Florida, in 1853. Through his work he was able to struggle for liberation, basing his social consciousness, as well as Cuban consciousness, upon a faith in Christ.[5]

In spite of a few voices like Varela, the church remained complicit with the colonial power structures, turning the average Cuban away from the church. *Españolidad,* a love for customs, traditions, and things from Spain, sustained and maintained the Cuban colony. When Catholics did practice their faith, their pride in their Spanish roots led them to prefer a more traditional approach to their religious expressions, rather than the radical changes being advocated by younger clerics like Varela or his superior Bishop Juan José Diaz Espada y Landa. Serving the see of La Habana from 1802 to 1832, Espada y Landa condemned the practice of slavery, criticized Spain's extensive landholdings, and called for a more modern and liberal approach to La Habana's lax clerics (Kirk 1988, 20).

The rise of the Spanish liberals of the 1830s and their anticlerical measures greatly affected the Cuban Catholic community, and the hopes of clerics like Bishop Espada y Landa and Varela failed to materialized. Because the liberals expelled priests and confiscated church property, the Cuban church lost a significant portion of its clergy. Religious orders were suppressed, hampering educational programs and social ministries. Furthermore, the see of La Habana remained vacant for fourteen years (1832–46), while the see of Santiago de Cuba remained vacant for fifteen years (1836–51). The unwillingness of the Spanish authorities to fill the two most important ecclesiastical posts on the island revealed that the church was not only irrelevant to the general masses, but also unimportant to the Crown. Left deprived of leadership and common support, the church, in order to survive, found itself supporting Spain's interests over against Cuban interests. The strategy adopted by the Catholic Church included avoiding any confrontation with Spain by ignoring injustices like slavery and colonialism, and by reestablishing their presence on the island, specifically in La Habana, at the expense and neglect of the rural areas.

Spurred by the French Revolution, the elite, educated, and affluent of Cuban society adopted both its ideology and anticlericalism. In reaction to these anticlerical and liberal attacks, church leaders strengthened their ties with groups they deemed sympathetic, specifically conservative parties, landowners, and the old aristocracy (Smith 1991, 13). A dichotomy developed between those wishing to usher in modernity and its democratic ideals, and those within the church clinging to absolutism, who were still recovering from the horrors the church faced during the French Revolution. Father Varela attempted to overcome this dichotomy by becoming the first person of importance to make a serious call for Cuban liberation, specifically while a delegate to the Cortes de España. An exception to the clerical norm, Varela fought for those residing on the underside of colonial rule, raising their awareness of widespread injustices and holding those with power and privilege responsible for their abuses. He criticized the Cuban elite for thinking more "about sugar and coffee sacks" than about patriotism, human rights, and fidelity to God. Varela equated liberation with equality and constitutional rule, hence repudiating any form of inequality and calling all Cubans toward revolutionary change by creating a society governed by reason and justice.

The contribution of Varela to the creation of a Cuban-based theology comes in his active pursuit of consciousness-raising. He taught Cubans that in order to assume the responsibility for their existence, Cubans must learn to think with their own mind, apart from how Spaniards taught Cubans to think. Like the Brazilian educator Paulo Freire, whom Varela predates by a century and a half, he saw the need to awaken los humildes from a traditional lethargy reinforced by colonialism. Spanish rule provided all Cubans with false consciousness, preventing them from seeing themselves as Subjects with the ability to develop their own country. Through Varela's works a version of what Freire would eventually term *"conscientização"* was introduced in Cuba. Conscientização is the process by which an object becomes a subject through awareness of the social, political, and economic contradictions existing within the social structure and taking the necessary praxis (actions) to combat the oppressive elements of reality (Freire 1994, 17). Varela would insist that conscientização can be achieved through an understanding of a Christ whose purpose is to liberate.

For Varela, to deny the Deity leads the nation (or individual) to unhappiness and hopelessness, and ultimately leads to despotism. The secular government's anticlerical campaigns (as in other Latin American nations who were attaining their independence from Spain) undermined the moral foundation required for the success of nationhood. Such a foundation safeguards against blind nationalism. He wrote:

> Liberation and religion have the same origin, and they are never in contradiction because there cannot be contradiction in its Author. The oppression of a people is not distinguished by injustice, and injustice cannot be the work of God. The people are truly liberated if they are truly religious, and I assure you that to be made a slave is precisely to begin by making one a fanatical. So distance is true religion from being the foundation of tyranny! (1974, 67)

Varela's understanding of the *imago Dei*, that is, the imprint of the image of God on each individual, assured the dignity of all individuals and their divine right to exist as free, regardless of their race or class. Human dignity created a responsibility for the church to advocate liberation (specifically from Spain), and endowed each Christian with a duty to construct a social order incarnated with the principles of Christ. Unlike other Cuban clerics, Varela's thought attempted to find a balance between liberal democrats who included the church as part of the antidemocratic problem needing to be swept away, and the traditional elements of the church, which maintained its privilege through sovereign power.

Thus Varela contended that liberation requires the education of the people to learn how to synthesize themes from liberalism (that is, democracy) with transcendental divine truth. This synthesis enables a duty-based society to emerge, a society keen to insure that opportunities to perform are available for the people. His understanding of Christ compelled him to seek Christ's glory in everything he did. Yet in spite of individuals like Varela, the established church continued to be irrelevant in Cuban society. Varela, a nationalist, attempted to raise Cuban consciousness, allowing Cubans to see themselves, their country, and their Christ with their own eyes. It would take Martí, a postnationalist fighting against the colonialism of Spain and the impending dangers of U.S. imperialism, to move the perception of Cuban consciousness beyond the island, making Christ-based principles of justice universal. It is toward Martí that we now turn our attention.

The Martí Christ

Centuries of Spanish colonialism defined Cuban identity as an extension of Spain. During the early 1800s, voices like the one belonging to Félix Varela attempted to raise Cuban consciousness. Although nationalism encouraged Cubans to see themselves, their country, and their Christ with their own eyes, it failed to dismantle as normative the acceptance of the Spanish Christ that was brought to the island by the conquistadors. In order for Cubans to move beyond Spanish colonialism, Cuban consciousness had to be raised above the limitations of the Caribbean island. José Martí was instrumental in moving Cuban consciousness beyond the Cuba ethos, making universal the Christ-based principle of justice. Liberation was no longer sought for the inhabitants of just one island; rather it was sought for all of humanity.

For Cubans, José Martí is the nation's liberator from Spain. He is also recognized as a voice warning of the possible dangers from the United States. As he forewarned, deliverance from Spain's colonialism resulted in servitude to U.S. imperialism. The eve before his death, while physically battling to rid Cuba of Spain's dominance, he composed a letter to his friend Manuel Mercado. Referring to the United States, he wrote, "I have lived in the monster and I know its entrails, my sling is that of David." Historically, it has always been easy for Cubans to blame Euroamericans for Cuba's situation. Yet not all of Cuba's woes can be solely attributed to the United States and its neoimperialism, or to the present embargo, or even to global capitalism. Martí advises, "In Nuestra America [Our America] it is vital to know the truth about the United States. We should not exaggerate its faults purposely, out of a desire to deny it all virtue, nor should these faults be concealed or proclaimed as virtues" (1975, 49).

A rhetoric of blame develops when Cubans attack the dominant Euroamerican culture for being white, privileged, and insensitive to structures of oppression. The ignorance of North Americans to their own historical participation in establishing imperialist structures in Cuba cannot become the sole lens by which Cubans assess their relationship with the United States. To solely attack the United States for being complicit with racism and ethnic discrimination is not an alternative to blaming victims for their predicament (Said 1994, 14, 96, 228–30). Subscribing to a Cuban-type nativism accepts the consequences of U.S. imperialism and reinforces Cuban subservience, even while attempting to reevaluate the Cuban ethos. Regardless of Cubans' aggressive stance, they become trapped within a defensive role. Against Cuban nativism, liberation (not nationalist independence) becomes a new alternative. Any quest for economic justice is doomed to fail because both European capitalist models of development as well as Western-style Marxism serve as unreliable cultural guides for resistance. If Cubans are to participate in a search for Christ, the danger exists in falling prey to this "invidious universalism" that has connected Cuban culture to imperialism for centuries. Describing the historical dialectic between the United States and Cuba, which is held together by imperialism, becomes the first task in unmasking the existing power relationship (Said 1994, 279). Once this power relationship is exposed, it allows Cubans to search for their own understanding of Christ.

The proximity of Cuba to the United States creates a relationship in which neither could be ignored by the other (this continues to be true in spite of the embargo and in fact is its cause). Throughout the entire history of the United States, a covetous eye has gazed upon the island, as is revealed in the remarks of John Quincy Adams and Thomas Jefferson.[1] During the U.S. Revolutionary War, British troops used ports in La Habana to attack North America, a fact the strategic-minded new republic never forgot. The United States based policy toward Cuba on the proposition that Cuba was the first line of defense (offense) of the southern U.S. flank. Due to this unique relationship with the United States, the quest for the Cuban Christ becomes a quest for a Christ who can liberate Cubans from the consequences of imperialism, specifically the imperialism conducted by the United States for most of the twentieth century. Such a quest becomes an indigenous search for liberation through Cuban symbols. One such symbol, which can never be ignored, is the historical figure of José Martí. While Martí is not the incarnation of Christ (in spite of what some patriots claim), he does provide a Cuban way of seeing and understanding the Christ searched for. How, then, can José Martí, a severe critic of Cuba's church, be used as a cultural symbol by which the divine communicates to today's Cuban community?

Gustavo Gutiérrez, one of the founders of Latin American liberation theology, stresses the importance of using theology to communicate through the significant symbols of culture. For him, theology has something in common with the prevailing culture. Theologians would be greatly helped if they adopt the view of "theology as wisdom," that is, if they perceive theology as knowledge shot through with the "savored" experience first of God but then also of the people and the culture to which they belong. The use of national thinkers will precisely serve the purpose of communicating some of this "savor" (1993a, xxxv). National individuals like Varela and Martí, products of their own times, have been deeply involved in the sufferings and hopes of their people and have been able to express, as few others have, the soul of the nation. Resident Cuban theologian Reinerio Arce insists that the development of Cuba's own theological and philosophical reflection is not located within European systematics. Instead it is developed in Cuban literature, music, art, political discussions, cultural manifestations, and national symbols (1996, 10).

The revolutionary figure of Martí, venerated as "the apostle of Cuba," serves as the primary symbol communicating the "savor" of Cuban theological thought. Like no other Cuban writer before or since, Martí skillfully blended the religious, scientific, and artistic views of Latin America, Africa, Asia, and Europe to create an image of *patria* (fatherland) that can encompass the polycentric aspects of a complex and diverse Cuban people. So, it is not surprising that Martí, like Varela, constitutes a common sacred space shared by both Resident and Exilic Cubans. Carlos Montaner summed up the feelings of most Cubans when he wrote, "For us Cubans, everything can be debated, everything can be divided into opposing views, except the figure of Martí . . . to deny the validity of Martí is tantamount to renouncing an ingredient, possibly the most basic one, of the Cuban identity" (1971, 3). For this reason, both Castro in La Habana and CANF (Cuban American National Foundation) in Miami can claim Martí as the intellectual author of their separate and conflicting crusades.

All Cubans, including myself, read our own biases into Martí. Every generation of Cubans since the war for independence has focused on certain aspects of Martí while ignoring those features appearing either contradictory or uncongenial. Yet, by returning to Martí and rereading him, we can recognize both our blind spots and his. The quest for the historical

Martí can uncover new aspects of his work capable of informing and helping the search for the Cuban Christ.

José Martí, leader of the revolutionary movement for Cuban independence, poet, journalist, professor, diplomat, and precursor of *modernismo*
in Spanish letters, needs no introduction in the Americas, with the exception of the United States and Canada. Although his name is used in the
U.S. propaganda broadcasts to Cuba, known as "Radio Martí" and "TV
Martí," costing over $240 million annually, Euroamericans know almost
nothing about him. Yet when Latin Americans are asked to describe their
major struggles, the response can be: "Everything Martí predicted." Martí
gave voice to the dream of los humildes by calling for the construction of a
liberated society based on democratic social justice, racial harmony, labor
rights, and self-determination. This chapter will reappraise the significance of Martí as a moral agent who attempted to construct his idealized,
secularized vision of Christian love, a love rooted in the figure and mission
of Jesus Christ. Specifically, I will analyze the significance of Martí as a
Cuban symbol, the historical role he played as a forerunner to the present
Latin American theologies of liberation, and his importance as a postnationalist.

José Julian Martí was born in La Habana on January 28, 1853, to low-
income *peninsulares*. His father, son of a poor maker of ropes, was from
Valencia, Spain, his mother from the Canary Islands, and both met in La
Habana. Martí, the only male of eight children, was influenced by two
father-figures: Simón Bolívar, the liberator of South America, and Mendive, Martí's educator, who was a leading man of letters and a revolutionary poet. At the age of sixteen Martí was imprisoned and sentenced to hard
labor at the quarry for his pro-independence activities. This experience
profoundly transformed Martí from a thinker to a doer, from seeking
glory and fame to performing duty and sacrifice.

Because of his father's intervention, Martí only served six months of
his sentence. However, he was exiled to Spain, where he began to write
pamphlets advocating Cuba's independence. During his exile he completed
a doctorate in philosophy and humanities from the University of Zaragoza
in 1874. Subsequently, he went to France, Mexico, and Guatemala. He returned to Cuba in 1878 but was banished the next year for his revolutionary activities. In 1880 he arrived in New York City, where he spent the last
fourteen years of his life. He worked as a journalist for North and South
American presses, rapidly becoming Latin America's most widely read

chronicler of his time. He provided a "thick description" of North American culture, politics, education, and economics, similar to those of Alexis de Tocqueville or Viscount James Bryce.

His exile to the United States was in a time of world plunder by European powers and social ferment in U.S. cities. The United States wanted to be considered a coequal with Europe and began in earnest its imperialist venture into Latin America. Martí was among the first to see the economic transition in the United States from local competitive markets toward a more evolved brand of capitalism that encouraged the development of monopolies. He was keenly aware of the danger this new brand of capitalism posed in creating poverty and imperialism, specifically in its relationship with Latin America. Cuba was the key by which the United States could expand its "Manifest Destiny." He saw the danger to Latin American countries, rich in raw material and national resources, remaining underdeveloped if the highly developed United States were allowed to set the terms for trade. He was among the first to systematically warn Latin America of the United States's imperialistic aims and desires.

While in New York, he served as a diplomat representing monetary policies for Argentina, Paraguay, and Uruguay. Martí also organized the Cuban Revolutionary Party and founded its journal, *Patria*. He was responsible for organizing the armed invasion of the island and successfully carried it out in 1895. Shortly afterward, he was killed during a skirmish with Spanish troops at Dos Ríos.

Martí as Symbol

Unfortunately, the romanticizing of Martí's life has led to his apotheosis in a way that ignores his words and works. Every Cuban ruler has justified his own actions by claiming to continue Martí's dream. For example, two of Cuba's most ruthless "presidents," Gerardo Machado and Fulgencio Batista, were adept at quoting Martí. And Cuban president Carlos Prío Socarrás once wrote:

> I too, José Martí, have felt your presence, and in the harshest and more bitter days of *la lucha* (the struggle) which you dreamed of for Cuba and which liberated our generation, I have seen you watching over my dreams and caressing the little good that there was in me. I learned in time that I could not imitate you, because it is not possible

to compare oneself with you. But I did aspire to win for myself the approving silence of your august shadow. (1946, 391)

In contrast to Prío's extravagant lifestyle, a story is told by a Cuban patriot who, upon seeing Martí carrying his suitcase in New York, asked why he didn't take a carriage. Martí replied that the money saved by walking could instead be used for the Cuban cause (Gray 1962, 186). It is safe to say that no ruler of Cuba has ever earned the "approving silence of [Martí's] august shadow." Jorge Ibarra, a Resident Cuban historian, shows how Martí refused large sums of money from Cuban highway robbers even though his revolutionary organization lacked funds. He insisted that the political structure of the revolution was more than a party charged with freeing Cuba from Spain. For Martí, the liberation of Cuba could only come forth through clean roots (Ibarra 1972, 172).

Richard Gray, reviewing the literature on Martí, documents his portrayal to the Cuban people as a quasi-deity, referred to as the apostle, the saint of the Americas, the mystic, the second son of God, the Captain of Archangels, Saint Joseph, the Redeemer, the American Christ, the Savior, and Jesus-Martí. Martí becomes the mythical prototype for the ideal Cuban, containing all possible Cuban virtues. To question or challenge Martí's thoughts, or those who claim to be continuing his work, is to risk righteous condemnation, for his works are quoted with the same reverence reserved for Holy Scripture.

Yet great misunderstanding exists as to what Martí said or believed. His words have been manipulated to justify the actions of everyone who has held or wanted to hold power in Cuba. In fact, we are left with the task of first conducting a search for the historical Martí, which may then inform our quest for the Cuban Christ. I propose that the historical usage of Martí as a Cuban symbol can be understood as having developed during the course of three overlapping stages. The first stage is Martí as a *marginalized symbol,* embracing the period from his death in 1895 through 1933. During the first years of the republic, Martí was basically ignored, reduced to one of several symbols of independence. Although appreciated by the intelligentsia, no popularization of his image existed. Ironically, Martí first gained attention in the other countries of the Americas, then in Spain, and finally in Cuba. By the time of the centenary of his birth in 1953, he was honored in both Washington, D.C., and Moscow.

The second stage, Martí as *sacred symbol,* began around 1933 and continues in the present Exilic Cuban experience. I chose 1933 because it was a pivotal year in Cuban history, during which major sociopolitical changes occurred. This year marked the end of the bloody dictatorship of "president" Gerardo Machado, thus ushering in hope for a democratically ruled Cuba freed from U.S. imperialism. The revolt was made possible because of the political space created by the United States: less overt political strategy to exert pressure in protecting its economic interests and the so-called Good Neighbor Policy. Failure to establish patria, however, contributed to *pistolismo* (gangsterism) from 1934 until 1952.

In this second stage, Martí emerges as a mythical figure deserving of reverential awe. However, the deification of Martí ignores his shortcomings in the area of "family values." His failed marriage, owing to his obsession with patria and the consequences of expatriation, led to an affair with Carmen Miyares de Mantilla, the Cuban woman who operated the New York boarding house where he stayed. Her daughter, María, born November 20, 1880, was considered to be the product of that union (Mañach 1944b).

His image as sacred mythical figure served as a weapon against the imperialistic influence of the United States. Martí, as a sacred symbol, afforded psychological compensation for the disenfranchised middle class by providing a spiritual figure that contrasted with U.S. materialism. As romantic hero, Martí becomes important more as a moral example and less for his works or words. During this stage, Martí was transformed from a postnational political radical to a national hero. As mythology, Martí gave legitimacy to an illegitimate Cuban elite, who neither had power nor were in radical rebellion against U.S. imperialism. While legitimizing the elite, Martí's mythology provided "false consciousness" for oppressed Cubans throughout the island. His revolutionary anti-imperialist, antiracist, and anticlassist tenets were reduced to Keynesian ideas, welfare strategies, and hostility toward *vendepatria* (traitors), all of which found minimal justification in his writings (Kapcia 1986, 58–60). Hence, a Martí void of his thought was presented to and venerated by Cubans.

The third stage, Martí as an *adulterated symbol*, developed alongside the Martí of sacred symbol. These two stages both falsify the historical Martí. Whereas Martí as sacred symbol *masks* his words and thoughts, Martí as adulterated symbol *misrepresents* his words and thoughts. Martí became the poster child of political propaganda, an exploited symbol for those who wished to gain political power by using his writings on morality as a weapon against the corruption of those in power. If one were an Exilic Cuban, then Martí loved the United States. If, however, one were a Resident Cuban, then Martí hated the United States. For Exilic Cubans, Martí symbolizes *la lucha* against Castro. His writings become proof texts for a pro-U.S. stance. While most Exilic Cubans born in the United States know of Martí, few can describe his historical significance or quote his phrases. His symbolic worth is in denouncing Resident Cubans. Conversely, Resident Cubans demythologized Martí and reconstructed him as a Marxist, making him the intellectual author of Castro's revolution. As Castro stated, "I believe that my contribution to the Cuban Revolution consists of having synthesized Martí's ideas and those of Marxism-Leninism and of having applied them consistently in our struggle" (1987, 146). In spite of Martí's willingness to work with the rich class who achieve "*el honesto lucro*" (the honest profit) and his critique of class struggles, Martí becomes a Cuban Marxist symbol used to denounce U.S. imperialism. In reality, for him, a slave was one who worked for another, void of self-determination. He feared that freedom from being a slave to capitalists might lead to becoming a slave to the functionaries of the state.[2] Ironically, since Castro made his statement about his contribution to Martí's ideas, the Cuban National Assembly of People's Power voted in December 1991 to drop Marxist-Leninism from the Constitution as the official ideology of the state.

Manipulating the symbolic significance of Martí ignores his ambiguity toward the United States and the complexity of his work. In a March 25, 1889, letter to the *New York Evening Post*, Martí writes:

> [Honest Cubans] admire [the United States], the greatest ever built by liberty, but dislike the evil conditions that, like worms in the heart, have begun in this mighty republic their work of destruction. They have made of the heroes of this country their own heroes, and look to the success of the American commonwealth as the crowning glory of mankind; but they cannot honestly believe that exclusive individualism, reverence for wealth, and the protracted exultation of a terrible victory are preparing the United States to be the typical nation of liberty, where no opinion is to be based on greed, and no triumph or acquisition reached against charity and justice. We love the country of Lincoln as much as we fear the country of Cutting [Francis Cutting was a leader of the American Annexationist League]. (1977, 235)

His dream for a just society is betrayed by Cubans on both sides of the Florida Straits who mask their striving for power by claiming to be his intellectual heirs. This process makes Martí "all things to all men." The manipulation of Martí as symbol is not limited to the political sphere. The Cuban Catholic Church is also guilty of reconstructing him as a good Catholic, ignoring his strong anticlerical stance.

Martí's hostility toward the Catholic Church is unmistakable, a stance probably based on his affiliation with the Freemasons. In 1871 he severed his Catholic ties in order to join the Freemasons. He attacked the pope and called for the church to be stripped of all its power and influence within the sociopolitical Cuban community. Although he was anticlerical, he was not anti-Christian. He did not advocate the anticlerical fervor sweeping Mexico during his time. He attacked the church because it collaborated with the wealthy to oppress los humildes. A product of nineteenth-century liberalism, Martí was a free thinker who reconciled a respect for reason with the experience of religion, emphasizing human God-consciousness over divine revelation. For him, religious freedom was an integral part of Cuban existence. For Martí, Christianity had died under Catholicism and was in need of being saved from the priests (*Obras Completas* 34:111–32). Some scholars claim Martí underwent a mystical awakening during his travels through Latin America, rejecting Spanish scholasticism as he redis-covered his Hispanic roots (Vitier 1971, 238).

Martí accused Christianity, when it was aligned with colonialist powers, of being a "false religion." While rejecting the power of the church, Martí used Christianity as a foundation for patria. Resident Cuban Rafael Cepeda shows the biblical precepts used by Martí by correlating Martí's writings with the Bible (1992, 45–60). It appears that Martí called for the death of Christendom so that the birth of the church could occur. He saw the Catholic Church as being in an unholy alliance with Spain, defending its power within civil society by means of the state. The majority of the church blessed colonialism, class stratification, indigenous genocide, and the subordination of los humildes. Against these historical trends, Martí called for churches to follow the example of New York priest Father McGlynn, who, against the archbishop's orders, supported social pro-grams. For Martí, Father McGlynn was *"un cura de verdad"* ("a true priest") because he was censured by Rome for defending and standing with the poor, leading Martí to ask the question: "who then is the sinner?" Is it Christendom who misuses authority to protect its position of power, or is it the local priest who disobeys the church to side with the poor and with their bitterness so that they could be comforted? He attacked all structures that create poverty and believed in the ability of churches to address social problems. Consequently, Martí welcomed the religious who practiced their faith in the construction of patria. He fervently admired Father Félix Varela, whom he met in New York in 1848, considering this priest to be the first revolutionary intellectual of Cuba. He agreed with Varela that political liberty could never be achieved apart from spiritual liberty. Hence the latter needed to be guaranteed (*Obras Completa* 25:183–85; 1975, 270–86).

Martí Reveals the Christ of los Humildes

As an indigenous Cuban symbol, Martí serves us as a precursor to liberation theology. For Pablo Richard, Martí's postnationalist project—against economic, political, and cultural dependence—is the thesis to the antithesis of developmentalism—against economic, political or cultural underdevelopment—creating a synthesis of Latin American socialism in the 1960s—against economic, political, and cultural capitalist domination (1987, 75). Historian George D. H. Cole makes a similar argument: "The Cuban Revolutionaries were hardly Socialists; nor did their principal theorist, José Martí, put forward any specifically Socialist doctrine. . . . But his nationalism was very Radical and rested on a conception of racial equality which links him to the later developments of Socialism and Communism in Latin America" (1960, 838).

Martí moved away from the negative liberalism of his time, which simply criticized the misuse of power. An Oxford idealist, Martí saw poverty as an instrument utilized by the state to maintain structures of oppression. He condemned the blind materialism of Euroamericans, which he interpreted as the "money cult." Referring to them he wrote, "That is how the people die, like men, when because of brutality and abjectness they prefer the violent joys of money to the easier and nobler object of life: Luxury rots" (*Obras Completa* 12:70). Accordingly, his proposals, strongly influenced by the economic theories of Henry George, moved away from a laissez-faire economics toward the idea of a controlled economy empowered to protect los humildes (whom he also referred to as "*los pobres de la tierra*," the earth's poor), namely, an economy based on small producers.

Writing half a century after Latin America's wars for independence, Martí could see how these economies were taking shape as the assigned suppliers of commodities to industrialized countries, specifically Great Britain. He attempted to construct an alternative devotion to patria, rejecting the liberal-dependent view that sought independence from Spain in favor of dependence upon the United States. Martí's struggle was to prevent a Latin American type of independence where the island-born Cuban bourgeoisie replaced the departing Spaniards as the new dominant class. As he repeatedly warned: "To change masters is not to be free." He fought Cuba's Eurocentric elite, who sought to hold onto their money by turning the island into a client state of the United States. Ironically, the clientalism found repulsive by Martí is now advocated by Exilic Cubans. Many exiles look toward the United States, hoping they will "do something" about Cuba. Through organizations like CANF, Exiles lobby to tighten the U.S. embargo or, better yet, to initiate a military intervention.

Thus Martí is a forerunner to liberation theology. Martí can provide for Cubans their own cultural model of Christ the liberator. Even though his thoughts bear the marks of his own time, many of his core ideas remain valid. By exploring these core insights, Cubans can recognize the one-sided ways in which he has been presented to us and move toward a common Cuban understanding. Additionally, his *obra* (works) can provide a theological base upon which Cubans can construct an understanding of a Christ who, like them, is Cuban.

As a precursor to liberation theology, Martí advocated what later liberation theologians would term "a preferential option for the poor." Basically, this option asserts that God is not neutral in the face of oppression. Instead, God takes sides. The biblical narrative records the history of a God who seeks the liberation of those who are disenfranchised. For God to side with los humildes means that God stands against those with power and privilege, the pharaohs of this world. Rather than impassively watching the unfolding of human suffering in history, God decisively acts on behalf of those who are oppressed (Boff and Boff 1987, 50). This model is best revealed in the personhood of Jesus Christ and those willing to participate in his teachings.

Martí, following the model of Christ, makes the liberation of the oppressed central to his thoughts, whether the oppressors are Spaniards, North Americans, or fellow Cubans. Through his actions, Martí voluntarily lived an economically marginalized life, resisting the U.S. cult of conspicuous consumption. He would say, "With the poor of the earth, I want to cast my lot" (*Obras Completa* 16:67). The vice of the United States, according to him, was its "piling up of fortunes" and its "widespread lust for money," creating a "survival of the fittest" mentality and spurning its noble heritage. The perpetuation of this vice would eventually lead to the conquest of Latin America. He feared that the financial domination of Wall Street over the southern and western United States would be transferred, with time, to Latin America. Responding to the United States's all-seeing covetous eye, Martí called for the construction of patria.

For Martí, the disenfranchised possess the preferential option of God because they are closer to the truth of the gospel. He wrote, "As always, it is the humble, the shoeless, the needy, the fishermen who band together shoulder to shoulder to fight injustice and make the Gospel fly with its silver wings aflame! Truth is revealed more clearly to the poor and the sufferers! A piece of bread and a glass of water never deceives!" (1975, 271–72). To understand Christ, one had to experience Jesus's marginality. He further wrote, "To fully understand Jesus, it is necessary to have come into the world in a darkened manger with a pure and devout spirit, and to go through life touched by the scarcity of love, the flowering of cupidity, and the victory of hate. One must have sawed wood and kneaded bread amid the silence and transgressions of men" (1999, 78). Yet Martí's "preferential option for the poor," while normative, was not universal. He believed situations existed when those being oppressed did not have a right to organize a work strike against the oppressors.

The patria Martí envisioned is similar in principle and spirit to Latin American Christian base communities, known as Base Ecclesial Communities (BEC). BEC were grass-roots organizations fostering lay participation in the liberation theology movement. Martí similarly attempted to erect a grass-roots patria in which all Cubans could exercise their duty to participate in their political liberation. He attempted to create patria on ethical dimensions of equality, not on economic capitalism. Patria would have freedom of expression, legislative assembly, and a free press, none of which has ever existed in Cuba. Martí's egalitarian Cuba would be a just society without the exploitation of one person by another. He did not uphold a gospel of individual salvation. Rather, he encouraged building a "kingdom" of justice based on morality.

Martí was inspired by the conditions of poor Cubans in New York, marginalized by classism and racism. The organization he founded, and which eventually led to the invasion of Cuba, was established by and through those who were disenfranchised. His meetings for independence originated among the black émigré base communities in New York. The Patriotic League was started in 1890 by Martí and Rafael Sierra, a Cuban of African decent, to elevate the consciousness of Cuban blacks through education.

Martí's writings have always emphasized the importance of education. He would write, "the fundamental freedom, the basis for all others, is the freedom of mind" (*Obras Completa* 12:348). Only an educated Cuban community could work effectively for any and all social reforms. So crucial was education for Martí that it took precedence over the state's responsibility to feed the people. He called for "free day-care centers in all the poorest areas" (*Obras Completa* 12:459). He wrote, "When everyone comes to this earth, they have the right to be educated. Afterward, as a form of payment, they have the obligation to contribute to the education of everyone else" (*Obras Completa* 20:375). The liberation of Cubans would occur when self-actualization is realized through the process of consciousness-raising, through a new sociopolitical and historical awareness, facilitated by education. A liberated people would naturally create a liberated patria, a people determined to reconstruct their social reality. As Varela before him and as Freire would later articulate, Martí saw consciousness-raising as the means to a Cuba Libre (Freire 1995, 7–10).

Martí denounced Spanish colonialism and U.S. imperialism as unjust, immoral, and unchristian. He demonstrated an overriding desire to destroy oppressive structures by reducing abstract thoughts into concrete praxes, motivated by his religious commitment to duty (Ripoll 1984, 2). The creation of Cuban consciousness could not be reduced to political independence from Spain. It required a fundamental change or conversion within the essence of the Cuban identity. Such a conversion could occur only if compatriots undertook their responsibilities and duties in creating *cubanidad*. "To think is to serve," Martí would say, emphasizing orthopraxis over orthodoxy—"right action" over "right thought." Consequently Martí downplayed his intellectualism in favor of his actions to liberate all Cubans. Patria's existence depended on a consciousness-raising in which humans become ethically aware of and active in the establishment of justice. Martí was among the first to recognize that Cuba was the key to preventing U.S. expansionist actions. If Cuba succumbed to the United States, it would serve as a launching pad for other nations in Latin America.

Although Martí predates the expression "institutional violence," he saw sin and evil in both people and social structures. He saw the Spanish elite and the common Cuban as trapped within structures of oppression. He responded to the Spaniards' oppression with love, welcoming them to participate in the construction of patria after the war for independence.

In general Martí shunned violence. He admired Marx, but he rejected Marxism because it advocated a violent struggle. Martí maintained that the social changes advocated by Marx through class struggle constituted an immoral use of violence. For Martí, a classless society is one leveled both by education and economic status, brought about by a land tax (González and Schulman 1961, 385). In an 1883 eulogy to Marx he wrote, "He deserves to be honored for declaring himself on the side of the weak . . . [but] the task of setting men in opposition against men is frightening. The compulsory brutalization of men for the profit of others stirs anger. But an outlet must be found for this anger, so that the brutality might cease before it overflows and terrifies" (1975, 184–88). Martí abhorred violence. Yet, as pointed out by the liberation theologian Leonardo Boff, at times the need existed to pick up arms. Boff insists that Christians can never initiate physical violence; however, violence might become necessary for the sake of sociopolitical liberation. As José Comblin argues, no liberation theologian prefers violence, but at times one must decide when faced with the unavoidable dilemma of choosing between no action—hence condoning the violence of the oppressor—and action that risks fomenting a new violence (Ferm 1992, 30–31, 45).

Martí constructed an alternative to a military dictatorship by providing a democratic/civilian discourse that exercised control and discipline over caudillo elements. Witnessing the rise of General Porfirio Diaz in Mexico, Martí rejected all types of *personalismo* (charismatic authoritarianism). In an effort to prevent the "spoil system" government of the past, he proposed a republican form of government with four-year political terms modeled on U.S. government. Though rejecting personalismo, his role as *delegado* (delegate) in the revolutionary organization he constructed to overturn Spaniard domination portrayed him as an authority figure. Final authority in any matter was invested in the delegado.

In 1884 General Máximo Gómez insisted on placing the military over the civilian government. This insistence led to a temporary break with Martí, a breach mended when Gómez relented. Martí wrote Gómez, stating, "It is my determination not to contribute one iota—through blind love of an idea affecting my entire life—to bringing my country a government of personal despotism more shameful and regrettable than the political despotism it now endures. . . . A nation is not founded, General, the way one commands a military camp" (1977, 211–12). Martí's willingness to stand by his principles, even at the risk of jeopardizing the revolution, testifies to his uncompromising conviction to oppose personalismo and those who would exploit la lucha for selfish advancement.

Martí Reveals Christ as Victim

The Cuban national anthem contains the following stanza: *No temáis una muerte gloriosa, que murle por la patria es vivir* (Do not fear a glorious death: To die for Fatherland is to live). Cuban ethos is preoccupied with the inevitability of death. The ultimate sign of being Cuban is to die gloriously for one's beliefs while facing the sun. Martí reveals a fixation with death in his writings, second only to his obsession with creating patria. His well-known 1894 poem reads:

I wish to leave the world, By its natural door;
In my tomb of green leaves, They are to carry me to die.
Do not put me in the dark, To die like a traitor;
I am good, and like a good being, I will die with my face to the sun.

In another passage, where his attitudes toward death are better represented, he wrote:

Death! Generous death! Death, my friend! Sublime bosom where all
the sublime kingdoms are wrought; fear of the weak; pleasure of the
brave; satisfaction of my desire; dark passage to the remaining episodes of existence; immense mother at whose feet we stretch out to
gain new strength for the unknown way where heaven is wider, lim-
itless horizons, where unworthy feet are dust, truth at last, wings;
tempting mystery, . . . harbinger of liberty. (Gray 1962, 43–44)

Martí's pronouncements on death are more than mere romanticism. For Martí, death was not the opposite of life; rather, it was life's reward. It is through the existential act of death that the hidden salvation of humanity is achieved. Hence life and death exist as harmonious elements of a dual relationship.

Through death, life is achieved. Any attempt to explicate this paradox, aside from the suffering and tension it creates, is unacceptable to the Cuban ethos. Such tension must exist, for agony and suffering mean struggle, and as long as there are struggles there is glory and there is life, not death. For Martí, the main characteristic of life is suffering mitigated by grief. Reflecting on his teenage prison experience, Martí wrote in his essay "Political Prison of Cuba":

Prison, God [are] ideas as close to me as immense suffering and eternal well-being. Perhaps to suffer is to enjoy. To suffer is to die for the
stupid life we have created, and to be born to the life of the good, the

only true life. . . . To suffer is more than to enjoy; it is truly to live. (1977, 163)

The Cuban Christ dies so that life can occur. Christ becomes the ultimate tragic victim who dies, as do the innumerable humildes of Cuba, seemingly abandoned by God, as if God had turned God's back to them. Yet God is present not as a transcendent power standing triumphantly against earthly injustice, but as the self-negating Christ who lovingly surrenders his life in the struggle against the political injustices of his day. Death does not end with the cross but continues to exist within the daily afflictions of all who suffer. Those who, like Christ, suffer injustice find a Christ who carries the stigmata of oppression upon his flesh. The hope of the humildes who are crucified is in the Christ who was also crucified.

Martí Reveals a Postnationalist Christ

Martí distinguished liberation from nationalist independence. In fact, Martí can be characterized as a postnationalist along the lines of Garvey, Du Bois, and Fanon. Martí the postnationalist becomes a liberating voice challenging the mutual hatred and violence presently existing between the Cubans in La Habana and Miami, each fueled by nationalistic fervor. Nationalism is usually constructed by writers, poets, lawyers, and doctors who themselves are shaped by colonial powers. They usually attempt to replace the colonial structures of power with a replicated class-based structure. Because nationalism maintains oppressive structures, it is insufficient for establishing liberation (Said 1994, 223–24, 230, 264). Martí understood this and advocated a nationalism that was more than a political struggle. His nationalism meant a social revolution directed toward a multiracial celebration of Hispanic culture and articulated as Nuestra America.

The character of Nuestra America, in his mind, was superior to the "other America" (the Anglo-Saxon America), which has descended from glory since winning its independence from England. Martí best expressed this sentiment when he wrote, "But no matter how great is this land, or how anointed the America of Lincoln may be for the free men of America—for us, in our very heart of hearts where nobody dares to challenge or take issue with our secret feelings, the America of Juárez [president of Mexico from 1861 to 1871] is greater because it has been more unhappy, and because it is ours" (1977, 71). For Martí, Nuestra America was one patria that began at the Río Grande and ended in the muddy hills of Patagonia (Obras Completa 11:48). It consisted of an alliance among disenfranchised biracial Latin Americans, the enlightened middle classes, the working classes, and the peasantry united against U.S. imperialism and their cooperating Latin American landowning elite.

Martí seldom used words like "freedom" or "nationalist independence." He called for liberation and attempted to go beyond the mere creation of egalitarian structures. Not espousing a defensive cry for freedom, Martí advocated offensive actions on behalf of liberation. This praxis was undergirded and motivated by an unconditional love that contained no room for hatred or revenge. In his prison journal he wrote:

> God does exist, and I come in His name to break in Spanish hearts the cold and indifferent glass that contains their tears. God does exist, and if you people make me move away from here without having torn out of you your cowardly, unfortunate indifference, let me despise you, since I am unable to hate anyone: let me pity you in the name of my God. I will not hate you, nor will I curse you. If I were to hate anyone, I would hate myself for so doing. (1977, 152)

Martí's emphasis on love as the foundation for deeds could have served as a prototype to the Medellín Documents, the theological bases for liberation theology, which stated: "Love, 'the fundamental law of humanity's perfection, and the transformation of the world' (Vatican II, Gaudium et spes, No. 38), is not only the supreme commandment of the Lord; it is also the dynamism which ought to move Christians to realize justice in the world, having as a foundation truth, and as a sign liberty" (CELAM 1968, 53).

Consciousness of one's existence as objects to the foreign and/or national elite subject entails an epistemological break with the reality created by the oppressors. This awareness creates resistance to domestication. Political parties are formed, literatures calling for freedom are written, slogans are shouted, revolutions are started. Yet Martí foresaw the danger of a nationalist consciousness evolving into a new kind of oppression in which the foreign oppressor is only replaced by the domestic oppressor. He understood that liberation and reconciliation would only occur when Cubans transcended their traditional factionalism (white against black, Resident against Exilic, rich against poor). By constructing a *cubanidad* (a type of Cuban ethos) that raised the political and social consciousness of all Cubans, Martí attempted to avoid the pitfalls of nationalist consciousness. Unless the notion of national consciousness changes, once success is achieved in overthrowing the imperialist, momentary liberation will rapidly digress into a new form of imperialism. For nationalism to survive the departure of the colonist, the local bourgeoisie must be forced to surrender its own hegemonic authority. Hence, to avoid the pitfall of national consciousness, Martí portrayed Cuban history as a facet of an overall history of human subjugation, shifting the focus from freedom for the land and its inhabitants to human liberation.

His postnationalism envisioned liberation not just for los humildes of Cuba but also for all who are oppressed and all who are oppressing. He wrote, "Every man is to feel on his cheek the blow received on the cheek of any other man." More than merely reacting to colonialism, Martí forged an alternative narrative for interpreting history and thus constructing ethnicity, a narrative he termed cubanidad. Manuel Pedro González, expounding on Martí's commitments to liberation in its relationship with the United States, wrote:

> If the situation had been reversed and the United States had been the weak nation and Cuba or Latin America the oppressing power, he would have struggled with equal fervor and heroism in defense of the United States against the abusive country. Justice and freedom were indivisible for him. In spite of his intense patriotism, he would never have endorsed the doctrine of "my country, right or wrong." Such a creed would have been repugnant and barbarous to him, proper only to primitive tribes. (1953, 21)

Cuba's liberation would insure a Latin America free from what he termed "ultraeaglism," the spreading of the U.S. eagle's wing over much of the earth with the help of the local elite. In Martí's last writing from Dos Ríos, he wrote, "[The Cuban elite] are satisfied merely that there be a master—Yankee or Spanish—to support them or reward their services as go-between with positions of power enabling them to scorn the hardworking masses—the country's [mestizos], skilled and pathetic, the intelligent and creative hordes of Negroes and white men" (1977, 440). Although his earlier works looked toward the United States as a beacon of hope upon which to model patria, he was disillusioned by incidents like the 1886 Haymarket Riot, the U.S. "money cult," and the moral vacuum created by its entrance into imperialist ventures (Martínez Bello 1940, 159–60).[3] For Martí, the danger of Cuban independence from Spain would be the instantaneous loss of that independence to the United States. He hoped Cuba Libre's contribution to a "free Antilles will preserve the independence of Nuestra America, and the dubious and tarnished honor of English America, and perhaps may hasten and stabilize the equilibrium of the world" (1977, 403). By rejecting North American greed, Martí's patria became the synthesis of his conception of Christ, liberty, self-government, and sovereignty conceived in terms of his exilic experience and his Hispanic cultural values.

If Martí, as symbol, serves as a precursor to liberation theology and as an example for postnationalism, then he can be used here as a metaphor and catalyst for the quest for the Cuban Christ. From Martí we learn that the Cuban Christ, as victim, takes his stand with the poor and seeks a liberation that goes beyond nationalism. Yet Martí is not the only symbol. Another Cuban symbol is *Santería*, based on the religious beliefs brought to Cuba by African slaves. This phenomenon is usually ignored because of Cuban white supremacy, but is crucial in the continuous quest for a Cuban Christ. Hence we now turn our attention toward the black Christ of Cuba.

The Black Cuban Christ

Throughout the island, white men were recruited to defend the homeland from what was perceived to be the worst threat since the war for independence. The year was 1912 and a race war loomed over Cuba. It would be a battle for the future of la patria, a struggle between "white civilization" and "black barbarism." Thousands of white Cuban volunteers were given arms and paid by the government to rove across the nation and put down the revolt in any way possible. During *la guerrita del doce* (the Little War of 1912), thousands of unarmed black Cubans were deliberately butchered by these white Cubans, mostly for "resisting arrest" (a Latin American euphemism for the assassination of captured prisoners). Government officials in Santiago paid five dollars for every black cadaver brought to them. No one asked questions as to the identity of the black body or its involvement, if any, during the so-called uprising (Arredondo 1939, 66). In the central plazas across Cuba blacks were hung from the lampposts by their genitals (Casal 1989, 472).

According to official reports, a race riot was about to break. Blacks wanted to overthrow the newly formed republic and replace it with a Haitian-style dictatorship. White women everywhere were in danger of being raped by liberated black men bent on tearing down white Cuba. Decisive force was employed to combat the danger of a black revolt. Yet no trace of the rumored uprising could be found, no cache of arms was ever discovered, no demonstration occurred outside of Oriente, no white woman was ever raped or cannibalized (contrary to newspaper accounts), and no destruction of valuable property occurred. Although Cuban history books, written mostly by whites, still insist on referring to this incident as a race war, the fact remains that only one side had substantial weapons; hence, it was a race massacre. Bernardo Suárez, a witness to the massacre, wrote:

All the bitterness, all the hatred, all the ancestral prejudice of the white race against the black, were let loose. While the machine guns of the government troops were mowing down thousands of colored men, not alone those in arms, but the peaceful inhabitants of towns and villages . . . the larger cities and even in the Capital of the Republic: white men armed to the teeth went about ordering any and every black man to withdraw from the streets and public places on pain of death, and the mere color of his skin was sufficient reason to send a man to prison on the charge of rebellion. (1922, 43)

What could have triggered such a violent race massacre? Could it have been that Cuba's former slaves hoped for and believed in Martí's vision of a colorblind patria? After all, blacks had valiantly fought for la patria. Larger numbers of black Cubans died in the struggle for independence than did whites. Now they expected a fair share of the fruits of a new republic. After the war they believed they had earned sociopolitical recognition and a right to participate in establishing la patria. Black Cuban general Quintín Banderas serves as an example of what all Cuban blacks who dared to proclaim their humanity could instead expect. He bravely fought for independence during the war. Afterward, he sought work in a "free" Cuba. His white counterparts found government jobs and positions as rural officers, yet General Banderas was denied a government job as a janitor. When his money ran out he asked for help from President Estrada Palma. The president denied him an audience. He eventually joined a group to protest the fraudulent reelection of Estrada Palma and was consequently murdered by the rural guard, who mutilated his body (Helg 1995, 16, 105–6, 120).

The race massacre was a response to blacks who, through official channels, openly protested a Cuba that relegated them to a disenfranchised space. The massacre was violent and sadistic. It was neither the first nor the last time that the "black question" would be settled in this fashion. These massacres over real and alleged revolts and conspiracies occurred in 1792, 1793, 1795, 1814, 1844, 1912, and 1919. Historians disagree on how to interpret these episodes of Cuban history. Many historians assign blame to those of African descent for instigating the violence. Every massacre is portrayed as a preemptive response to a black revolution along the lines of the one in Haiti; others insist these "black revolutions" are Machiavellian fabrications initiated by the government to justify repressive measures. Although historians may argue about the causes of these massacres, one fact is certain: most of those who died in these "revolts" were unarmed blacks. Hence, these blacks were also los humildes of Cuba. They were powerless against forces that claimed their labor and life for the benefit of the privileged within a white Cuba.

This chapter will continue the quest for the Cuban Christ by seriously considering Christ's blackness as a source of liberation from the sin of intra-Cuban racism. Because racial categories are central to Cuba's collective identity, the blackness of Christ will be explored by briefly reviewing Cuban history from the underside—in short, from the African experience. To do this we must ask how Cuban blacks are seen by the dominant white Cuban culture. We must also consider the influence of Santería, the African-based religion, in the search for the cultural Cuban Christ. To ignore Santería because Cuban Christians insist it is not a Christian symbol would be to overlook the possible religious influence of one of Cuba's most marginalized communities.

Black Cuba

By 1524, Diego Columbus's term as viceroy had ended. In the aftermath of the Amerindian decimation more African slaves lived in the Caribbean than did Taínos; African slavery arose in Cuba as Amerindian enslavement declined.[1] Originally, because of a lack of precious metals and a stagnant island economy, few Africans were brought to Cuba. But by the 1640s, a sociopolitical change took place as the semifeudal settlements in Cuba gave way to plantation agriculture, specifically the harvesting of sugar cane. Such economic shifts furthered the institutionalization of slavery in colonial Cuba, creating one of the most brutal systems of all Latin America. It was upon sugar that Cuba was constructed. It was because of sugar that slavery endured. Expanding sugar production propelled the rapid growth of slave labor in the peripheral economy of Spain's colony while contributing to the rise of capitalism in the motherland. By the 1830s the jewel of the Spanish crown had become the largest single producer of cane sugar in the world.

For Spain to be enriched, slaves were forced to work eighteen hours a day, six days a week. Life expectancy for a slave arriving in Cuba was seven years. Slave deaths exceeded births, which necessitated the constant acquisition of new labor. It was considered more cost effective to work a slave to death and then to purchase a new one than provide adequate slave health care. This form of slave labor (and its accompanying white racism) created profit for the elite. After the Haitian revolution of 1794, planters turned Cuba into the world's sugar bowl. Prior to the 1790s, Cuba's slaves had been supplied by the English, who grew rich through the slave trade. But England's abolition of this trade led to the creation of direct slave routes between La Habana and Africa, allowing the merchants of La Habana to accumulate wealth by filling the void created by diminishing English slave traders. Since Cuba's economy depended on slaves, this practice insured the loyalty of sugar plantation owners to the Crown during the early wars of national independence, lest they jeopardize their privileged positions. Wars against the Crown failed because the revolutionaries could not overcome the privileged oligarchies who remained militarily, psychologically, and economically dependent on Spain.

During the inhumane treatment of Africans, especially during slavery, the church of Christ remained silent. Sadly, the church itself was a slaveholder, claiming its generosity in reaching these "savages" for Christ, which outweighed any work slaves might have to do in return; the soul's salvation prevailed over the body's destruction. A close relationship existed among the Spanish government, the sugar barons, and the church, to the detriment of the Africans. The church developed this relationship in the hope of carving out a space for Christian participation in society.

Legal slavery ended in the Caribbean when Cuba abolished slavery in 1886; however, abolition did not mean an end to racism or exploitation. Under "freedom," former slaves were hired only during peak seasons of the sugar cane harvest and left to themselves during the off-peak seasons from June through November. Slavery was replaced with the rural proletarization of black Cubans. For Esteban Montejo, a former slave, life remained the same. He was still confined to the plantation, lived like an animal in the *barracón* (slave quarters), and submitted to the white master. Thus, he wrote, "Some plantations were still the way they were under slavery; the owners still thought they owned the blacks" (1968, 96).

Racism in Cuba developed in an atmosphere of fear and insecurity. After the Haitian revolution, white Haitian exiles brought to Cuba stories of rape, murder, looting, and destruction, sufficiently scaring Cuban planters into tightening controls for nearly a hundred years. Spain skillfully used the memory of the Haitian revolution to frighten white Cubans into loyalty to the Crown. Every revolt against Spanish rule was presented as the start of a race war. "Remember Haiti" became the rallying cry against Cuba's attempt to liberate itself from Spain. Independence would leave white Cuba unprotected from black Cuba, threatening its property, security, and women. *La Guerra Chiquita* (the Little War—the 1879 premature war for independence) was interpreted by the Spaniards as the start of a race war led by black gangs of Haitian origins roving through Oriente. Whites feared a divided Cuba with a white west and a black east that would lead to a civil war culminating in a Haitian-style black dictatorship. The outbreak of the war for independence in 1895 was also labeled by Spain as a race war. Antonio Cánovas del Castillo, prime minister of Spain at the time, remarked, "The fact that this insurrection threatens Cuba with all the evils of Haiti and Santo Domingo, and with the triumph of the colored people and perpetual wars of races, virtually obligates the whites in Cuba to side with Spain" (Helg 1995, 49–56, 80–89).

Ironically, during the wars for independence, blacks and biracial Cubans, approximately a third of the population, made up over half of the insurgents fighting for Cuba's liberation from Spanish colonialism (Scott 1985, 112). More than 40 percent of the senior commission ranks of the liberation army were held by Africans and/or their descendants. The large proportion of Afro-Cubans in the army helps explain why the United States provided military aid long after the insurgents obtained a clear military advantage. Rather than needing these arms to fight Spain, white landowners, fearing a black-led race war, wanted protection from their own army. People feared what might occur if a predominantly Afro-Cuban army prevailed; specifically they worried about the impact on the existing racial hierarchy (Moore 1997, 22–23).

Throughout Cuban history, whenever the indigenous black population threatened to exceed the white population, a process known as *blanqueamiento* (whitening) occurred whereby land was freely given to white Spaniard families who would leave Spain and come to live on the island. Characteristic of Spanish colonial policy was the constant emigration of poor whites from Spain. José Martí stands out among late nineteenth-century thinkers who rejected blanqueamiento.

Martí went further than any of his white contemporaries in affirming the equality of the races. He became a nonblack voice who identified with the oppressed blacks. He attempted to die to his "whiteness" in order to create Cuba Libre, free from racist social structures. His response to slavery was forceful. Martí's revolutionary document, "Manifesto," is the only document of its kind in the Western Hemisphere mentioning blacks as a positive force for society. In an era when most whites believed the notion that blacks were inferior, Martí continuously stated that racism was a "sin against humanity." In the articles "Basta" ("Enough") and "Mi raza" ("My Race"), he proposed that there is no such thing as race. He viewed race as a social construction that allows one group to oppress another. Calling race categories "*razas de librería*" ("bookstore races"), he refused to connect inferiority and slavery, for, as he points out, "blue-eyed, blond-haired Gauls were sold as slaves in the Roman marketplace."

Martí insisted that race classifications are entirely artificial constructions. To be Cuban meant "*más que blanco, más que mulato, más que negro*" ("more than being white, more than being a mulatto, more than being black"). In Martí's attempt to create a colorblind society, he blames blacks for being racist when they attempt to develop black consciousness. He asks, "What must whites think of the black who prides himself on his color?" Then he answers his own question by stating, "The black man who proclaims his race, even if mistakenly as a way to proclaim spiritual identity with all races, justifies and provokes white racism" (Pérez 1999, 91).

Although Martí poetically wrote articles to combat racism, his rhetoric lacked substance. He maintained that an integrated liberation army would forge a single Cuban consciousness that would rise above the pettiness of racism. Obviously this integration failed to materialize. Later generations of Cuban whites would use Martí's rhetoric to claim that no racism existed, for if the colorblind society has been achieved then there can be no racism (Martí 1959, 14, 27). Undermining his own work, Martí's views included forms of evolutionism that created a human hierarchy of development. In his notes for a projected book, *La raza negra* (*The Black Race*), he insisted blacks must rise to the levels of whites through both education and intermarriage. He spoke of a "savage element" in blacks that prevented them from fully participating in civilized culture. With time, Martí thought blacks would embrace Western culture and reject their African heritage (Ortiz 1942, 346–47). These comments were cited by the early-twentieth-century Cuban cultural interpreter Fernando Ortiz in order to continue the very racism Martí intended to eliminate.

Ortiz capitalized on the black's "savage element" in his observation of the polarization of Cuban society.[2] In his work *Contrapunteo cubano del tabaco y el azúcar* (*Cuban Counterpoint of Tobacco and Sugar*), he expresses the normative assumptions of white Cuba. For Cuba's white supremacy, the existing polarity can be termed as "the Cuban counterpoint," where:

Tobacco and sugar contradict each other in economics and in society. Even rigid moralists have taken them under consideration in the course of their history, viewing one with mistrust and the other with favor. (1963, 1–2)

According to Ortiz, half of the island, like sugar, is sweet, refined, odorless, and white. The other half, like tobacco, is raw, pungent, bitter, aromatic, and dark. Tobacco requires constant care; sugar can look after itself. Tobacco poisons; sugar nourishes. Within the spiraling smoke of a good Cuban cigar exists something revolutionary. The tobacco's consuming anarchical flames protest oppression. Sugar, on the other hand, contains neither rebellion nor resentment. It is calm, quiet, beyond suspicion. Sugar is the work of the gods, a scientific gift of civilization. Tobacco is of the devil, a magic gift of the savage world (1963, 5–15, 46).

> Tobacco does not change color, it is born black and dies with the color of its race. Sugar changes color, it is born brown and whitens itself; it is syrupy mulatta that being blackish is abandoned to popular taste; later it is bleached and refined so that it can pass for white, travel the whole world, reach all mouths, and bring a better price, climbing to dominating categories of the social ladder. (1963, 7)

Even though Ortiz's metaphors accurately reveal how most white Cubans saw their black compatriots, the Cuban-African community claimed equality under the law. By 1910, black *mambises* (Cubans who fought for independence) were mobilizing to petition the government for their rightful share.[3] Unfortunately, whites interpreted black involvement in the fight for Cuba Libre as *dando ala a los negros* (making blacks uppity). The creation of El Partido Independiente de Color (The Independent Party of Color) served as the political vehicle to force the government to seriously consider its rhetoric of racial equality and to provide equal opportunities in power, employment, and services.

El Partido Independiente de Color did not advocate black separatism. Rather, it called for integration, specifically the elimination of racial discrimination, equal access to government jobs, and an end to the blanqueamiento policies. By the end of the Spanish-American War, 50 percent of the rebel army and 40 percent of the officers were of African descent. Most lost their land to foreign investors and white *criollo* entrepreneurs. These former soldiers formed El Partido to pressure the government into establishing justice. In effect, El Partido threatened the hierarchical power structures based on race and class, and thus was perceived as a dangerous threat to the republic.

In 1910, after not even a year of existence, El Partido was outlawed by a bill presented by the only black senator of Congress, Martín Morúa Delgado. Blacks were indiscriminately rounded up, jailed, or killed. This persecution culminated in the 1912 race massacre. For a black person to question the white government was sufficient grounds for death. Even if the person were fortunate enough to escape brutal treatment, the knowledge that violence could arbitrarily occur again pervaded the relationship between blacks and whites. The "success" of the massacre settled the black question for the remainder of the twentieth century. The massacre of Afro-Cubans who challenged those with power and privilege annihilated future social protest by terrifying the surviving blacks into conformity. The Cuban worldview became white once again because the black voice was effectively silenced.

Africans Reveal a Black Crucified Christ

The Cuban African shares a sacred bond with the Amerindians. This element of Cuban culture, epitomizing los humildes, represents God's "crucified people," literally bearing the sins of Cuba. As a crucified people they provide an essential salvific perspective to Cuban history. How? Liberation theologians insist God habitually chooses those oppressed in history and makes them the principal means of salvation, just as God chose the "suffering servant," the crucified Christ, to bring salvation to the world (Sobrino 1993, 259–60). Historically, God has always chosen the disenfranchised as agents of God's new creation. It was not to the court of the pharaohs that God made God's will known; instead God chose their slaves, the Jews, to reveal God's movement in history. It was not Rome, the most powerful city of the known world, where God chose to perform the miracle of the incarnation, nor was it Jerusalem, the center of Yahweh worship; rather it was impoverished Galilee where God chose to first proclaim the message of the Gospels. Nazareth, Jesus' hometown, was so insignificant to the religious life of Judaism that the Hebrew Bible never mentions it. This theme of solidarity between the crucified Christ and the victims of oppression is supplemented by atonement for the recipients of society's power and pretensions.

Because the Cuban black experience closely resembles the lot of los humildes, God's crucified people, their lucha becomes central in the search for a Cuban Christ. Christ, for Cubans, has always been seen as *blanco* (white). To be blanco, like sugar, is to be pure, sinless, and unblemished. But this blanco Christ has been used to justify the oppression of los humildes. The blanco Christ who condones or remains silent in the presence of slavery, in the death of los humildes, and in the numerous massacres is a false Christ, an anti-Christ. A black Cuban Christ stands against the supposed historical duty of superior Cuban whites to care for and religiously instruct their presumed inferiors. Yet, because of los humildes, all Cubans are provided the opportunity to discover the Cuban Christ, who happens to be black. To see Christ as black appears heretical to those Cuban blancos who possess power and privilege. It seems to them blasphemy to color Christ with the color of tobacco, the color of evil, soil-ness, and impurity. Hence, to look for a black Cuban Christ (or an indigenous Taíno Christ) subverts the normative white Cuban Christ of power and privilege.

In order to sever the bond between barbarism and blackness, Christ must be recognized as physically and/or symbolically black. Just as white Cubans have worshiped a Christ in their own image, it becomes significant to see the divine in the color of los humildes. The white Christ of Cuban history has been the Christ who justified the historical reality of slavery, racism, oppression, and numerous massacres. It was in the name of the white Christ, the Christ who symbolized the protection of white Christian civilization from so-called black barbarism, that atrocities against los humildes were committed throughout Cuban history.

The black Cuban Christ is informed by the historical identification of Jesus with those who suffer under oppression. Christ's blackness is not due to being "politically correct," nor to some psychological need among Cuba's black community. Jesus is black because the biblical witness of God is of one who takes sides with los humildes against those who oppress them. In a white Cuban racist society, blacks were the ones being oppressed, the ones who were hungry, thirsty, cast out, naked, afflicted, and incarcerated.

In the famous biblical parable of the sheep and the goats as recorded in the Gospel of Matthew (25:31–46), Jesus divides those destined for glory (the sheep) from those destined for damnation (the goats). The salvation of those with power and privilege is contingent upon how they treated those who were starving, thirsty, foreigners, unclothed, ill, and imprisoned. Usually, los humildes occupy this space. The dominant culture finds its life (salvation) when it struggles along with those who are oppressed by attempting to alleviate, if not eliminate, the structures that cause death. Crucial to the understanding of this passage is the radical revelation made by Jesus. He ends the parable by stating (verse 45), "Then [the Lord] will answer [the condemned], saying, 'Truly I say to you, inasmuch as you did not do for one of these, the least [los humildes], neither did you do it to me.'" To "see" Jesus within Cuban history is to see him within God's crucified people, those most oppressed by Cuba's structural racism. But to seek Christ within black Cuban spirituality, we must examine how that spirituality is manifested. Hence, the quest for the Cuban Christ leads us to Santería.

Santería as a Christian Symbol

In the previous chapter we saw Martí as a symbol that facilitated an understanding of a Christ who is Cuban. Another symbol that contributes in our quest for a Cuban Christ is Santería. Even though Santería, due to racism, has historically been alien to white Cuban Christians, it is part, if not central, to the Cuban identity as a whole. As such, Cubans must come to terms with the African-based religion reformulated within the depths of Cuban culture. By seriously reevaluating Santería, we can find rich resources for understanding Cuban ethnicity and the Cuban Christ. As such, Santería cannot become subordinate to European Christianity nor to the African Yoruba faith. It is a separate reality with an equal voice in any dialogue concerning the Deity. Cuban Christians can disagree theologically with the tenets of Santería without disavowing its influence upon their essential identity or its contribution toward the quest for the Cuban Christ.

Santería is a Cuban religious expression that enables the survival and self-affirmation of a people whose roots are African. In reality, four religious-cultural structures originating in Africa live within the overall national Cuban culture. They are the palo monte of Kongo origin; the regla Arará of Ewe-fon origin; the Abakuá Secret Society containing Ejagham, Efik, Efut, and other Calabar roots; and the regla de Ocha of Yoruba. The latter, as Santería, is the most popular among Cubans. Santería, the "worship of saints," also known as the Lucumi religion, is the product of a religious space created by those who were subordinated to the arbitrary exercise of power imposed by Catholic Spaniards upon their African slaves. Specifically, Santería was influenced by European Christianity expressed as a counter-Reformation, Spanish folk Catholicism, African orisha worship as practiced by the Yoruba of Nigeria, and nineteenth-century Kardecan spiritualism as originated in France and popularized in the Caribbean.

Santería recognizes the existence of a supreme God. Olodumare, the supreme being, is a transcendent world force or "current" known as *ashé*. This sacred energy becomes the power, grace, blood, and life force of Olodumare and nature, embracing all mystery, all secret power, and all divinity. Ashé is absolute, illimitable, pure power, neither definite nor definable. It is a nonanthropomoporphic form of theism (Verger 1966, 36–39). Orishas are quasi-deities serving as protectors and guides for every human being, regardless of the individual's acknowledgment of the religion. They were the first to walk the earth, and from them all humans are descended. Hence the orishas are the first ancestors. Created by the supreme God, Olodumare, they are specific parts, forces, or manifestations within Olodumare. They govern certain parts of the universe, for Olodumare is an absentee ruler. Because the universe is so vast, Olodumare has no time to become directly involved in the affairs of humans. Consequently, when an animal is sacrificed to Babalu-Aye (who governs the sphere of illness), the practitioner is worshiping the part of Olodumare exemplified in this particular orisha. Olodumare created the orishas to allow the divine form and will to be manifested to humanity via nature (De La Torre and Aponte 2001, 128–30).

The elaborate belief system of the Yoruba became part of the Cuban culture when colonial Cuba began to import subjugated African slaves to develop the urban centers and work the mines and sugar estates. These Africans were not ignoble savages captured in the slaver's nets, but patricians and priests who had been disloyal to the ascendancy of new rulers, specifically in the kingdoms of Benin, Dahomey, and the city-states of Yoruba. The vicissitudes of monarchic power struggles resulted in the enslavement and expatriation of those opposing the new regimes, especially in the Yoruba city-states. Captives of war were routinely enslaved, but slavery was also imposed as a debt payment for a period of time or as a judicial decision for committing a legal infraction (Brandon 1997, 19).

Tragically torn from their ordered religious life, Africans had no time to ponder philosophically the spiritual response to their tragedy. They were compelled to adjust their belief system to the immediate challenges presented by colonial Cuba. This transition created a nascent state for Santería, in which Yoruba's ethos survived by manifesting itself through Spanish Catholicism. According to a study done by the Catholic Church in 1954, one out of every four Catholics occasionally consulted a Santería priest (ACU 1954, 37). Even when Cubans reject Santería and insist solely on their Christianity, they still observe the adage *"Tenemos que respetar los Santos"* ("We have to respect the Saints").

Santería can be classified as a popular religion, not because of its widespread appeal but because it is a product of Cuba's most marginalized community. The term "popular" does not refer to popularity, but to a sociohistorical reality. The religion is "popular" because the disenfranchised are responsible for its creation, making it a religion of the marginalized. The emphasis is on *el pueblo* as opposed to the elites. Popular religion becomes the expression of the popular classes' creativity rather than the "true" Christianity of the "official" church (Espín 1994, 65–67). Clearly Santería can be classified as Cuba's "popular religion," and as such cannot be ignored. In constructing an understanding of Christ indigenous to the Cuban culture, care must be taken to avoid the error made during the early stages of liberation theology, when Catholic theologians disregarded the possible contributions that could be made by the religion of the people (*religiosidad popular*). While claiming to represent the Latin American periphery, early liberation theology ignored their ethical views, concentrating instead on the Eurocentric ethics of Vatican II.

Cuban whites legitimate their religious practices by labeling Christianity a religion, while disqualifying the black beliefs as syncretistic, if not demonic. Many practitioners of Santería, facing persecution, maintained an outward appearance of Catholicism. With time, both faith traditions began to share quite similar sacred spaces. Practitioners of Santería see their faith as an authentic search for the reality of God; however, the Catholic priest sees his role as correcting the practitioner of Santería so that she or he can enter the official faith of the church. Others voice harsher criticism, claiming Santería adulterates the mostly white form of Catholicism (likewise, a movement known as "Yoruba Reversionism" exists among African Americans who attempt to expurgate Spanish Catholicism from Santería). For Protestants, specifically Pentecostals, Santería is a satanic cult. For Exilic Cubans, especially those attempting to assimilate into the North American culture, Santería is a source of embarrassment, appearing both backward and primitive (De La Torre 2001, 840–41).

Throughout the Americas, the widespread phenomenon exists of cultural groups simultaneously participating in two diverse, if not contradictory, religious systems. Christianity, when embraced in the context of colonialism or slavery, creates a new space where the indigenous beliefs of the marginalized group resist annihilation. Yorubas refer to their culture as a "river that never rests." This metaphor reveals the ability of a people to flow with the constantly changing currents of life. This flexibility becomes evident in the unique hybrids that developed as the religious traditions of Yoruba slaves took root on Caribbean soil.

The vitality of the Yoruba belief system found expression through Catholicism as Voudou in Haiti, Shango in Trinidad and Venezuela, Candomble in Brazil, Kumina in Jamaica, and Santería in Cuba. Modern examples of orisha worship are not limited to the exchange that took place between Catholicism and the Yoruba religion. Examples of this African faith combining with Protestantism can be found in the Jamaican Revival and Pocomania groups. A similar example can be noted in the Trinidadian group known as Spiritual Baptist, or Shouters, where the Yoruba's faith found expression through Christian Fundamentalism. And religion need not be the only lens by which to look at Santería. Another example is articulated by the Resident Cuban Magdalena Campos, who finds no conflict between Santería and atheist Marxism. For her, Santería expands the frontiers of Marxism while enriching it. Furthermore, for Marxism to function in Cuba, it must incorporate Cuban reality as defined by the traditions of Santería (Camnitzer 1994, 211).

Yet white Christians usually portray Santería as the dialectical product of the Yoruba's belief system and Iberian Roman Catholicism, in which a "confused" and idiosyncratic merging of the saints with the orishas occurred. The official Cuban church places itself above the other's religion through rhetoric designed to reduce Santería to a sphere of ignorance and impurity. Power is thus exercised in the way that Catholics, operating from doctrinal knowledge, look down on blacks, who are confused. White beliefs are pure; blacks' are impure. The task of whites is to correct blacks' confusion. Seeing blacks as "confused" relegates Santería to an inferior social position while elevating Catholicism to an authoritative location from which paternal correcting can originate.

The *santera/o* (priest of the religion) is not "confused." L. Ernesto Pichardo, the santero whose actions led to the 1992 U.S. Supreme Court decision protecting animal sacrificial rituals of Santería, maintains that Santería is not the product of confused imagery and that distinctions between their religion and Catholicism have always been clearly recognized (1984, 14). Practitioners understood the need of placing Spanish masks over the black faces of the orishas so as to defend themselves from religious repression, an act made possible because the universality of the Yoruba faith allows the orishas to manifest themselves in other religions.

Santería's internal structure allows for the incorporation and assimilation of new deities. For Pichardo, when a "seeker" is unable to comprehend a concept because he or she lacks a Catholic background, the santero/a may substitute a saint with a compatible icon from the seeker's own religious tradition. For example, if the seeker were Hindu, the creator of the world, Obatalá, as the Mother of God (our Lady of Mercy), and the war-orisha Oggún, as St. Peter, both would easily be explained as Brahma the creator and Shiva the destroyer. While insuring fidelity to the original faith, this method also guarantees that the seeker is not proselytized. According to santeras/os, the seeker is enlightened by a newer and deeper understanding of the original faith and a knowledge of how to manipulate its spiritual power to survive life's hardships and struggles (De La Torre 2001, 841–42).

Santería and the Twentieth Century

Throughout Cuba's history, santeras/os have faced religious persecution, and Afro-Cuban religions have been portrayed as the principal cause for Cuba's problems. Slavery was considered a curse, not for the Africans who were oppressed and mistreated, but for the whites who were contaminated with barbarism. Prostitution, laziness, superstition, and criminality all supposedly originated with Cuba's black religion. During 1919 (seven years after the 1912 race massacres), a *brujo* (witch doctor) craze swept the island. Mass lynchings occurred, fueled by rumors of santeros/as kidnapping white children in order to use their blood and entrails in religious practices. These reports began to circulate after a white girl was found dead, presumably cannibalized by brujos. White mobs descended upon blacks with "righteous indignation." One newspaper, *El Día*, praised the lynchings, commending their violence as a "step forward that we take toward civilization." Middle- and upper-class blacks abandoned Santería and internalized the myth that racism did not exist in Cuba, while disassociating themselves from the lower class masses in order to assimilate into the white mainstream (Helg 1995, 238–45).

Fernando Ortiz's ethnographic research, conducted under the rubric of racial theorizing, was an attempt to prove the moral inferiority of blacks to whites. The assumption of black malefaction is evident in the title of his book, which primarily dealt with criminality by focusing on Santería (complete with police mug shots): *Los negros brujos: Apuntes para un estudio de etnología criminal*, translated as *The Black Witches: Notes for a Study on Criminal Ethnology*. In this book Ortiz insisted that African immorality was "in the mass of the blood of black Africans," a contamination affecting lower-class whites. The fetishism of Santería had to be eliminated, and so he suggested the lifelong isolation of its leaders. The movement from African fetishism (and its white forms, palm-reading and spiritualism) to Western scientific reasoning could be accomplished by providing a solid scientific education for all blacks and low-income whites. Expressions of African culture (such as African festival dances) had to be heavily policed to prevent the incitement of lust and immorality, or the stereotypical "black rapist." As a congressman, he proposed legislation during the 1919 brujo craze against what he deemed superstitious and antisocial practices.

During the presidency of Alfredo Zayas (1920–24), all Santería ceremonies, including playing drums and dancing during the gathering of Afro-Cubans, were strictly prohibited by law. Until 1940 Santería was a punishable crime in Cuba and a source of ridicule by the general populace. Persecutions resumed in 1962. Termed "folklore" rather than religion, Santería became subject to a growing number of restrictions, including bans against practicing the rituals or participating in the festivals. By the mid-1960s, santeros/as were arrested, imprisoned, and, in at least one case, executed. Authorization from the CDR (an adjunct of the state police) was needed to celebrate any ceremony, even though such authorization was routinely denied. Lack of official authorization resulted in arrest; Catholics needed no such authorization. The final declaration of the first National Congress on Education and Culture in 1971 stated that juvenile delinquency is partially caused by "religious sects, especially of African origin" (Moore 1988, 100–102). It was reminiscent of the days of the republic when Cuban cultural interpreter Ortiz stressed the "criminality" embedded in Santería.

During the 1980s persecutions eased. An increased interest in Santería developed because of the numbers of black Cuban soldiers returning from Angola and the 1985 publication of Castro's bestseller *Fidel y la religión* (*Fidel and Religion*). Adding to this interest was the 1987 visit by His Majesty Alaiyeluwa Oba Okunade Sijuwade Olubuse II, the Ooni of Ife. The Ooni is the spiritual authority of the Yoruba of Nigeria and all who worship the orishas in the Americas. The Castro regime also initiated an unprecedented campaign to court the practitioners of Santería. The Castro government now found value in the folklorization of Santería for the benefit of tourism. The bizarre and dangerous cultural features of Santería were domesticated and commodified to produce tourist dollars. By 1990 the Religious Affairs Department provided economic and political support to state-friendly santeras/os (De La Torre 2001, 842–44).

Santería Reveals a Christ of Resistance

In this final section, I will elucidate how Santería, as the faith of a segment of the Cuban population that is composed mostly of los humildes, contributes to the underlining (organic) function of religion and the understanding of the Christian Christ. As previously mentioned, Olodumare is the one supreme being. As creator, ruler, and judge of all, Olodumare is immortal, omniscient, and omnipotent. Olodumare consists of many facets. For example, he is Elemi, owner of life, Olorum, owner of the sky, or Olojo Oni, controller of daily occurrences. Olofi represents humanity's personal god. God on earth is Olofi, and, as such, Olofi is most commonly worshipped by believers. Jesus Christ, in the minds of the worshipers of Santería, is Olofi. While Olofi is mentioned in every prayer, he relegates all earthly matters to the orishas (González-Wippler 1992, 9–10).

Santería can never be understood solely by examining its tenets, rituals, or beliefs. Unlike traditional Western expressions of Christianity, Santería is a practical religion that promises power for dealing with life's hardships, and its power is manifested in a variety of ways depending on the cultural context of the practitioners. Santería cannot be explained by describing sacred forces like the orishas; rather, it is concerned with how these universal forces can be used for the betterment of all humans, specifically the practitioner. As a Cuban way of being and living, Santería is part of the Cuban ethos, an indigenous symbol of cultural resistance. To explain Santería theologically reduces the religion to a view of life rather than a way of survival, survival by way of cultural resistance.

Wherever oppression exists, there too is resistance. Every oppressed group creates from its sociological location "hidden transcripts" representing a collective critique of power spoken in the absence of the oppressor. These hidden transcripts are usually expressed openly, although disguised so the oppressors are kept in the dark (Scott 1990, 51). In this way, Santería meets the psychological need of accessing power within a powerless milieu. While the practitioner is impotent, Olofi (Christ), working through the orishas, possesses the power to protect los humildes and humble the powerful. Santería therefore becomes a resistance religion whose rituals critique the dominant power.

For example, a decapitated white dove found on the front steps of the Christian overseer was a sign of forthcoming disaster. He might, in turn, change his previous treatment of blacks to elicit a reversal of the spell. The powerful are thus warned that their behaviors and attitudes toward those they oppress are more grievous than can be tolerated by the laborers. Another example of resistance can be found in the figure of the trickster, the orisha Elleguá. Although portrayed as weak, he always outwits his adversary. According to numerous stories (*patakis*) concerning the origins and interrelationships of the orishas, as well as the role they play in determining the destiny of humanity, he successfully navigates treacherous situations and solves the most difficult of problems. He succeeds by hearing and seeing the powerful, learning their weaknesses, and proceeding to take advantage of their supposed infallibility, their greed and gullibility. Thus Elleguá is a model for all who live under oppression.

One pataki has the creator sick in bed with all the orishas attempting to cure him. After all have failed, Elleguá appears to attempt a healing. The other orishas are shocked that the weakest among them would have the gall to try what they all failed to do. Elleguá is successful, and as his reward, he becomes the first orisha to be honored in every ceremony. Thus the weakest among the powerful becomes first. In another pataki, Elleguá's powerful brother, war-orisha Oggún, is continuously raping their mother, Yemmu. Elleguá overcomes his brother, not by the strength of his body, but through his wits. Another pataki shows how he saves another brother's life while defying the authority of his father, who orders him to bury his brother. By literally obeying his words and burying him up to his waist, he avoids the intent of the command to kill him. In short, Elleguá is essential for survival, theologically teaching los humildes how to survive their own condition and how to overcome those who are stronger.

Another form of resistance is found in the *bembe*, where the participant is mounted by the orisha. The bembe is a drum and dance festival performed in honor of the orishas. Santería as a dance religion uses percussion rhythms to invite the orishas to manifest themselves by "mounting" or possessing the participants, who are dancing to the beat according to a choreographed tradition. This form of spiritual possession provides a sacred space where the practitioner can express hostility towards the oppressors. Under normal conditions such outbursts would not be tolerated. Yet the voiceless can openly protest their circumstances within a "hidden transcript," within the safe outlet of possession. The protest comes not from the subordinate individual but, under the cloak of possession, from the powerful orisha.[4]

As a catalyst for resistance, Santería has always played a role in the political development of Cuba. In the summer of 1958 Fulgencio Batista spent thousands of dollars to convene a meeting of santeras/os to summon the orishas to aid him against the forces of Castro's revolution. For many Cubans, the battle between Batista and Castro was as much a spiritual war as a military one, and Castro won because of the *ebbos* (incantations conducted through a sacrifice offered to an orisha) done on his behalf. Ebbos done by the vulnerable disenfranchised became a safe alternative to challenging the dictatorship of Batista, and thereby also allowed them to participate safely in the triumph of Castro.

Castro's revolution symbolically tied itself to Santería. The revolutionary guerrillas were based in Oriente, the colonial haven for runaway slaves and a stronghold for African religions. Many of the guerrillas, upon entering La Habana, wore *elekes* (beads) and waved the red and black flag of the 26th of July Movement. These colors are significant because they belong to Ellegúa, the trickster, who determines destiny and fate. Ellegúa is also considered first among the trio of holy warriors (Oggún and Ochosi being the other two). As these colors triumphantly arrived at La Habana, spectators familiar with Santería saw Ellegúa (the appropriate symbol for what was to be a self-proclaimed guerrilla society) enter the city, ready to protect Cuba and her people. Crucial was the date of the rebels' entry into La Habana: January 1, Niño de Atocha's day, the holiest day of the orishas when the course of history is set for the rest of the year.

The most often cited evidence of Castro's being chosen by the orishas occurred on January 8, 1959, during his first national speech from Camp Columbia: while he pleaded for unity and peace, a white dove landed on his shoulder. In addition to being a symbol for the Holy Spirit, the white dove is also a symbol of Obatalá, the son of Olodumare. One pataki states that during a physical battle between the brothers Changó and Oggún, Obatalá appeared on the scene. Suddenly a white dove hovered over the combatants, bringing an end (however temporarily) to the brothers' feuding. Castro symbolically occupied a dual religious persona. For Christians, he assumed the role of the Son of God, the Prince of Peace (Matt. 3:16–17). For santeros/as, he appeared as Obatalá, the divine provider of peace. Obatalá is particularly important because in one of his *caminos* (paths, ways, avatars), known as Oshacriñán, he is manifested as the crucified Christ. Even Cuba's oldest daily newspaper, the conservative *Diario de la Marina,* did not miss the religious significance of the moment, referring to the incident as an "act of Providence."

A more recent example of how Santería has had an impact upon the Cuban communities is the Elián story, the boy found off the coast of Florida surrounded by dolphins on Thanksgiving Day 1999. One of the side stories to the Elián saga told of a note Lazaro González, the boy's great-uncle and Miami guardian, wrote to Elián's Cuban grandmothers. He entrusted the note to Sister Jeanne O'Laughlin, host to the boy's grandmothers in late January 2000 during their trip to the United States. Sister O'Laughlin forgot to pass the note on, finding it in her pocket days later. The note was a warning to the grandmothers that Castro wanted the child so that he could make a Santería sacrifice of Elián. This concern was based on the most-repeated rumor on the streets of Miami, that Castro was forewarned of a child saved by dolphins in the sea who will overthrow his regime. Castro had to acquire the boy to prevent the fulfillment of this prophecy. Elián (Jesus) was being sought by Castro (Herod), who wanted to kill the messiah who threatened his rule. Even Miami's Auxiliary Bishop Agustin Román was quick to make the comparison between Castro and Herod after reading the Scriptures about Herod wanting Jesus killed to preserve his reign. According to Resident and Exilic practitioners of Santería, Castro participates in this Afro-Cuban religion, even traveling to Africa to be initiated into its mysteries. But according to the annual oracles, Castro offended quasi-deity Ellegúa, the first and most powerful orisha.

Throughout Cuban history Christ has been represented by cultural symbols. The Cuban quest for Christ thus requires a serious consideration of historical symbols in order to comprehend how the Deity communicates to the Cuban people. So far, we have seen how the Cuban understanding of Christ has been influenced by the oppression experienced by the Taínos, by the rebellion against Spanish colonialism as advocated by Varela's nationalism, and by the desire to thwart U.S. imperialism of Martí's postnationalist quest to establish a just Cuba. In this chapter, Cuba's black community—its history, culture, and religious expression—also become important ingredients for construing the Cuban Christ. A Cuban Christ that is black unmasks oppressive racist structures that are normative in the white Cuban mind. The black Christ represents the sociohistorical location of Cuba's most marginalized, providing them with a voice in the overall discourse of Cuban spirituality. The black Christ teaches all Cubans, black, biracial, and white, how to survive and how to overcome those stronger. Finally the black Cuban Christ serves as a guide to dismantling ingrained structures of Cuban racism in order to create a reconciled and just Cuban society. To ignore Christ's blackness is to ignore a major aspect of the Christ who is accessible to all Cubans.

Thus far, we have explored a Taíno and a black Christ, that is, a Christ who is in solidarity with Cuba's most disenfranchised communities. Although the investigation of Cuban racism, and by extension classism, is crucial in understanding the Cuban Christ, we have yet to consider the largest marginalized segment of Cuban society. For this reason, we now focus our attention on Cuban sexism. To ignore a Christ who is female limits the influence of Cuban women in the continuous search for the Cuban Christ. To consider only a Christ who is male confuses the divine with patriarchy, and hence justifies gender oppression. For this reason, our quest progresses in the next chapter to an examination of the female Christ.

The Female Cuban Christ

The conquest of Cuba began when the original inhabitants awoke to discover lost ships anchored off their coasts. Their first perception of Christianity came in the form of a cross emblazoned on the sails of these ships. Within a generation, they would discover that the cross was an instrument of death upon which los humildes are crucified. At first, the Taínos gawked in bewilderment at these new wonders and strange people, not fully aware of what would soon befall them. The Spaniards upon these ships stared back, assessing the island they would soon possess. These were the first Europeans to gaze upon the naked bodies of the indigenous people and the virgin land under their feet. Christopher Columbus's first comments about the inhabitants in his travel journal dealt with their naked bodies. He wrote, "They all go naked as their mothers bore them, and the women also . . . they were very well built, with very handsome bodies and very good faces" (1960, 22–24).

Columbus's first reaction was not to the lack of political organization of the island's inhabitants nor to the geographical placing of these islands within the world scheme. Rather, he noticed naked bodies, and specifically naked female bodies. The naked Amerindian woman signified the romance of conquest, which was simultaneously erotic and aggressive. Columbus and his men saw themselves as being invited to penetrate this new continent that offered herself without resistance. The titillating fantasies of the conquistadors intersected with their lust for political dominance (Mason 1990, 170).

The concept of virgin land represents the myth of empty land. The land awaiting violent possession of the would-be colonizer is conceived by the dominant conquistador as female, fertile, and wild. If land is indeed virgin, untouched, then the indigenous population has no aboriginal territorial claim, allowing for the colonizer "the sexual and military insemination of an interior void" (McClintock 1995, 30). On this momentous occasion, when the soon-to-be oppressors first gazed upon los humildes, their immediate conquest of the naked female bodies paralleled the eventual conquest of the land. Before Cuba was taken and ravished, women had to be reduced to the status of representational objects. Succinctly stated, the Spaniards' conquest of Cuba began with the literal sexual conquest of the Amerindian woman. These women were the spoils of war, and like the land were regarded as nonhumans in need of taming. Upon their bodies the act of colonialism began, as the so-called primitive virgin land willingly awaited insemination from the European male seed of civilization.

The colonialists' act in relation to the naked Amerindian women allowed Columbus to appropriate the role of reproducer. A "he" gives birth to the land, forgetting that the land has already been used by others before being "discovered" by the colonizers. Columbus named the erotic Other "Juana," ignoring and attempting to erase the Taíno's name for the island, Cubanacan.[1] The colonizer plants his flag upon her body and claims all the fruits she has to offer. Naming the naked island "Juana" reinterprets the indigenous culture and presents her as a virginal body to the European. Women, symbolized by land, need to be vanquished.

So complete was the sexual conquest of the island that prior to their return to Spain after the success of his maiden voyage, Columbus records in his diary accounts about an island called Matino believed to be entirely peopled by women (January 15, 1493 [1960, 150–51]). Rather than visiting it, Columbus immediately returned to Spain, possibly indicating that he and his crew had had their fill of erotic native women. Yet, once in Spain, Columbus immediately planned for a second expedition. In September 1493, he returned with seventeen vessels manned by fifteen hundred conquerors.

Accompanying Columbus on his second journey was an acquaintance named Miguel de Cuneo. As a reward for loyal service, Columbus gave him an indigenous woman (as though Columbus "owned" these women and was able to provide them as gifts). Cuneo proceeded to seduce his new "possession." When she resisted, he whipped her and commenced to rape her (Todorov 1984, 48–49). The violation of the unnamed possession of Miguel de Cuneo illustrates how the oppression of women is tied to the very fabric of the Cuban ethos. Conquistadors distributed Amerindian women among themselves to serve as permanent servants and gratifiers of sexual urges. In fact, the first generation of "Cubans" was the product of the Spaniard's rape of the Amerindian woman. Through the bruised and abused body of indigenous women like Cuneo's unnamed possession, Cubans were birthed.

This unnamed possession of Miguel de Cuneo was neither willing nor passive. She resisted. She, along with numerous other anonymous Amerindian women, fought against the invading Spaniards. They struggled and died along with their men for Cuba's liberation from armed invasion, testifying to their heroism and spirit of sacrifice. These dehumanized sexual possessions are among the first humildes of the island, humildes with whom Christ identifies. Additionally, they are the prototypes for the first Cuban *mambisas* (female freedom fighters).

Cueno's taking of the Amerindian woman also illustrates the Spaniards' attitudes toward race and sex. The Spanish understanding of racism was unlike that of other Europeans in North America, where laws were passed prohibiting racial mixing during their colonialization of the northern continent. For Spaniards, sexual relations were as natural as breathing or eating. Spanish men took indigenous women as bed partners, concubines, or wives. The children of these unions, claimed by the Spanish as their own, took their father's name. It is estimated that by 1514, 40 percent of Spanish colonizers had indigenous wives. By 1570, in accordance with the Council of Trent's elevation of marriage to a sacrament, the Crown forbade married men from traveling to the Americas for more than six months without their family. This edict resulted in more single men heading west, stimulating the rise of a miscegenational population (Mörner 1967, 35–52; Sauer 1966, 199). The blood of the conquerors and los humildes converged in the veins of Cubans. From this biological space, the quest for Christ continues. But how can a male Savior understand the sacrifice of the maltreated women who gave birth to Cubans? How does machismo inform the Cuban understanding of a male Christ? And how did this *machista* neurotic state develop?

In Cuba, unlike in other Latin American nations where the indigenous people were enslaved, the Spanish nearly exterminated the Taínos. To replace this vanishing population, the Spaniards imported Mayans and Africans as slaves. Later, they sought Chinese. The only concern of the slaveholders was the acquisition of cheap labor. Hence, slave merchants did not bother bringing women of color to the island, contributing to a predominately male society. By the same token, the white overlords were also mostly men, searching for gold and glory. Cuba was a stopoff point to the fortunes awaiting on the mainland. Few women had accompanied these conquistadors. Since the beginning of Cuban European history, its population lacked sufficient women of any color. This absence of women contributed to the creation of an excessively male-oriented society.

Furthermore, Cuba was the last Latin American nation to gain its independence from Spain. Rather than having a century of nation-building, Cuba spent the nineteenth century preoccupied with military struggles, contributing to a hyper-macho outlook. The physical bravado that characterized a century of bloody struggle for independence fused manhood with nationhood. Machismo became ingrained in the fabric of Cuban culture. Those who are victors of Cuban history inscribe their genealogies upon the national epic, genealogies emphasizing military victories and political achievements. These deeds are rooted in an anthropocentric memory reconstructed for a male-oriented future. This history becomes the official account, mirroring the actions and values caused by the forward thrust of predominately white, elitist Cuban men. Nevertheless, Christ is not found, nor understood, in the conquering male subject, nor in the subject's machista history. Christ is found in the locus of the conquered Other, in this case the feminine Other. Now, if all forms of structural oppression that eventually developed in Cuba found their roots in this machista-based male-female paradigm, then by seriously considering Cuban feminism, a process of liberation for los humildes can occur.

Seeking the voice of those who do not inhabit history critiques those with power and privilege who substitute their memory for forgotten history. Recalling history from the feminine underside forces the male subject to view the object as in fact external rather than simply a projection of the masculine ego's subjectivity. On the other hand, ignoring the voices of history's neglected justifies yesterday's sexual, racial, and economic domination, while it normalizes today's continuation of that oppression and prevents tomorrow's hope for liberation. This chapter specifically examines the oppression of Cuban women in order to understand a Christ who, like them, is female and as such can liberate los humildes.

Christ as Woman

The word "theology" literally means "the study of God." Theology attempts to understand the mysteries of the Deity, and traditionally theologians have emphasized God as the object of their discipline. Absent from such investigations is the role played by those doing the studying. Theology may aspire toward eternal and universal truths about the nature and essence of God, but all theology is contextual, done by human beings, limited by their finite identities and their place in society, culture, and history (De La Torre and Aponte 2001, 42). Traditional theologies, as done primarily by men, necessarily differ from the theology done by women. Yet theologies done by men have positioned themselves as more objective and more legitimate, while relegating theologies done by women to the periphery. What would happen if theology were done from the experience of women, specifically Cuban women? What if the experience of Cuban women became a resource for understanding the Deity? How could a male Christ become a female figure to inform and liberate the female social space? While a full investigation of a feminist Christology remains beyond the scope of this work, it is still important to have a basic understanding concerning how Christ can be appropriated by Cuban women to inform the continuing search for the Cuban Christ.

When I state that Christ is female, I am not denying the historical fact that Jesus, the Palestinian Jew who lived over two thousand years ago, was born with male genitals. Nor am I suggesting that Jesus was somehow androgynous. The Christmas story is the revelation of the Deity incarnated in male human form. If this is true, what then do I mean when I refer to the female Christ?

Throughout this book, I have relied on the biblical story that shows how Jesus seeks solidarity with the outcast of society. As previously mentioned, Jesus, in the parable of the sheep and the goats as recorded in the Gospel of Matthew (25:31–46), divides "the saved" (the sheep) from the "damned" (the goats). The salvation of those with power and privilege is contingent upon how they treated those who are the least within society, those who are excluded from full participation in the community. As this book has argued, it is los humildes who usually occupy this space. Counted prominently among los humildes, within all racial classes, are women.

Toward the end of the parable Jesus states (verse 45), "Then [the Lord] will answer [the condemned], saying, 'Truly I say to you, inasmuch as you did not do for one of these, the least [los humildes], neither did you do it to me.'" To see Jesus within Cuban history (or world history) is to see him among God's crucified people, those most oppressed by Cuba's structural sexism. To hear the voices, and to consider the plight of women denied the experience of full humanity, is to find Christ among them, for Christ will always identify with those most disenfranchised. Yes, even though Jesus was physically a male, Christ is symbolically female. Specifically, Christ is a Cuban woman, for within Cuban culture, historically and presently, women have always been "one of the least of these."

The experiences of these Cuban women as nonpersons become the subject of theology in the quest for the Cuban Christ, as their historical struggles become one of the sources that informs the understanding of a Christ who is Cuban. Such a process challenges the historical understanding of Christ that gives power and privilege to men because of their exclusive identification with Christ's maleness. It matters little if Christ's incarnation was manifested as male or female. Rather, the emphasis of the incarnation is the identification of Christ with the world's crucified people, los humildes. Although the totality of the incarnation has been reduced to the physical maleness of the body appropriated by God in God's revelation to humanity, the basic Christian understanding of Christ's body has always been the composition of the community of believers, male and female, acting as one body. As the Apostle Paul succinctly writes in his letter to the Galatians (3:28), "There is neither Jew or Greek [racism], slave or free [classism], male or female [sexism], for you are all one in Christ Jesus." For feminist theologian Elizabeth Johnson, "The guiding model for the [image of Christ] is not replication of sexual features but participation in the life of Christ, which is founded on communion in the Spirit . . . [but] when Jesus' maleness . . . is interpreted to be essential to his redeeming christic function and identity, then Christ serves as a religious tool for marginalizing and excluding women" (1998, 72, 151).

Mambisas Reveal Christ as Suffering Servant

Sexism is a social construction that assumes that males are inherently superior to females, and hence the very structures by which society functions are arranged to perpetuate this assumption. Operating from this premise, religion teaches that God made man in God's own image and women, a deficient copy, in the image of man; thus man is given divine authority to rule over women. Religious views such as these pervert human relationships by creating religious systems and social structures that advocate the domination of the group dismissed as defective. As feminist theologian Mary Daly reminds us, "If God is male, then the male is God" (1975, 38). As an elite group, men insist on their superiority over women, and justify their actions of domination and domestication in order to enhance their own social standings. Laws, established mostly by men, reinforce these so-

cietal assumptions about the nature of genders in order to establish a
power structure that becomes normative and legitimate in the minds and
hearts of the community, including the women abused by the system.
Women learn to perceive reality through the eyes of men (a type of false-
consciousness) and at times become the most vocal defenders of the status
quo.

Feminism was nonexistent during colonial Cuba, as women were limited to the domestic sphere (de Caturla 1945, 155). Like other Latin American nations, the husband/father in Cuba was the head of the family, solely
responsible for its wealth and all public relationships, under the patriarchal
legal concept known as *"patria potestad."*[2] Upon marriage a dependency
relationship was created as women forfeited their personhood before the
law. Their husbands assumed control over all their properties and legal
authority over women and children, while women, bound by law, were
required to obey and submit to their husbands. Under such an arrangement, women, through marriage, were "saved" from having to work as
domestic servants or prostitutes. As *"el bello sexo"* ("the beautiful gender"), women were taught, via church and social norms, a prescribed be-
havior of gracious submission to the authority of their fathers and husbands. A well-bred Cuban woman was considered desirable if she was
weak, beautiful, and meek. In theory Cuban women were to devote themselves to the finer aspects of life (the arts, charity, and so forth); in reality,
however, this was a privileged space of upper-class Cubans. For the vast
majority of Cuban women living in poverty, exhausting labor fended off
starvation.

As progressive as José Martí was in his political thoughts, he typified
the reigning chauvinism existing among Cubans when he equated the
manipulation common to political maneuvering to womanlike qualities.
Although he despised and challenged Euroamerican racism, he glamorized
North American sexist mores. He disliked the women of the United States
because they appeared "physically and mentally stronger than the young
man who courts her." For men like Martí, the future women of Cuba Libre
were to serve as a repository of inspiration, beauty, purity, and morality
lest the unleashed powers of female passion generate the destructive passion of men (Foner 1975, 36).

He ignored the role women could play in a new society by idealizing
them as mothers, mothers who produce male warriors to fight *la lucha*
(the struggle) for Cuban independence. Martí honored Mariana Grajales
Maceo (mother to Cuba's greatest general and military genius, Antonio

Maceo), whom he called *"la leona"* ("the lioness"), for her procreation of impressive male patriots. She, like most Cuban mothers, was responsible for teaching her boys to wield a machete, hate tyranny, and dream of a nonracist Cuba. Martí would comment, "Easy to become heroes with mothers like these." But while Martí sang the praises of la leona, he glossed over, if not totally ignored, the efforts of Cuban women of all colors who raised funds, aided refugees, outfitted insurgent forces, attracted Euroamerican support, fought as mambisas, started hospitals, and served as spies and couriers (Hewitt 1995, 23–32).

The participation of women in la lucha for national liberation coincided with their quest for personal liberation. Forty-nine women's clubs participated in Martí's coalition of revolutionary parties, the Cuban Revolutionary Party (PRC). Their presence assured them about forty percent of the delegates assigned to the task of making Cuba Libre a reality (Pérez 1999, 48–49). Many others served as soldiers in the field of battle, achieving commissioned status due to their skill and valor. For example, Magdalena Penarredonda y Doley rose from within the ranks to serve as general. Maria Hidalgo Santana, a poor black woman who rose to the rank of captain, fought in eight major battles until her death on the battlefield. About twenty-five women held ranks as officers, including a general, three colonels, and about twenty captains (Caballero 1982, 24, 32–46, 123–24). Many other women (including the mother and wife of Maceo) accompanied their men into battle, risking their lives to rush into the heat of combat to drag their wounded husbands and sons out of the crossfire.

Those who did not fight offered their meager food and possessions to freedom fighters that passed by their *bohíos* (shacks). In some cases, they turned their simple homes into field hospitals and convalescent homes for those wounded in battle. Women like the Afro-Cuban Rosa Castellanos, known as Rosa la Bayamesa, and Isabel Rubio, known as the Cuban Florence Nightingale, organized networks of field hospitals. With scarce resources, they fabricated weapons, tools, and other items needed by the revolutionary armies (de Caturla 1945, 156–57, 183, 185). There is no doubt that women played an indispensable role in la lucha for Cuba's independence.

These mambisas joined the list of patriots and martyrs, breaking through the socially prescribed model of womanhood, namely to be uneducated and male-dependent. The mambisas engulfed themselves in la lucha. Like their male counterparts, one in four died of starvation and disease in the last year of the war for independence (Stoner 1991, 13–17).

They were equal victims of the horrors of Spanish colonialism. As such, a spiritual union developed between men and women who fought, suffered, and died as a result of Spain's brutal attempt to hold onto the island.

These revolutionary women, having participated in the liberation of their land by becoming transforming agents of society, concurrently fought for their own liberation. Their heroic acts, sacrifices, and patriotism during la lucha against Spanish colonialism proved their ability and their right to participate in creating a new social order. Because of the blood women shed for Cuba Libre, they expected a voice in the construction of patria, a role beyond staying in the home birthing patriots. These women insisted that a newfound commonwealth would lack civilization unless women actively participated in the process of nation-building (Boloña 1905, 76). Their fathers and husbands had to admire their valiant service to la patria. To castigate the role women played as mambisas, regardless of how much their actions contradicted male notions of machismo, would undermine male virility and commitment to la lucha.

Yet, after the war for independence, the position of women within patria became unimportant. Women who lacked privilege (that is, women not of the elite social class) faced a dismal reality. The war shattered homes, forcing many women to be the sole source of family income. Nevertheless, only 9 percent of all women at the close of the nineteenth century were gainfully employed, representing 10.6 percent of the labor force. The majority of women were presumably housewives and older women. Those who were employed worked mostly as domestic servants (63 percent), followed by manufacturing, agriculture, and prostitution (Pérez 1988, 207–9). The latter was a consequence of (1) a lack of marketable skills, (2) a lack of education, (3) a need for income in order to survive, (4) limited opportunities, and (5) a result of being expelled from the countryside due to the reconcentration policy during the wars for independence. Undoubtedly, these women represented los humildes.

In paternalistic fashion, Cuban men, influenced by the so-called Age of Enlightenment, attempted to implement legislation favoring the status of Cuban women. By 1918, legislation favorable to women's rights was established, specifically in the areas of (1) free public education, which opened opportunities in teaching the young, including girls, a role previously delegated to the religious institutions; (2) labor rights, passed because of economic crises (not women's rights) that allowed women to comprise the cheapest labor pool, working as office clerks, nurses, minor bureaucrats, and unskilled labor in factories (specifically tobacco and textile); (3) property rights, which overthrew the centuries-old "patria potestad," not out of concern for women's rights, but because of the concerns of the gentry class to protect their privileged status during a time of economic uncertainties; and (4) no-fault divorce, as a way of driving a wedge between the church and state. During the passage of these reforms, "women's rights" was used as a battle cry by men to support or oppose the legislation. Yet few women participated in the discussions because no effective women's movement existed during this time (Stoner 1991, 34–53).

During the early 1910s, the first women's organizations began to be established, the most important being the Partido Nacional Sufragista, established in 1915 to secure civil and political rights through the vote, and the Club Femenino de Cuba, founded in 1917, followed by the creation of the Comité Pro Igualdad de la Mujer. By 1921 the last two groups mentioned, along with Congreso Nacional de Madres, Asociación de Católicas Cubanas, and Asociación Nacional de Enfermeras, organized an umbrella group called the Federación Nacional de Asociaciones Femeninas, which held its First National Women's Congress in La Habana in 1923. More women participated in public affairs as they became gainfully employed, reflected in an increase of 35 percent within the labor pool since the turn of the century. Yet their share of the total labor market declined from 10.6 to 9.4 percent (Pérez 1988, 237). Like the earlier mambisas, these women were concerned with creating patria by exercising their emerging voice. These women were interested in influencing legislation, particularly in the struggles for the vote; for equality of educational opportunity; for the development of cultural activities; for the protection of motherhood, and by extension, the family; for the improvement of employment prospects; for equal rights under the law; and for the elimination of the prevalent political corruption that existed during the early twentieth century. Their lucha for liberation was not viewed as solely applicable to women. Rather, their protest against the U.S.-backed governments during the republican years sought the liberation of the entire society, women and men, integrated as one cubanidad (de la Cruz 1980,2).

Yet Cuban feminist leadership constituted an elite group who did not need to work for a living. Many came from the propertied families. Because of their economic status, they tended to be more conservative, unwilling to challenge the normative societal structures that protected their class. Hence they did not radically oppose their husbands or the church, but rather attempted to influence reform from within their constructed space, a space that strived to preserve gender-specific roles, insisting that women were equal to, and distinct (due to motherhood) from men. Central to feminist thought was the proposition that a woman did not need to leave the household to claim her liberation; her liberation within society and her role within the household were not mutually exclusive (Barinaga 1931, 15). Yet, can it be that the ability to be active in both the public and private sphere remains a privilege of wealth as "darker" or poorer women assume the menial chores of the household?

The wealth, education (most had college degrees), and political connections (daughters or wives of politically powerful men) of these early feminists created a framework from which to advance their agenda. Yet their agenda dealt with the concerns of white middle- and upper-class Cuban women. All had at least one servant, lived in exclusive neighborhoods, and were married with children. Missing from the discourse were the voices of poor white women and women of color, or, in other words, the voices of their servants. Unlike the vast majority of Cuban women, none of these feminist leaders had any experience in being a domestic servant, a factory worker, a farmer, a low-level bureaucrat, or a sales clerk. As Stoner concludes, Cuban feminism only applied to privileged women (1991, 78–86).

By 1933, with the ouster of the Machado regime, Grau San Martín formed the first government without U.S. sanction or support. Under the slogan "Cuba for Cubans," many of the demands made during the 1920s became law. Among them was the abrogation of the Platt Amendment (by which the United States maintained a semblance of legality in its imperialistic venture toward the island), reduction in utility costs, eight-hour workdays, and a minimum wage for cane cutters. Also of importance was the granting of the vote to women. Yet the legal improvement of women did not necessarily translate into economic improvements. According to sociologist Lowry Nelson, during the early 1950s women composed a large number of the beggars stationed at the steps of churches throughout La Habana. For many, prostitution was the only option for earning a living. By 1958 nearly 11,500 women were prostitutes in La Habana, with some as young as fourteen years old. Suicide rates for women reached four hundred a year by the mid-1950s; an additional three thousand attempted it. By 1957 almost 70 percent of all children entering public orphanages had been abandoned in hospitals. Female poverty, prostitution, suicide, and mendicancy were visible manifestations of the condition of women prior to Castro's revolution (Pérez 1988, 304–5).

After the revolution, women were called upon to make the transition toward socialism. With the creation of the Federation of Cuban Women

(FCW), an important segment of the population was employed to combat the threat of counter-revolution. The FCW was a feminine organization, not a feminist organization, as self-described by its leaders. Women also joined the civilian militia, composing 44 percent of the Committees for the Defense of the Revolution's members by 1964. By the late 1960s, women were fully mobilized into the labor pool, specifically with the need to accomplish the "ten-million-ton sugar crop campaign" of 1969, working both in agriculture and in industry so as to free up men to cut cane. Women who had never worked outside the home now found themselves traveling across the island as teachers, administrators, and agricultural workers. Women were also incorporated into the early educational goals of the revolution. Over 56 percent of those who learned to read during the literacy campaign were women (Pérez 1988, 369–74).

Yet despite the attempts of women to influence and affect the creation of patria, its construction has always remained man's work. Even today, more than a century since mambisas shed their blood on the Cuban battlefield and forty years after the revolution, women are still denied positions of power. A double standard remains. While women may help achieve the goals of the state, they still must face a glass ceiling. Fidel Castro shared his machista views about the creation of revolution when he stated, "[Revolutionary Cuba] needed strong men to fight wars, sportsmen, men who had no psychological weakness" (Lumsden 1996, 53–54). One is left asking what role women play? Must they become, like Martí's "la leona," pseudomachos?

Sexism and machismo are not limited to just one side of the Florida Straits. Exilic Cubans also consider patria building the task of real men of valor. The majority of the women who immediately immigrated to the United States after the revolution belonged to the privileged class. The traditional role of staying in the household was shattered due to economic needs. Like other Latinas, Cuban women arriving in the 1960s found only dangerous, low paying, and degrading jobs. These women were able to gain employment faster than their male counterparts because the unskilled jobs that were available in Miami preferred women who could be given lower wages. By 1970, Exilic Cuban women constituted the largest proportionate group of working women in the United States. Their role as wage earners was more a response to economic survival than a response to the feminist movement for equality (García 1996, 109).

Eventually, the establishment of an economic ethnic enclave in Miami shielded more recent arrivals from the predicament still faced by other non-Cuban Latinas. Obviously, Exilic Cuban women still face discrimination, especially outside of Dade County. But the existence of an ethnic economic enclave, which facilitated the establishment of a Cuban power base in Miami, assisted Exilic Cuban women in obtaining otherwise unavailable higher status jobs. Today, among some Exilic Cuban women, status and social prestige are again measured by the ability to hire *una negrita* (a black girl, regardless of age) or *una india* (a mestiza) to come and clean house, raising issues on how race and class impact intra-Latina location and oppression.

Cuban women have nonetheless suffered for centuries under the ideology of machismo. These "suffering servants" contribute to the overall quest for the Cuban Christ. While many Christians historically referred to the "suffering servant" passage found in Isaiah 53 as messianic, that is, a foreshadow of the coming Christ, it has also been used as a reference to all of God's servants who suffer unjustly, as in the case of los humildes. Women, like Christ, represent suffering servants because manmade history has classified them as nonpersons.

Even though it is argued that God is beyond gender and that Christ can be symbolically understood in feminine form, Christ in the male figure of Jesus, as a model for women struggling to liberate themselves from patriarchal structures, may prove to be an ineffective paradigm. After all, women have suffered centuries-long servitude to men with the approving support of Christian churches operating in Christ's name. The question before us is whether or not God can be signified through a feminine symbol, a symbol indigenous to the Cuban culture. The Cuban form of Marianism, expressed through the veneration of La Virgen del Cobre, becomes one expression of Christ as God, not just for Cuban women, but also for Cuban men.

Liberation theologian Leonardo Boff makes a similar claim, insisting that the maternal face of God is represented by the Holy Spirit. The Spirit, as a member of the divine Trinity, appropriates the feminine aspect of God. The feminine dimensions of the Spirit—as counselor, advocate, and unconditional self-giver—emphasizes characteristics that have traditionally been ascribed to women. The feminine dimension of God, as manifested through the personhood of the Holy Spirit, is realized within the human experience of Marianism (Boff 1987, 101). The functions of the Spirit, as outlined by the biblical text, have been ascribed to Mary by the faithful.

Several U.S. Latino theologians have made a similar argument. They suggest that Marianism is not necessarily a veneration of the historical

Mary of Nazareth, Jesus' mother; rather, Marianism is a pneumatological issue. The manifestations of Mary in Cuba, or La Virgen de Guadalupe in Mexico for that matter, are acts of God's Spirit and not the historical Mary. The Holy Spirit reveals the divine to those historically oppressed in Cuba through La Virgen de la Caridad del Cobre. The encounter between los humildes of Cuba and La Virgen del Cobre is an experience of "God-who-is-for-us." These images become the authentic language by which God's Spirit communicates grace to the oppressed, a grace that confronts the reality of daily oppression and dehumanization (Espín 1999, 137–41). La Virgen del Cobre becomes a bearer of Cuban cultural identity, and as such serves as a rich religious source of empowerment, a resource that helps Cubans define and understand the Cuban Christ.

But to speak of La Virgen del Cobre requires us also to consider the African orisha Ochún. The female representation of the divine's presence has become a shared symbol appropriated both by the Catholic Church and the practitioners of Santería. It is an ambiguous symbol which, while not Christ, can serve to inform the shape of a Cuban Christ. For this reason, we turn our attention to Ochún as we continue our quest for the Christ who is a female Cuban.

Ochún Reveals the Ambiguous Christ of Mystery

Santería, the African-based religion of resistance and survival, contributes to the understanding of the Cuban Christ through the quasi-deity Ochún, known to Catholics as La Virgen de la Caridad del Cobre. Our quest for the Cuban Christ can be enhanced by exploring this feminine symbol. She serves as a religious model that underscores the divine as mystery. St. Augustine said it best: "If you understood, it is not God." Christ as mystery means no group can claim a monopoly on the normative view of Christ. To claim total comprehension and realization of the Deity is a delusional proposition, for God is beyond the conception of human minds. The final section of this chapter does not imply that La Virgen del Cobre/Ochún is a manifestation of Christ, rather, that the Virgin, specifically its African manifestation, helps us understand an aspect of Christ which, as mystery, uplifts los humildes.

Although Ochún and La Virgen del Cobre are two separate entities, in the minds of many Cubans they inhabit the same religious space. Ochún becomes the African Yoruba manifestation of the European Catholic La Virgen del Cobre. Ochún/La Virgen del Cobre, as a religious model, becomes one of the great representatives of Cuban identity and as such, may be one piece to the puzzle of understanding the Cuban Christ who is feminine.

As Ochún, we discover that there exist many *caminos* (paths) to her because she represents different realms of human life. Rather than a one-dimensional entity, Ochún, the youngest of all the orishas, has multiple meanings adaptable to the changing social milieu. As Ochún Yeyé Moró, she signifies the sensuous saint, knowledgeable in the art of lovemaking, akin to the Greek goddess Aphrodite or the Roman's Venus. As Ochún Kolé Kolé, she signifies the saint of poverty, the owner of one faded yellow dress who eats only what the vulture brings to her door. She represents and defends all women suffering at the hands of abusive men. She epitomizes both joviality and seriousness. She signifies frolicking, enjoying night-long dancing and parties as well as domesticity, sewing, and keeping house.[3] Like most Cuban women, she represents their different facets.

As La Virgen del Cobre, we discover a Catholic saint who made her appearance in Cuba early in Cuba's European history. According to the traditional Catholic version, around 1610 two Taíno Native American brothers, Juan and Rodrigo de Hoyos, along with a ten-year-old black slave named Juan Moreno (whose last name means "person of color"), went rowing on Nipe Bay in search of salt. Nipe Bay is not far from the copper mines of Cobre on the northwestern tip of the island. At about 5:30 in the morning, while paddling their canoe, they came upon a carved statue of the Virgin Mary floating on a piece of wood. Miraculously, the statue was dry. At her feet was inscribed "I am the Virgin of Charity." She was, in effect, *la primera balsera* (the first rafter) to be rescued.

During the time of her apparition, there were approximately twenty thousand inhabitants on the island of Cuba. This was a population in flux, composed of Spaniards, Amerindians, and Africans. The decimation of the Amerindians had reduced that group to less than two thousand, while the African population, at five thousand, was increasing because of the expansion of the slave trade. The Spaniards, comprising the rest of the population (about thirteen thousand), came to Cuba in search of fortune and glory, many only stopping over on their way to more exploitable lands on the continent, specifically Mexico. European women comprised less than 10 percent of the population, an imbalance persisting throughout the seventeenth century (Perez 1988, 45–47). This skewed European male-female ratio led to the taking of the indigenous and slave female populations by Spaniards, giving birth to the Cuban people and their ethos.

Cobre was a mining town where innumerable Amerindians died tunneling for copper. African slaves were beginning to replace them as Amerindians approached extinction. While these two peoples of the Cuban ethos suffered grave oppression, La Virgen del Cobre appeared to the "least" of Cuban society. Her apparition accomplished two tasks. First, she symbolized the birth of Cuban identity, the birth of cubanidad. Cuba's patron saint ceased to be a European white figure. Instead, the divine appeared in the form of a bronzed-colored woman, a color symbolizing death (the color of the mined copper responsible for the death of Amerindians and Africans), as well as life (the color of the Cuban new race). Second, to the oppressed she gave dignity. Rather than appearing to the white Spaniard religious leaders, she identified with the economic and racial outcasts, appearing in the color of oppressed Cubans. A biracial saint thus severs the bond between inferiority and non-whiteness, for the divine is represented as colored. Her presence allowed the two Juans and Rodrigo to become companions with the divine, and with them, all Cubans. Not surprisingly, the earliest devotees of the Virgin were the slaves working in the copper mines. For a time, the statue was housed in a slave hospital adjacent to the shrine at Cobre. Also, it was in Cobre where slaves were first emancipated.

Nonetheless popular modern icons of the Virgin represent her as white and blond. And in modern statues, one of the Amerindians has been replaced with a balding, bearded, and white-haired Spaniard. Rodrigo was transfigured into a white Spaniard named Juan, creating "los tres Juanes" (the three Johns) one white, one black, and one Amerindian. It is unlikely that a white Spaniard would have accompanied slaves on such an arduous and demeaning journey. He probably would have been too busy increasing his wealth through managing the mines. This bearded patriarchal figure rewrites itself into tradition, inserting and incorporating the oppressor into the drama and presenting him as an equal, thus masking the power relation existing at this time.

During the nineteenth century wars for independence, Mary became a crucial symbol. Latin American leaders credited her as an effective weapon in their struggle for autonomy, and she became the protector of numerous independence movements. The wars for Cuban independence were no different. These struggles elevated the Virgin's prominence among all Cubans. Freedom fighters wore her image on their clothes while their families sought protection for them by making promesas (vows). For her intervention in Cuba's struggle for independence, veterans petitioned the pope to declare her officially the Patron of Cuba. On May 10, 1926, Pope Benedict XV honored their request.

Nevertheless, Exilic Cubans tragically separated from the land of their birth by Castro's 1959 revolution felt that they lost their "virgencita," who has always been tied to Cuban soil. In 1973, in order to rectify this separation, Exilic Cubans built on Biscayne Bay in Miami, Florida, a tent-like shrine for La Virgen de la Caridad, to serve as both a political and a sacred space. She faces the ocean, a beacon for those who cross over to the United States. According to a pamphlet titled "Our Lady of Charity Shrine," which is distributed at the site, "[the shrine] is situated with its back toward Cuba so that prayers may be offered by the faithful looking toward Cuba." Besides praying to Cuba, Saturday evening masses are broadcast to the island on Sundays via Radio Martí. Upon this sacred ground Exilic Cubans construct the image of a nation while living in a foreign land. This substitute shrine, interwoven with Cuban patriotism, is illustrated by the mural behind the altar and icon.

This impressive mural, painted by Exilic Cuban Teok Carrasco, merges religious and patriotic emotions (figure 1). The mural, titled *The History of Cuba in a Glance*, retells the story of Cuba, beginning with Columbus (hence history begins with European penetration) and ending with the Exile (hence ignoring the events that have taken place on the island since the Exilic Cubans' departure). Besides ignoring Amerindians and Resident Cubans, it also ignores the effects of Spanish colonialism and U.S. imperialism (the Statue of Liberty appears as a symbol of hope). The image of the Virgin occupies the central position as Cuban history swirls around her. José Martí (father of Cuban independence) also occupies a prominent spot (directly to her right), ensuring the bond between nationalism and the sacred. Forgotten are Martí's sharp critiques of the Catholic Church. His reincarnation as a child of the church is crucial in the construction of "*la Cuba de ayer*" ("the Cuba of yesterday") myth. This mural provides a vision of nationhood that can only be realized with the return of the Exiles to the island. Standing in the shrine, one can simultaneously occupy space in both la Cuba de ayer and the Miami of today. This illusion, created by the physical presence of the Cuban shrine of Cobre reproduced on U.S. soil, provides the Exilic Cuban with the temporary and illusory luxury of avoiding the reality of Exilic status.

The presence of Cuba's patron in the Miami shrine indicates that she too came from Cuba as an exile, just as in the Bible the divine left the

Fig. 1. Teok Carrasco, *The History of Cuba in a Glance,* courtesy of Bishop Agustin A. Román.

rightful habitation of the "defiled" Jerusalem to reappear before the exiled Ezekiel. Glory lives in the exile, with humiliated and abandoned people. From exile, God begins a new history. This is not the first time she is manifested as a wandering symbol of her people. As Ochún, she journeyed from Africa when her African children were forced by slave traders to go to Cuba. She consulted the quasi-deity Yemayá, who admitted the orishas' powerlessness in preventing this catastrophe.[4] Because of Ochún's love for her children, she decided to accompany them to Cuba. She first asked Yemayá to straighten her hair and lighten her skin to the color of copper, so that all Cubans might join together in worshiping her. Just as the Yoruba slaves found a source of support and comfort in Ochún when facing the difficulties of colonial Cuba, Exilic Cubans today discover the same support and comfort in La Virgen del Cobre when facing refugee status in a foreign land (De La Torre 2001, 847–56). Ochún/La Virgen del Cobre becomes more than a national symbol; she is also sacred. Christ, like Ochún/La Virgen del Cobre, becomes a model for women seeking their humanity, apart from patriarchal structures created by Cuban machismo. Her role within the Cuban ethos signifies liberation for all Cubans, particularly Cuban women.

Yet Christ, as we have seen, has been used and abused to advance the political agenda of those with power or desiring to capture power. This abuse is evident throughout the twentieth century, when three different images of Christ emerged in Cuba. In the next chapter, the search for the Cuban Christ continues as these three Christs are unmasked in hopes of revealing the Christ of los humildes.

Three Christs for the Twentieth Century

The twentieth century was a century of nation building for Cuba, characterized by sociopolitical, economic, and cultural turmoil. The radical transformations that Cuba experienced resulted in an ongoing search to construct and define Cuban identity. Cuba was the last country in the Americas to break free from traditional colonialism. Most of Latin America overthrew their Spanish colonizers and began constructing their own brand of nationalism by the early nineteenth century. With each defeat in the Latin American wars for independence, large numbers of reactionary Spanish troops and upper-class royalist refugees came to Cuba with tales of dislocation and misery. As the Spanish empire withered, Spain held on to Cuba, nicknamed *"siempre leal isla Cuba"* ("the ever-faithful isle of Cuba"), with blinding tenacity. Yet under the mask of loyalty existed discontent. Spain was determined to maintain Cuba's subservient role, committing troops and resources to thwart all attempts at self-determination.

In spite of the odds, Cuba fought for liberation. Yet the hope of gaining total and complete independence from Spain was quickly subverted by the rise of the U.S. empire. The neocolonialization of Cuba also had its religious counterpart, as the Euroamerican Christ became part of the Cuban religious ethos. Rebellion against imperialism gave rise to Cuban nationalism, concluding with Fidel Castro's assuming of political control in 1959. Again, Christ and sword merged, this time to serve the revolution. With the Castro regime came a new theology known as theology in revolution, and with it, a continuation of the attempt to create an indigenous Cuban Christ.

Castro was initially supported by a large segment of the Cuban population, but another faction fled, settling mostly in Miami, Florida. This latter group went into the diaspora, hoping and praying for a quick return. More than four decades have passed and they are still hoping and praying. During their exile, they too merged Christ with the sword to create the Christ of el exilio. La lucha against Castro became a holy war against the forces of darkness, in which the defeat of Castro represents the eventual eschatological defeat of Satan. This chapter will attempt to examine these three manifestations of Christ and his church as we continue our quest for the Christ of Cuba.

The Euroamerican Christ of Imperialism

The first Euroamerican Protestant worship service in Cuba (excluding the brief English occupation in the 1700s) was held on a U.S. gunboat in 1871 in La Habana Harbor, officiated by Bishop Benjamin Whipple, an Episcopalian. This event characterizes the relationship that eventually developed between the United States and Cuba, a relationship that understood the political through the spiritual. Once again, the sword and the cross joined forces to create a Christ more concerned with establishing, justifying, and defending political reality than with spiritual piety. John Sayles's fictional story humorously illustrates the relationship between Cubans and Euroamericans. He writes:

> [Liborio was] a zafrista, a poor cane-cutter, in the days just after la Guerra de Independencia [War of Independence].[1] One afternoon he is alone in the cane field, still cutting as others ate their meager lunch, and he chops through a row of cane to discover God, sitting in an expensive white suit on a little stool, the type colonos [sugar planters] used when they stopped to survey their property.
>
> "Buenos días, Liborio," said God. "I have come to see how my Cubanos are doing."
>
> Liborio stood with his clothes soaked with sweat, his hands cracked and bleeding, his feet bare and filthy. He stuck his machete into the ground, spit out the piece of cane he had been chewing on, and thought for a long time about what he should say to God.
>
> "First of all, Señor," he said, "we are no longer subjects of the King of Spain. We are free men."
>
> "I can see that," said God, looking at Liborio from head to foot. "The difference is astounding."
>
> "But I wonder something," Liborio continued, "why life is still so hard?"
>
> God smiled at him. "My son, nothing on this earth can be perfect, or nobody would want to go to Heaven. Sugar is sweet, but man has

to labor to take it from the ground. The ocean is wide and bountiful, but it has sudden storms and dangerous currents to pull you under and drown you. This Cuba is so beautiful, the pearl of all my creation, so I had to make the pests, the mosquitos, the sea urchin, the thorn of the marabú, all so life here would be less than Paradise. Nothing can be perfect in this world."

Liborio pondered this, trying to fathom the wisdom of God's ways. "But nothing can mar the beauty of freedom," he said finally. "Surely freedom is perfect?"

God smiled again, "For that," he says, "I created los yanquis [the Yankees]." (1991, 258–59)

After Teddy Roosevelt "saved" Cuba from the Spanish empire, U.S. Protestants attempted to save Cuba from Roman Catholicism. Modern Euroamerican nationalism took shape when the United States asserted itself beyond its borders, beginning with Cuba. Upon the safe domain of Cuban land, the United States launched its venture into world imperialism. Earlier conquests of northern Mexico represented the expansionist ideology of extending U.S. boundaries and physically possessing and re-populating the new lands. Cuba represented a shift in this strategy toward imperialism.

Maturing as an empire, the United States was less interested in acquiring territory than in controlling peripheral economies to obtain financial benefits for itself. A dependency relationship with Cuba, masked under the guise of Cuban independence, was preferable to incorporating an "undesirable" people into the Union. Then Senator John M. Thurston, advocating U.S. involvement in Cuba's War for Independence, bluntly expressed the anticipated benefits for United States businesses. He correctly prophesied the future when he said:

War with Spain would increase the business and earnings of every American railroad, it would increase the output of every American factory, it would stimulate every branch of industry and domestic commerce, it would greatly increase the demand for American labor and in the end every certificate that represented a share in any American business enterprise would be worth more money than it is today. (Thomas 1971, 371)

Martí recognized the threat of what he called the "New Rome." From New York he wrote a letter to his friend Gonzalo Quesada:

We need to know the position held by this avaricious neighbor who admittedly has designs on us before we rush into a war that appears to be inevitable, and might be futile, because of that neighbor's quiet determination to oppose it as a means of leaving the island in a state enabling it to lay hands on Cuba at a later date . . . And once the United States is in Cuba, who will drive it out? (Martí 1977, 244–46)

Possessing Cuba did not entail annexation. By 1906, there was no desire on the part of the United States to incorporate into the Union what they perceived to be an "inferior" people. In his September 16, 1906, letter to President Roosevelt, Senator Lodge sums up Euroamerican attitudes when he writes:

Disgust with the Cubans is very general. Nobody wants to annex them but the general feeling is that they ought to be taken by the scruff of the neck and shaken until they behave themselves. It is a great disappointment to me and I had hoped better things of them . . . I would think that this Cuban performance would have the anti-imperialist think that some peoples were less capable of self-government than others. (Lodge 1925, 232–33)

A recurring theme found in the writings and speeches of Euroamericans in Cuba dealt with Cubans' supposed incompetence for self-government. Exilic Cuban historian Louis Pérez lists a chorus of quotes to substantiate the Euroamerican attitude toward Cubans. For example, General Young, division commander in the Spanish-American War, said, "[The Cuban] insurgents are a lot of degenerates, absolutely devoid of honor or gratitude. They are no more capable of self-government than the savages of Africa." General Shafter, field commander in the Spanish-American War, said, "Self-government! Why those people [Cubans] are no more fit for self-government than gunpowder is for hell." Major Barbour, U.S. sanitary commissioner for Santiago de Cuba, said, "[The Cubans] are stupid, given to lying and doing all things in the wrong way . . . Under our supervision, . . . the people of Cuba may become a useful race and a credit to the world." Major Brodie said, "The Cubans are utterly irresponsible, partly savage, and have no idea of what good government means." Governor General Brooke said, "These people cannot now, or I believe in the immediate future, be entrusted with their own government." Governor General Wood said, "We are dealing with a race that has steadily been going down for a hundred years and into which we have to infuse new life, new principles and new methods of doing things." And one New York journalist wrote, "If we are to save Cuba, we must hold it. If we leave it to the Cubans, we give it over to a reign of terror—to the machete and the torch, to insurrection and assassination" (1988, 180–81). When the Cuban army requested to be present during the ceremonies witnessing Spain's departure from the island, the United States rejected the request. Thus on January 1, 1899, noon, the Spanish flag was lowered and the U.S. flag was raised. It was the United States, not Cuba, who bid Spain farewell and was present during the symbolic "transfer of power." Even when the military departure of the United States eventually occurred, subservient puppet officials were chosen to serve as leaders of the new Cuban Republic. Yet, there was no doubt as to who was in charge.

The Spanish-American War reduced Cuba to a wasteland, yet a new generation of Euroamerican carpetbaggers saw Cuba as virgin territory. By 1905 they had acquired title to 60 percent of all rural property. Another 15 percent of rural land remained in the hands of resident Spaniards (Pérez 1988, 195–96). Economically, the United States was able to step in and replace the bankrupt Cuban ruling class. The war for independence created widespread indebtedness, providing cheap land and labor for the Euroamerican capitalists. Bankrupt properties were easily acquired by paying back taxes. Cuba's traditional oligarchies virtually disappeared as they were replaced by those friendly to the new U.S. forces, usually Spaniards who remained after the war. During military occupation, Military Governor Wood granted 218 tax-exempt mining concessions, mostly to U.S. firms.

Between 1909 and 1929, U.S. capital investment in Cuba increased by 700 percent. Approximately 80 percent of Cuba's imports and 60 percent of her exports came from or went to the United States. During the 1920s, 95 percent of Cuba's main crop, sugar, was bound for the United States, while 40 percent of all raw sugar production was owned by Euroamericans; two-thirds of the entire output of sugar was processed in U.S.-owned mills (mostly located in Baltimore and other U.S. cities), and the product left the island through the Havana Dock Company, also in U.S. hands. Additionally, 23 percent of non-sugar industry, 50 percent of public service railways, and 90 percent of telephone and electric services were owned by U.S. firms. Nickel deposits were mined and processed by Nicaro, a U.S.-built plant. Of the four oil refineries, two were owned by U.S. companies, a third by Royal Dutch Shell. All banks were in U.S. and British hands, with one-quarter of all deposits located in foreign branches. Approximately 90 percent of the export trade of Havana cigars went through Euroamerica, which controlled half of the entire manufacturing process (Thomas 1971, 466; Newman 1965).

The U.S. domination of the Cuban market bordered on the absurd. Cuba exported raw sugar to the United States while importing candy. It exported tomatoes, and imported all its tomato paste. Cuba would export fresh fruit to receive canned fruit. It would export rawhide and import shoes. It produced vast quantities of tobacco, yet imported cigarettes (Benjamin et al. 1984, 13). Regardless of this economic arrangement, Cuban national elites were able to amass wealth, power, and privilege even though they did not control the means of production.

U.S. control of Cuba's economic and political affairs occurred in order to help "civilize" the Cuban people. This tutelage encompassed a religious dimension. Like the priests who came with the conquistadors four hundred years earlier, Protestant missionaries accompanied the U.S. occupational army, despite the fact that Protestant communities had existed on the island since the early nineteenth century. Cuba is the only Latin American country where the first permanent Protestant congregation was founded by nationals and not by Europeans, because of Cuban converts in New York (1866), Tampa, and Key West (1870) who returned to the island after the signing of the so-called peace treaty ending the first war for Cuba's independence (1868–78). Exilic Cubans like Díaz and de la Cova (Southern Baptist); Moreno, Duarte, Báez, and Peña (Episcopal); Someillán and Silvera (Methodists); and Collazo (Presbyterian) are but a few of the individuals who formed churches whose members were entirely Cuban (Ramos 1986, 91–106). Although Cuban Protestants may proudly claim that the first Cuban congregation was founded by Cubans, the fact remains that 95 percent of the resources needed to build and maintain these Protestant churches in Cuba came from the United States.

The appeal of Protestantism lay in the array of social services provided, especially in the neglected rural areas. Protestants started orphanages, created grade schools, distributed food and clothing, dispensed agricultural equipment and tools, established clinics, provided free vocational classes, and gave English-language instruction. Besides the material sustenance, Protestants offered an alternative moral system that implied modernity, prosperity, and progress. Like those who came to govern, missionaries also saw their role as agents for civilization, perceiving the Cuban as morally deficient and intellectually backward. Euroamerican missionaries operated during the transition from Spanish colonialism to U.S. imperialism. They served the important role of confronting the Cubans with their supposedly defective character by offering redemption within normative Eurocentric structures (Pérez 1999, 58, 248–51).

Cuban Protestantism ceased to be Cuban with the end of the Spanish-American War. Unlike other Latin America countries where missionaries came from both the United States and Europe, the vast majority of Cuba's Protestant missionaries came exclusively from the United States. U.S. Mission Boards, which before the Spanish-American War had limited themselves to economically helping the efforts of local Cubans, now took over the Protestant movement, relegating Cubans, who until then had led the movement, to secondary positions. While Cubans may have maintained some influence over missionaries, Euroamericans always had the last word (Ramos 1989, 23, 29).

But why the need to send missionaries to a country where the vast majority claimed to worship Christ? Because Cubans were worshiping the "wrong" Christ. To be a Christian meant more than the acceptance of the Euroamerican Christ as Lord and Savior; it also encompassed the acceptance of U.S. political, economic, and cultural institutions and practices. If the United States represented the new Jerusalem, then part of Manifest Destiny was to spread the Euroamerican Protestant Christ in order to overcome the "heresy" of Roman Catholicism. Protestant Christian magazines at the turn of the century described the military intervention in Cuba as an "act of providence," a response to a "Macedonian Call." Euroamerican imperialism was masked by a zealous understanding of Christ's mission in regards to Cuba, as illustrated in the following typical comment expressed in church newsletters during the late 1890s:

> The Churchmen of our [U.S.] land should be prepared to invade Cuba as soon as the army and navy open the way, to invade Cuba in a friendly, loving Christian spirit, with bread in one hand and the Bible in the other, and win the people to Christ by Christlike service. (Hageman 1971, 21)

The imposition of the Euroamerican Jesus resulted in neutralizing Cuban spirituality in the same way that imperialist policies emasculated the nation politically.

The true intents and assumptions of the United States were reflected in the operational practices of most Protestant denominations. They normalized the dominant position of the United States by placing the missionary activities conducted in Cuba under the auspices of denominational "home" mission boards as opposed to the foreign mission boards. Some Cubans converted to Protestantism as a devout spiritual response to the missionaries' message, while some converted because it seemed a prudent economic and social response to the Euroamerican presence in Cuba.

Since military occupation, immediately following Cuba's war for independence, approximately fifty denominations were established in Cuba. In 1902 an interdenominational conference convened in Cienfuegos to divide the spoils of war. Northern Baptists were given Oriente and Camagüey; Southern Baptists acquired Las Villas, La Habana, and Pinar del Rio. Eastern Cuba was divided between Quakers and Methodists, while western zones were allotted to Presbyterians and Congregationalists. Episcopalians were awarded Matanzas and Santiago de Cuba. Cities in excess of six thousand inhabitants were declared open territory.

Their ties with Euroamerican capitalists were obvious. For example, the Methodist Candler School in La Habana was funded by and named after the founder of Coca-Cola. John D. Rockefeller helped establish a boarding school for boys in El Cristo. The United Fruit Company in Banes and the Cuban-American Sugar Company in Puerto Padre subsidized the Quakers. The United Fruit Company provided three hundred rent-free acres to the Methodist Agricultural and Industrial School in Preston, Oriente. And Hershey funded a Presbyterian agricultural school in Aguacate. Graduates of these schools usually took managerial jobs representing the interests of their Euroamerican benefactors (Pérez 1995, 63–71). Mainline churches brought their liturgical, theological, and architectural styles. Those who converted to Protestantism tended to be of modest social origins from the working and lower-middle class, living U.S. lifestyles and supporting Euroamerican issues. They were presented with a pietist Christ who was mainly concerned with conservative individualism.

The Catholic Church did not exactly provide a patriotic alternative. Cubans were indifferent toward the church. According to the Exilic Cuban Jesuit Calixto C. Masó y Vazquez, the Cuban population during the early twentieth century "always gave little importance to religious problems, being neither atheist nor fanatical, nonetheless their religiosity, above all else the practice of their religious duty, almost bordered on indifference" (1998, 467). Additionally, the church followed the lead of Pope Leo XIII, who supported Spain in its conflicts with the Cuban insurgents. The Catholic clergy were more committed to the Crown. The church's decision to side with Spain left freedom fighters no alternative but to battle the church also. On the eve of Spain's defeat, the bishop of La Habana, fearing a Protestant invasion, wrote a pastoral letter "for civilization, against barbar-ism," that is, for colonial rule instead of independence (Dewart 1963, 93).

Coinciding with the Euroamericanization of Cuban Protestantism was an intense Euroamericanization of the Catholic Church under the leader-ship of individuals like the apostolic delegate Archbishop Chapelle and ar-riving Euroamerican priests who opened schools (Ramos 1989, 25). The Vatican further assisted with the Euroamericanization process by appoint-ing Donato Raffaele Sbarretti as the new archbishop of La Habana. Sbarretti had recently served as auditor of the apostolic delegation in Washington, D.C., and had excellent contacts with U.S. government officials. Moreover, while direct ties between the Catholic Church and Spain were weakened, priests continued to go to Cuba from Spain. Throughout the republican years, the priesthood, which was predominately Spanish and white, be-came an important voice on the island by catering to and identifying with the economically powerful elite of La Habana. Their respectability lay in their Spanish roots. Of the three thousand Catholic priests in Cuba on the eve of the revolution in 1959, approximately twenty-five hundred were from Spain, trained during the Franco dictatorship and highly influenced by the bitter Spanish Civil War victory over communism that had clothed itself in heavy religious overtones. Some of these priests went to Cuba as ecclesiastical exiles, sent from Spain as a form of punishment for church-related infractions. These priests were not the best and brightest Spain had to offer, and almost all considered Cuba a post to avoid (Thomas 1971, 683–84). Most of these priests concentrated on running schools, which were also staffed by foreigners, located in the cities, and, due to their high tu-ition, excluded people of both color and low-income (Maza 1982, 65).

Most religious institutions in Cuba before the revolution, Protestant and Catholic, were controlled by foreigners hostile to leftist perspectives. Furthermore, in an effort to increase their political power, these churches attempted to establish and maintain links with the different conservative political regimes that ruled Cuba, regardless of corruption and disregard for socioeconomic justice.

The Resident Christ of Revolution

Although Cuba is rich in fertile soil and minerals and boasted the highest per capita income (after Venezuela) in Latin America during the 1950s, the majority of its relatively small population (6.4 million in 1957) lived in desperate poverty. La Habana had one of the world's highest cost-of-living indexes. Because most of the Cuban economy operated within the economic framework of the United States, it would be misleading to compare Cuba's per capita income with that of other Latin American nations; comparison must rather be made with the United States. Such a comparison reveals Cuba's per capita income late in the 1950s to be $312, less than half of that of the poorest state of the Union, Mississippi, at $829, and about one-sixth of the richest state, Delaware, at $2,279 (Huberman and Sweezy 1989, 5–7).

Who benefited from Cuba's relationship with the United States? The Cuban elite, who developed a desire for Euroamerican goods. It would be erroneous to assume that U.S. imposition was opposed by all Cubans. Exilic Cuban historian Louis Pérez documents how Cubans willingly participated in creating the social structures by which the Euroamerican hegemony was maintained. The success of the United States in Cuba was less a function of political or military control than a cultural condition designed to construct Cuban identity via the Euroamerican ethos (1999, 9–10). This becomes evident in the religious sphere, where Christ became defined by Euroamerican religious sensibilities.

The ability to succeed in Cuba economically required an ability to speak English (during the early military occupations by the United States, English was the primary language taught in schools). Handpicked financial advisors were needed to manage the assets of absent Euroamericans. The advisors were mostly white, educated in the States, and pro-United States. Their collaboration, instead of confrontation, provided opportunities for exploitation within their own satellite population, the Cuban rural periphery. La Habana developed at the expense of the economically declining countryside (a historical norm even under Spaniard colonialism). The rural areas had almost no schools or churches. Years would pass between church masses and the administration of the sacraments. More than 90 percent of the area lacked electricity, milk, fish, meat, or bread. Illiteracy in rural areas was four times that of urban areas. While La Habana boasted one doctor for every 220 persons, rural Oriente had one doctor for every 2,423 persons. Total wages during the 1950s rose by 22 percent in La Habana while the rest of the island experienced a decline (Huberman and Sweezy 1989, 5–7; Newman 1965; and Thomas 1971, 557, 601).

Hence, the rise of Cuban nationalism during the 1920s directly related to U.S. economic and political domination. The political elite were reviled for willingly submitting to the United States. Fervor for national independence fanned anti-imperialist fires and began to play a central role in Cuban politics. Disgust at Cuba's subservient position meant that any revolution conducted during the 1950s would be anticapitalist and anti-Euroamerican. When Castro forces succeeded, a frustrated United States hoped to bring Cuba into line. It resorted to the 1933 tactic of suspending Cuba's sugar import quota. Such a move would normally have suffocated Cuba's attempt to implement nationalist economic policies; however, a new element was added to the old equation. The Soviet Union offered an alternative market for Cuban sugar and, as such, a way to resist the hegemonic power of the United States.

Admission into the Soviet bloc, however, exchanged one hegemonic power for another. Different organizational principles and economic paradigms were required to insure Cuba's survival and constructed an indigenous form of socialism. The rapid reorganization of Cuba's economy, the external pressure of the United States, the legacy of centuries of colonialism, the development of unrealistic economic goals, the mismanagement caused by inexperienced personnel in turn caused by departing high-management-level Cubans, the constant flow of administrative improvisations, and the switch in priority to industrialization over the island's economic dynamo, sugar, created inevitable economic failures during the attempt to build socialism.

There were also, however, some successes. Submitting to the Soviet Union and becoming the sugar bowl of the Eastern bloc resulted in economic growth measured by a sustained rise in productivity. During the 1970s and early 1980s Cuba's economy enjoyed respectable rates of growth because (1) the Soviet Union allowed Cuba to sell on the free market any Soviet oil not domestically consumed; (2) Cuba improved planning techniques; and (3) Cuba began to grant material incentives for laborers rather than expecting an increase in production based on moral obligation.

Nevertheless, the world's rejection of Marxism, symbolized by the crumbling of the Berlin Wall, sent Cuba into an economic tailspin as the foundation of the "socialist paradise" ended. The end of Soviet subsidies, euphemistically called the "special period," was marked by the abrupt end of about 85 percent of Cuba's foreign trade with the Soviet Union and the Eastern European community, causing imports to drop by 75 percent and the gross national product to drop by 60 percent. Sugar production dropped to less than four million tons (the lowest since 1963), while factories produced at 30 percent capacity.

With the end of the Soviet Union, Cuba experienced "independence" for perhaps the first time since 1492. But this form of independence from foreign powers came at a price. The new world order has forced Cuba to abolish the Central Planning Board responsible for piloting the state-directed economy. By the end of 1994 Cuba had signed joint ventures with 185 foreign corporations. As a result, tourism increased (17 percent between 1991 and 1993) and Western consumer products were introduced. These measures have contributed to the island's turning a crucial financial corner since the economic collapse of 1993. While the economic free fall has been stopped by cracking a window to the economic breeze of the free market, inequalities caused by these latest initiatives may threaten Cuba's boast of providing the most equal distribution of wealth among Latin American countries. Recent events have undermined some of the basic health care and educational accomplishments of the revolution as Cuba reverts toward its capitalist past.

The dollarization of the economy has increased the inequalities between the races. Because whites have access to diaspora capital due to their Miami family connections, their ability to survive the "special period" is enhanced. The most vocal pro-Castro patriot is forced into a new form of segregation as capitalist tourists receive privileges denied to Cubans. A two-tier society is in the making: those with dollars and those without. Usually those without dollars are non-white (Bulmer-Thomas 1994, 12, 321, 347; Donghi 1993, 305–7, 373; and Fedarko 1998, 181–83).

These radical economic and political changes that have occurred on the island of Cuba throughout the twentieth century have affected all aspects of Cuban culture. How Jesus is understood and portrayed has also undergone several transformations within the Castro regime. As elucidated in a previous chapter dealing with the Black Christ, the most often cited evidence of God's hand resting upon Castro occurred on January 8, 1959, during his first national speech from Camp Columbia. As Castro called for unity and peace, a white dove landed on his shoulder. For Christians, he assumed the role of Jesus, who underwent a similar experience during his baptism, as recorded by Matthew:

> And having been baptized, Jesus immediately came up out of the water. And behold, the heaven was opened to him, and he saw the Spirit of God descending as a dove and coming upon him. (3:16–17)

Shortly after the victory of the revolution, the deification of Castro became a phenomenon throughout the island. For example, the August 1959 issue of the magazine *Bohemia* published a sketch by Luis Rey portraying Castro under a Christlike halo and with a heavenly countenance. An accompanying article by Mario Kuchilán wrote of the revolution's "miracle" and the "resurrection of (Fidel) faith." Fidel was more than just Fidel; he was "Jesus Christ incarnate, who came to put the affairs of Cuba, and other places, in order" (Quirk 1993, 255; Szulc 1986, 516–18). During a speech to the coordinators of sugar cane cooperatives in La Habana on August 11, 1960, Castro said, "Those who condemn this Revolution are condemning Christ, and they would be capable of crucifying Christ, because he did what we are doing." Similarly, a Presbyterian minister preached, "Fidel Castro is an instrument in the hands of God for the establishment of his reign among men!" (Moore 1988, 63). Like Martí before him, Castro embodied Christ.

During the revolution, both Catholic and Protestant chaplains actively served in the columns of the Castro brothers and Juan Almeida. Many Protestant leaders cooperated with the guerilla forces. Two early martyrs of the revolution were Frank and Josué Pais, Baptists who were killed by Batista's soldiers for leading an uprising in Santiago; Esteban Hernandez, a Presbyterian, was also tortured and killed by Batista's police. The boat that brought the rebels to Cuba, *Granma*, was purchased with the help of a $10,000 donation from a Presbyterian staff member with the National Council of Evangelical Churches. Additionally, homes of Protestant leaders served as underground headquarters for the Revolution.

Catholic leaders also took part in the insurrection. For example, Father Sardiñas served as chaplain to the rebel army and was promoted to the rank of comandante, Father Madrigal was treasurer of the July 26 Movement, and Father Chabebe relayed coded messages to the rebel forces via his religious radio program. Although the church hierarchy remained silent during the insurgence, a significantly large percentage of Catholics, like the martyred Catholic student leader José Antonio Echevarría, participated in the uprising, fighting the forces of Batista as Cubans who happened to be Catholics (Kirk 1988, 48–49). Those who professed a strong faith in Christ participated in the revolution as an expression of their commitment to Christ, which they understood to be essentially grounded in their action against socioeconomic injustices. If Christ's mission was to bring about a just social order, then as followers of Christ they too were commissioned to this task. They saw the revolution as the vehicle by which to place their faith into action, specifically through solidarity with those who were marginalized and oppressed in Cuba.

But while Protestants and Catholics chose to live out their faith through the revolution, others saw the revolution as a threat to their basic understanding of Christ. Almost all Protestant foreign missionaries and religious schools packed their bags and left the island. The failure of Protestantism to become integrated within the island life, and its success in maintaining a Christ that was more Euroamerican than Cuban, can be noticed in the near extinction of Protestant churches after Castro obtained power. Months after the 1959 revolution, these missionaries returned to the United States, followed by many Cuban pastors and their middle-class congregations. Entire congregations disappeared. Those congregations that stayed, which had previously held close ties with their U.S. counterparts, tended to reject the revolution. They became a social space of political resistance from which to criticize it (Cepeda et al. 1996, 95, 99–100).

Since the revolution, the trajectory of Cuban Protestantism has differed from that in the United States. First, Cuban law forbids the establishment of any new churches. Consequently, unlike those in the United States, churches experienced no schisms. When congregations reached a point where they might split, they were forced to work out their differences and stay together. Pentecostalism grew, in spite of the "no new church" law, by ignoring the spirit of that law and creating "home churches." Second, by 1960, Cuba's Protestant churches were independent from the mother churches. Besides struggling with feelings of abandonment, these churches were forced to interpret the biblical text apart from the "guidance" of Euroamerican churches. This break with the U.S. missionary movement meant an end to the neocolonial trend within the church. And finally, the U.S. embargo and the hostility of the Cuban government have isolated the Cuban churches from the theological changes and challenges occurring in the larger religious sphere (Cepeda et al. 1996, 95–116).

Many churches were at first pleased with the government's initial move to end gambling, prostitution, and political corruption. After helping to eliminate Batista, they returned to their church ministries. However, the early optimism of church and state cooperation gave way to disillusion as the new regime took a more leftist tilt. A closer relationship with the Soviet Union, the promoters of "godless communism," along with land and education reform (which curtailed church autonomy), led to the eventual break a few years after overthrowing Batista. Catholics as well as Protestants became engaged in counterrevolutionary activities, openly supporting and praising the United States, which was intent on ending the revolution and reestablishing its authority on the island.

Cuba needed to be "saved" from atheism. By Christmas 1960, Archbishop Enrique Pérez Serantes, a social reformer and critic of the Batista regime, wrote a pastoral letter that presented Cubans with an ultimatum, titled "With Christ or Against Christ." He laid out the existing dichotomy in eschatological tones: "The battle is to wrestle between Christ and the Anti-Christ. Choose, then, each to who they prefer to have as Chief" (Maza 1983, 91). By 1961, the government nationalized all church schools and declared most foreign clergy persona non grata, in response to three Spanish priests and at least one minister (Methodist) who participated as chaplains in the April Bay of Pigs invasion. One of the priests, Father Ismael de Lugo, was to read a communiqué to the Cuban population:

> The liberating forces have disembarked on Cuba's beaches. We come in the name of God. . . . The assault brigade is made up of thousands of Cubans who are all Christians and Catholics. Our struggle is that of those who believe in God against the atheists. . . . Have faith, since the victory is ours, because God is with us and the Virgin of Charity cannot abandon her children. . . . Long live Christ the King! Long live our glorious Patron Saint! (Kirk 1988, 96)

The most notable protest against the revolution occurred on September 8 (the day of La Virgen del Cobre), 1961. An anticommunist march (riot) was begun at the Cathedral of La Habana by the auxiliary archbishop, Eduardo Boza Masvidal, the revolution's most outspoken critic. About four thousand faithful participated in the march. Church forces clashed with revolutionary supporters, resulting in several injuries and the death of a passing seventeen-year-old. Within two days priests were rounded up, and on September 17, nine days after the event, one hundred and thirty-five priests, along with Msgr. Boza Masvidal, were expelled from the country and all religious acts outside of the church were prohibited.

Castro's December 1, 1961, declaration that he was a Marxist-Leninist sent further shock waves throughout churches in Cuba, as well as the rest of Latin America. Christians' worst fear was realized in the fall of a supposedly Catholic nation into the hands of an atheist communist regime. Catholics, influenced by the views of communism as presented in the encyclical *Divini Redemptoris*, understood Catholicism and Marxism as mutually exclusive. This 1937 pontifical document was written as a reaction to the excesses of the Spanish Civil War and the religious persecutions that also occurred in Mexico and Russia. Catholic priests who came from Spain, influenced by the denunciation of communism that accompanied Franco's victory, transplanted an atmosphere of a crusade to Cuba. No room existed for dialogue; instead Cubans were forced to choose between "*Roma o Moscú.*"

An I-told-you-so attitude prevailed among those Christian groups that had always opposed the radically leftist path of the revolution. It mattered not that the Marxism declared by Castro manifested his unmistakable stamp, molded within the Cuban ethos. In fact, it could be argued that Castro was more a Jeffersonian Democrat than a Marxist, and that Cuba's revolution was more a product of Two-Third World nationalism than Marxism. The early reforms implemented by Castro were not really all that radical. Initial agrarian reforms were based on moderate principles borrowed from Bolivia and Mexico and on rent-control policies that were already in place in many Latin American countries. It remains debatable how much of Cuba's drift into the Soviet orbit was in order to survive U.S. aggression.

Regardless of what motivated Castro's true ideologies, Christian churches challenged his power. To remain in power, he had to decisively deal with this threat. The proclamation that was supposed to be read by the priest involved in the Bay of Pigs invasion, and the participation of churches in protests against the revolution, led Castro to believe that an organized strategy existed among Christians to overthrow the revolution. In his speech concerning the September 8 showdown between the government and the church, Castro returns to the Cuban understanding of Christ as being in solidarity with the marginalized and oppressed. He said:

> [The counterrevolutionaries] want to paint the Revolution as an enemy of religion, as if that had anything to do with the things that interest the Revolution . . . The doctrine of Christ was a doctrine that found an echo among the slaves, among the humble people. It was persecuted by the aristocracy, by the dominant classes. These gentlemen, in contemporary times, completely abandoned the essence of the Christian doctrine, dedicated themselves to taking religion as an instrument to hide all the vices and all the defects of the present dominant classes, forgetting about the slaves of today, the workers, the peasants without land. These gentlemen separated themselves from the interests of the exploited masses, and from the humble masses, in order to carry religion on a silver platter to the great exploiters, to the dominant classes. They divorced themselves from the people, and they prostituted the essence of primitive Christianity. (1971, 130–32)

Returning to the image of Hatuey, Castro echoed the words spoken four hundred years earlier as he chastised the church for criticizing the revolution:

Did (the Cuban hierarchy) ever issue a pastoral against graft? Did any of you ever read a pastoral defending the sugar-plantation peasants? Or demanding schools for the children of peasants? Or condemning the murder of labor leaders and students? Or protesting the (exorbitant) prices (charged by the) electric and telephone companies? Did they ever protest against politicking? Against profiteering in food? Against high rents? Against smuggling? . . . So now I say: if the latifundistas go to heaven, we do not want to go; if the imperialists go to heaven, we do not want to go; if the criminals . . . (and) the exploiters go to heaven, we do not want to go. (Dewart 1963, 163)

Additionally, in an article responding to church opposition, Castro went on to define Christianity as follows:

A true Christian is one who loves his neighbor, who makes sacrifices for others, who obeys the doctrines of Christ and gives what he has in order to go serve his fellow human being. Let these "Christians" leave their temples and go to the fields to help the sick, plant trees, build houses, assist the Agrarian reform, sew smocks for children who have no clothes. That's what being Christian means. On the other hand, going to church to conspire against our fatherland is the action of a Pharisee—never a Christian. (Kirk 1988, 107)

It appears as if both sides, the church and government, claimed to be doing the work of Christ; both sides created a Christ that justified their political goals.

Opponents of Cuba's new Marxist orientation, either Catholic or Protestant, faced expulsion. They were not allowed to run schools, which cut deeply into the churches' financial resources, and the churches' formerly private media were nationalized. Church members were routinely watched by political organs of the government. Bishops, priests, and ministers were placed under house arrest. Christians were refused entry into the Communist Party, a route to economic advancement, and were denied high-level government and university positions. Hence no sociopolitical or economic reason existed to be a Christian. Many, mostly the middle class, chose flight rather than fight, creating a brain-drain on the island and furthering weakening the churches' power base.

Between 1965 and 1968 thousands of artists, intellectuals, hippies, university students, and homosexuals were abducted by the State Secret Police and interned, without trial, in Unidad Militar de Ayuda a la Producción (U.M.A.P., Military Units for Assistance to Production) reeducation labor camps. Also interned were Jehovah's Witnesses, Gideonists, and Catholic or Protestant activists. Even the Nicaraguan priest Ernest Cardenal, who had been friendly to the Castro regime, criticized the Cuban government for its treatment of Christians in his book *En Cuba*.

Monsignor Pérez Serantes, a combative critic of Castro's Marxist leaning best summed up the church's predicament: "All that is happening to us is providential. . . . We believed more in our schools than in Jesus Christ" (Büntig 1971, 111). With churches decimated, silence became essential to self-preservation. An era of "internal exile" began. However, as tension between the church and government subsided, and as the church ceased to challenge Castro's authority, tolerance for religion reemerged. The Catholic Church in particular began to be reconciled with the Castro regime under the leadership of Cesare Zacchi, the Vatican's emissary appointed in 1962, who criticized pre-revolutionary Cuba and the clergy who abandoned Cuba while praising Castro's social reforms. Eventually several expelled priests were allowed to return.

On April 10, 1969, a decisive break with the past occurred when the Catholic Church published the Cuban bishop's letter denouncing the U.S. embargo. Influenced by the theological developments occurring elsewhere in Latin America, specifically by liberation theology, the Catholic Church, for the first time, committed itself to work for the development of Cuba without condemning the ideology of the regime. The church began to come to terms with the context in which it found itself.

Castro also showed interest in establishing a Christian-Marxist dialogue, and he pondered a strategic alliance. He was influenced by priests like Camilio Torres, who in 1966 ceased to say the mass in order to join the people's struggle in carrying out a revolution in Colombia. The 1979 success of the Sandinista revolution in Nicaragua further affected Cuba's attitudes toward religion; several Catholic priests and Protestant leaders, motivated by their religious convictions, partook in the struggle against Somoza and assumed important governmental positions.

Protestants also sought a rapprochement. In 1977 the Confession of Faith of the Presbyterian-Reformed church declared, "The Church lives joyfully in the midst of the socialist revolution" (Kirk 1988, 139). Baptist minister Jesse Jackson visited Cuba in 1984; at that time Fidel Castro gave a televised speech from the pulpit of a Protestant church flanked by church leaders. Additionally, the 1985 publication of Castro's bestseller *Fidel y la religión* (*Fidel and Religion*) began a public dialogue concerning areas of cooperation between Marxists and what Castro called "honest" Christians. Because Castro's revolution occurred prior to the rise of liberation theology in Latin America, however, the church and the leftist government lacked a framework for dialogue.

The relationship between the churches and the political systems of Latin America has been volatile throughout the last quarter of the twentieth century. The radicalization of the churches of Latin America followed the Second Vatican Council (1962–65), convened by Pope John XXIII and concluded by Pope Paul VI to deal with the challenges of the modern world. The major contribution Vatican II made to the history of Christianity was the encyclical *Gaudium et Specs*, one of many documents that emphasized the responsibility of Christians toward the poor and afflicted. By divorcing the church from any particular social, economic, or political system, the church assumed the duty of passing moral judgment against those institutions creating structures that oppress the most vulnerable segments of society.

In 1968 Latin American clerics gathered in Medellín, Colombia, to consider the implementation of Vatican II. For European churches, Vatican II dealt with the confrontation between faith and science. Latin Americans instead entered a phase known as liberation in its struggle to confront faith and revolution. The conference focused its attention on the Latin American situation, asking itself what it ought to say as Christ's agents about the massive suffering of the people. Among its conclusions, the church made a "preferential option for the poor," choosing to accompany those oppressed in their struggle for liberation and salvation, even unto martyrdom.

Because the Cuban revolution preceded Vatican II, the trajectory of the church in Cuba differed from that of the other churches in Latin America. Although Cuban representatives participated in Vatican II and the 1968 Medellín reunion of Latin American bishops, Cuba developed its own form of theology. Cubans refused to import foreign models historically designed to advance the interests of the privileged class, as was done during Spain's (specifically Catholic) colonial venture and the United States's imperialist adventures (specifically Protestantism). Theology in revolution became a homegrown means by which some Resident Cubans began to understand Christ. Unlike liberation theologians of Latin America who read their experience through the lens of the biblical book Exodus, where a liberating God guides God's people toward the promised land, Resident Cuban theologian Israel Batista maintains that Resident Cubans are liberated and already live in the promised land. Consequently, the task facing Resident Cubans is not liberation, but constructing and building society. Praxis-based reading requires a "prophetic reading," providing the people with the necessary praxis for a revolutionary society. "Prophetic" does not mean the right to criticize the revolution; it simply means breaking open the sacred space occupied by theologians so that they can be in step with the people (Batista 1988, 102–17).

Resident Cuban theologian Sergio Arce Martínez makes it clear that when Christians reflect theologically on the revolution, they do not do it for the benefit of revolutionaries or to provide a service to the revolution. Rather, their reflection is done for Christians and the church so that they can render a service to both of them. He insists that they do not speak for the revolution, which is not Christian; they speak for the Christian revolutionary who plays an active part in Christ's church located within a socialist county, as well as for their socialist patria where a Christian church exists (1971, 193). While this theological perspective contains some commonalities with liberation theology, it is still vastly different, rooted in the Resident Cuban experience.[2]

Yet liberation theologians like Gustavo Gutiérrez expressed concern that revolution-type theologies have the tendency to "baptize" the revolution by placing it beyond criticism. Castro's well-known phrase, "Everything within the revolution, nothing outside of the revolution," fixes limits of acceptability on all discourse, including Christianity. Gutiérrez accuses theologies of revolution of "reductionism," where the gospel is reduced to sociology, economics, or politics. Faith becomes a justification for Christians to participate as actors in achieving the goals of the revolution (1984, xiii, 44). Similarly, Clodovias Boff states that the overall process of revolution tends to be confused with just one of its moments, the moment of breakage where the people are dragged by the yoke through "vanguardism." Fulfilling basic needs is not the end, but the means to a full realization of humanity (1990, 101).

Today Cuba is experiencing a spiritual revival. The fastest-growing churches (excluding those who practice Santería) are Pentecostal. The Bible has become the top seller; seminaries like the one in Matanzas have seen a jump in enrollment from fewer than five to one hundred and fifty students, and churches like the Methodist have seen their congregations increase threefold. Catholic churches have witnessed a renewal in popularity as thousands attend open-air masses inspired by the pope's 1998 visit. As Cuba suffers the economic effects of the "special period," caused by the collapse of world communism, church pews are beginning to fill. These new religious converts are academically prepared. Although ignorant of the church, they are educated and willing to participate in the life of the church. They are returning after years of absence, bringing with them the experience of secularism. Some are Marxists who have never been churched. These new parishioners are more critical, more questioning and demanding. This revival has created a meeting ground for those who have been opposed to the revolution and those who have served it.

The Protestant revival is attempting to restore a sense of community and its values within the "special period." After the fall of the Berlin wall, the Resident Cuban community experienced an aimlessness caused by the end of "utopias." Many who chose careers based on the needs of society found their vocation obsolete in a rapidly dollarized economy. Pentecostals, in particular, explained world events and the spiritual revival in Cuba as the "signs of the time." The normative Spirit-filled conversion experience gave new meaning to a life confused by the new world order and provided hope for those attempting to survive the economic fallout of the special period. Even non-Pentecostal churches experienced charismatic responses to conversion by those returning to church. Yet Pentecostals credit their growth to the fact that the Catholics and the pro-revolution Protestants failed to satisfy the Cuban "thirst" for Christ. The lay leaders who replaced the departing clergy (who left during the exodus) consider themselves closer to the people and view pro-revolution churches with suspicion. In turn, pro-revolution Protestant leaders, like Israel Batista, accuse Pentecostals of "spiritual machismo." He states that they place individualistic ethics above social commitment. For Batista, the Pentecostal response to Christ is emotional, private, reductionist, apocalyptic, and overbearing. The Pentecostals operate apart from the state, hence threatening the established professional clergy (1988, 104).

Notwithstanding the different ways Christ is worshiped on the island, one factor remains constant. Since the revolution, Cuba's churches have evolved into an indigenous expression of faith. The break with the United States and the effects of the embargo have isolated the Cuban Christian community, forcing it to find its own expression of religiosity. Regardless of these churches' political views, ranging from accommodation to aloofness toward the revolution, the Cubanization of Christ and the church has been a century-long process of resisting the Euroamerican Christ that came with the U.S. military forces.

The Christ of El Exilio

Every Exilic Cuban has heard Celia Cruz sing the popular tear-jerker "Cuando salí de Cuba" ("When I left Cuba"). No other song better summarizes the pain of the Exilic Cuban existential location. "Never can I die, my heart is not here. Over there it is waiting for me, it is waiting for me to return there. When I left Cuba, I left my life, I left my love. When I left Cuba, I left my heart buried." Written by a Chilean and sung as a hymn of faith, this popular ballad illustrates that Exilic Cubans deny the reality that they will almost certainly die on foreign soil. U.S. invasions and U.S. exploitation of Cuba's natural resources indirectly fostered the Castro revolution in 1959. Exilic Cubans find themselves as refugees in the very country responsible for their being there. These Cubans have lost the land of their birth and are coming to the realization that when their bodies are finally laid to rest, it will be as foreigners interred in an alien soil.

Historically, el exilio has always been a place for opposing whoever was in power on the island. Exilic Cuban Gerald Poyo develops this theme by demonstrating how each separate Cuban Exilic community, whether they were in New Orleans in the 1850s, Tampa in the 1890s, New York in the 1930s, or presently in Miami, assumed that their view of Cuba was shared by those who remained on the island. Their view provided moral justification for the struggle to change the island's ecopolitical reality. We can add to Poyo's list Fidel Castro, who in 1955 came to Miami to raise money for his successful Sierra Maestra campaign. Exilic Cubans "take actions, make decisions, and feel concerns, and develop identities within social networks" that simultaneously connect them with both Cuban and U.S. society (Poyo 1975, 76–98).

Influenced by Martí, el exilio equates morality with nationality. The assumption that Resident Cubans desire to be rescued by Exilic Cubans is rooted in Martí's words and actions. Martí's plight as an Exilic becomes central in his construction of Cuba Libre (Liberated Cuba). The concept of two Cubas (the real Cuba that is *aquí*, here, as opposed to the morally degraded Cuba *allá*, there) and the responsibility of Exilic Cubans to continue la lucha to "save" la Cuba de allá, is illustrated in his speech in Tampa, Florida, on November 26, 1891:

> You [Exilic Cubans] must create, allá where the corrupt proprietor
> rots whatever he looks upon, a new Cuban soul . . . Aquí where we
> keep watch for the absent ones . . . where we create what must replace
> the things destroyed for us allá—aquí, no word so closely resembles
> the light of dawn, no consolation enters our hearts with greater joy,
> than this ardent and ineffable word: Cuban! . . . To our fatherland
> crumbling to pieces allá, and blinded by corruption, we must take the
> devout and farseeing country being [constructed] aquí. (Martí 1977,
> 249–64)

Martí's words, repeated over a hundred years later, remain accurate for
Exilic Cubans' sense of duty toward la patria. Living in exile is a sacrifice
constituting a civic duty representing a grander moral basis. Nonetheless,
the danger of exile is the end of history, for a people without land will
eventually cease to exist as they assimilate to the dominant culture.

When dictator Fulgencio Batista departed from Cuba on New Year's
Eve, 1959, he triggered panic as partygoers rushed to their houses to collect
their sleeping children, money, and anything of value. Those who were
able to leave arrived in this country still in their tuxedos and dress uni-
forms, their wives in formal gowns and high heels. These first refugees
arrived with "class"—not so much in the elegance of their attire, but in
their high economic and social status. Unlike other contemporary refugees, the U.S.-bound Cubans belonged to the privileged upper class.

The first wave (1959–1962) of refugees brought approximately 215,000
Cubans. Demographically, these new Cubans were quite homogeneous.
The vast majority were composed of elites or former notables; most were
white (94 percent), middle-aged (about thirty-eight years old), educated
(about fourteen years of schooling), urban (principally La Habana), and
knew English. They were united in their bitterness over their lost status
and their commitment to overthrowing Castro in order to regain their assets. While I do not want to minimize the trauma and hardship of existing
in the diaspora, those who settled in Miami held an advantage denied other
immigrating groups because they relocated to a place made familiar
through years of prior travel and business dealings.

The second wave (1962–1973) brought approximately 414,000 refugees, predominately white, educated, middle-class, and willing to work below minimum wage. In Cuba they had largely relied on economic links
with the United States. In the United States they generally found semi-
skilled working-class jobs within the economic enclave being established

by the first-wave Cubans. Although all strata of Cuban society were represented in these first two waves, most came from the upper echelons and the middle class, that is, those who had most benefited from the pre-Castro regime.

The assertion of their cultural distinctions paved the road for their eventual capture of Miami's power structures. By the 1990s, the majority of Miami's city commissioners were Exilic Cubans, as were the city and county mayors and two of the three Congressional representatives. The superintendent of Dade County public schools, state chairs of the Florida Democratic Party, and local chairs of the county's political parties are Exilic Cubans. Also, the presidents of several banks (about twenty), Florida International University, Dade County AFL-CIO, Miami Chamber of Commerce, the Miami Herald Publishing Company, and the Greater Miami Board of Realtors (a post I held) have been Exilic Cubans. It is common to find Exilic Cubans occupying top administrative posts in City Hall, the *Miami Herald,* and the city's corporate boardrooms, a privilege not found among any other first generation community.

This success was made possible because the Miami Exilic community constructed an ethnic economic enclave dependent on a large number of immigrants with substantial business experience acquired in Cuba, access to capital through "character loans,"[3] about $2 billion in government-sponsored resettlement aid,[4] and access to labor drawn from family members. This enclave was organized to serve the needs of their own ethnic market. The enclave allowed Exilic Cubans to avoid the economic disadvantages usually accompanying racial segregation. The creation of an Exilic Cuban economic enclave fostered upward mobility not available to African Americans or other Hispanic groups. Not only did the original entrepreneurs benefit, but later arrivals found established community networks providing opportunities for employment and further entrepreneurship. For example, six years after the 1980 Mariel boat lift, about half of the refugees were employed by Exilic-owned businesses while 20 percent became self-employed (Portes and Clark 1987, 14–18).

Especially during the late 1980s but also in the 1990s, Exilic Cubans made substantial inroads into high-profile jobs and positions. Yet large numbers of the Exilic Cuban community still find themselves in lower-paying service jobs. Thus, the "golden exile" appeared to have applied mostly to the emerging Exilic Cuban elite, many of whom had previously belonged to the pro-Euroamerican Cuban elite of the first wave (Pérez-Stable and Uriarte 1993, 141–58).

El exilio on Miami's soil created a landless Cuban territory with its distinct cultural milieu and idiosyncrasies that served to protect Cubans from the pain of the initial economic and psychological difficulties caused by their uprooting. Cuba, as *la Cuba de ayer* (the Cuba of yesteryear), became more than just the old country; it became the mythological world of Exilic Cuban origins. Cuba became an ethereal place where every conceivable item *es mejor* (is better), where the sky is bluer, the sugar sweeter, the bugs less pesky, and life richer. Everything *aquí* (here), when contrasted with *allá* (there), is found lacking. Unlike the stereotypes of other immigrant groups who left painful memories of the old country behind, joyfully anticipating what they perceived as a new country where "the streets were paved with gold," Cubans did not want to come to what they perceived to be an inferior culture. In their attempt to avoid the pain of displacement, they created a mythical Cuba where every *guajiro/a* (country bumpkin) had class and wealth, where no racism existed, and where Eden was preserved until the serpent (Fidel) beguiled Eve (the weakest elements of society: los humildes), bringing an end to paradise.

This image of Cuba requires a religion and a new understanding of Christ. As previously mentioned, the creation of such a religion provides the psychological reassurance of legitimacy. When Exilic Cubans compare their own position with the less privileged lives of Resident Cubans they fail to be content with their success. They desire "the right to their happiness" (Weber 1963, 107). No matter how mythical the "golden exile" may appear to be, the "success story" is crucial in its construction. It allows Exilic Cubans to visualize their success as the result of their own hard work and moral superiority, pulling themselves up from their bootstraps in order to occupy positions of power in Miami.

Their consciousness thus dictates that their present wealth and privilege were earned. Equally, the economic misfortune of Resident Cubans is the direct consequence of their support for Castro or their laziness and incompetence in implementing Euroamerican capitalist paradigms. Their failure proves their illegitimacy as Cubans, making them envious of Miami's success and thus potentially dangerous objects.

Exilic Cubans create a required religion that takes the form of *la lucha* (the struggle), a counter-memory established as the starting point for their sacred space. La lucha, also known as *la causa sagrada* (the sacred cause), ceases to be a struggle for liberation and becomes instead a religious crusade. La lucha has its roots in the nineteenth-century struggle against Spain for liberation. Later it became la lucha against the United States as represented by Machado and Batista. Today, Exilic Cubans understand la lucha as a continued struggle against Castro and all who are perceived to be his allies. La lucha becomes a sacred space representing the cosmic struggle between the "children of light" (Exilic Cubans) and the "children of darkness" (Resident Cubans), complete with a Christ (Martí), an anti-Christ (Castro), a priesthood (the Cuban American National Foundation [CANF]), a promised land (Cuba), and martyrs (those who gloriously suffer in the holy war against the evil of Castro).

Those who suggest a dialogue with Resident Cubans are labeled traitors, communist, *vendepatrias* (sellouts), *tontos útiles* (useful idiots), and/ or *mariposas* (butterflies, a euphemism for homosexuals) by Miami's Exilic Cuban radio stations and *periodiquitos* (tabloids). Because the Castro government is understood as an atheist regime, any cooperation with it is tantamount to dealing with the anti-Christ. During the 1970s, Reverend Manuel Espinosa, pastor of the Evangelical Church in Hialeah and former captain in Castro's military, used his pulpit to preach on themes of intra-Cuban reconciliation. His sermons earned him the label "comunista" and a severe beating in 1975. By 1980, the reverend publicly admitted he was a secret agent for the Castro government. His admission only confirmed in the hearts and minds of the émigré community that anyone who actively sought or supported any dialogue with Resident Cubans must somehow be connected with the regime (García 1996, 139–40). Because such individuals are perceived as being against all that is good and holy, it becomes a Christian responsibility to silence them.

Like their Resident counterparts, Exilic Cubans are also experiencing a spiritual revival. Exilic Reverend Maros A. Ramos (a Protestant) and auxiliary Bishop Agustin Román (a Catholic) estimate that Exilic Cubans have a higher level of religious participation than when they lived on the island. For example, about 15 to 20 percent attend Catholic services compared with 5 to 8 percent prior to Castro's revolution (Ramos and Román 1991, 121). These followers of Christ tend to be more conservative, both religiously and politically. Their hatred of Marxism and the financial support provided to those of refugee status facilitated their adoption of the dominant culture's value system. Soon they became exaggerated "American" patriots, wholeheartedly committed to the morality of Reaganism. They merge their allegiance to Christ with their anticommunism fervor, making the latter a sacred cause.

This phenomenon of merging ultra-rightist political views with Christ can be seen in the international incident between Cuba and the United

States over the child named Elián. On Thanksgiving Day, 1999, a small boy of five years of age was found in the Florida Straits clinging to an inner tube. Within a few months, Elián's name became known throughout the entire world. This child was soon at the center of a custody battle between the Exilic and Resident Cuban communities. Surrounding Elián's Miami home, both young and old gathered to pray. Signs written in aquamarine, the color of Ochún—the quasi-deity of the sea—asked the nation to "Pray for Elián." Exilic Cubans held hands and surrounded the house to recite the rosary. These same worshipers were preparing to unclasp their praying hands and instead lock arms to prevent the U.S. government from taking this child. Some worshipers even claimed to have seen the Virgin Mary hovering over the house or peering from a window, while others referred to Elián as the miracle child or Miami's Jesus. Across the street from Elián's uncle's house lived a santera, a practitioner of Santería. For her, Elián is a child of Ochún. Followers of Santería believed that Ochún spared Elián's life to bear witness that Ochún is still the mother of all Cubans. To return Elián to Cuba would be tantamount to handing over the baby Jesus to Satan. To suggest that Elián belongs with his father is to publicly oppose Christ and his cause. The Elián story becomes a religious drama whose subtext illustrates how religion, politics, and power are fused and confused within Miami Exilic community.

The Cuban Christ Reveals a Biblical Response

How can a Jew who lived two thousand years ago be relevant to the Cuban experience of the twentieth century? How do we seek a Christ who knows what it means to be Cuban? Yet the danger of searching for a Cuban Christ is to create a Christ in the image of cubanidad, where twenty-first-century ideas of the community are projected upon a two-thousand-year-old historical figure in order to justify the ideologies of different aspects of the Cuban community. How do Cubans avoid looking into the well of history in their search for Christ only to discover their own reflection? While every interpretation of Jesus reflects the life of the author, how can Cubans remain faithful to the biblical narrative while exploring aspects of the text that might indicate how Christ would understand and sympathize with Cubans? Who then is this Jesus who bears upon his flesh the stigmata of being a Cuban?

Anyone approaching the Bible does so from a particular social location. The idea of reading the text from a position of complete objectivity is a myth constructed to protect the privileged space of those with power. Objectivity is the dominant culture's subjectivity, cloaked as academically and spiritually purer than any reading from the periphery. Interpretations of the Bible do not occur in a social vacuum. We are all born into an ongoing society that shapes us. When we turn our attention to the biblical text, we participate in a dialogue, a dialogue between the written word and the meanings our community taught us to give to these words. We are informed by the text after we inform the text as to what we bring to the reading. We become part of the reading as done through our own eyes (De La Torre 1999b, 5).

Latino biblical scholars have attempted to illuminate the text by methodically reading the Bible through Hispanic eyes. In reading the text with Hispanic eyes, the reader necessarily claims a Latina/o identity, and looks to the text from within the Hispanic context of struggles in order to learn what God wants them and the world to be. Yet, which Hispanic eyes do we use? Are Puerto Rican or Mexican eyes synonymous with Cuban eyes? For Justo González, an Exilic Cuban theologian, experiences of Hispanics are different; all Hispanic eyes are not the same. Hence he refuses to provide "the" Hispanic perspective. Instead, he provides "a" Hispanic perspective, while hoping such a perspective resonates among all Latinos (1996, 19, 28–29). The task before us is to narrow González's paradigm to Cuban eyes.

Hispanics in the United States usually read the Bible as aliens from the position of marginality, poverty, and *Mulatez*. For the vast majority of Latina/os in this country, life exists under these conditions. But for Exilic Cubans, this model falls short of the Miami reality. Unlike any other group of immigrants who came to this shore throughout this country's history, Cubans have risen to the top echelons of a city's sociopolitical structures within one generation. While poverty exists among Exilic Cubans, their national average family income is closer to that of Euroamericans than that of any other Hispanic group. Although they are a Mulatez people the vast majority (over 95 percent) claim whiteness, hence rejecting the other elements of their multiculturalism.

How then do Exilic Cubans read the Bible? For that matter, how do Cubans in general, Exilic and Resident, read the text? Frankly, the vast majority do not read the Bible at all, hence the need to turn to art in the next chapter to discover how we "see" the divine. Those who do look to the text read it through a methodology of popularizing narratives. To read the text as popularized biblical stories merges the biblical narrative with other religious traditions, for the purpose of providing a lesson that instructs on how to live and survive. This type of reading is usually discarded by theologians as being a distorted reading of the Bible; however, for many Cubans, it represents how the text is understood in their daily lives. Because many Cubans seldom read the biblical text, they often express their deeply held religiosity through customs and traditions. This approach leads to popularizing versions of the biblical stories, combining at times African traditions for the purpose of stressing a spiritual point.

When Exilic Cubans do read the text from their Exilic space, they read their pain as refugees within the biblical story. Like the Psalmist (137), they sit by the streams of this country, singing about their inability to sing God's songs. Due to different occupied spaces, Resident Cubans read the Bible differently from Exilic Cubans. As previously mentioned, during the repression of Christianity in the 1960s and 1970s, a secular/sacred dualism resulted in a revolution/Christian faith dualism. Such a reading created a space within the Christian faith from which one could protest and reject the revolution. Some Resident biblical scholars have called for a break with this perspective, insisting that the hand of God continues to work in history through the revolution.

These Resident scholars maintain that the need for social change in Cuba created an emotionally charged situation in which the Bible was misused to provide solutions to these new social problems. Cuban pastors became psychologists as they attempted to minister to people who were having difficulties with the human conflicts developed by the revolution. Such a reading overshadowed the mission of the revolution (Batista 1988, 102–17). They call for an action-based reading, where the Bible is read from the actual experience of the revolution, a reading grounded in the "liberation" brought about by the revolution.

Obviously divergences exist in how the Bible is read by Exilic and Resident Cubans, but commonalities also exist, of which the most important, I maintain, is the figure of Jesus. Yet reading the text solely through Exilic or Resident Cuban eyes raises concerns about masking intra-Cuban repression and obscuring the Christ who is Cuban. The danger of reading the Bible to justify political position over those of others is real.

In using the Bible as the source for discovering a Cuban Christ, we must acknowledge that it has also been used as the source of alienation, damnation, and subjugation. Liberation from oppression is achieved not by the Bible but by the justice-based call for action rooted in the reading of the

Bible, a reading made Cuban when done from a Cuban perspective. Such a reading requires turning away from Eurocentric theological triumphalism and looking instead to a search within the Cuban community for an understanding of who Christ is (De La Torre 1999b, 6). This can be accomplished through what Gustavo Gutiérrez, the liberation theologian, calls "a militant reading," one from the perspective of those dwelling on "the underside of history" (1984, xi). For Gutiérrez, reading the text from the perspective of those residing in the underside of history reveals two implicit themes. The first is the universality of God's love. The second is God's preferential option for those who are poor and oppressed (1991, 116). To read from the underside of history is not limited to Cubans being oppressed by Euroamericans; rather it recognizes that God's crucified people, los humildes of Cuba, are oppressed by their fellow Cubans who are privileged with whiteness, maleness, or economic class.

If reading the text implies application, then God's crucified people can only hear God's word in the context of their own suffering, which makes their oppressed existence part of the text's interpretation. This subversive way of reading the text emphasizes the interpretational privilege of los humildes. Because they have learned how to function in a powerless realm constructed by those with power and privilege, they know more about the overall Cuban experience, which includes the sphere occupied by the Cuban elite, than those with power know about the subjugated Others. This situation does not confer truth exclusively on those oppressed; it only states that they are in a better position to understand the biblical call for justice than those who deceive themselves into thinking justice already exists between the oppressed elements of Cuban culture and the privileged elements (De La Torre 1999b, 6).

Seeking a Cuban Christ requires moving away from forty years of siege mentality and away from the hostility it has fostered. Until now, the attitudes of Exilic and Resident Cubans, each toward the other, have hampered any serious consideration of transforming the possibilities for community and entering common spaces for all Cubans. But sociopolitical remedies alone will never heal. Considering the Cuban spiritual dimension as a people will help in the healing process.

Throughout Cuban history, Christ has been used to justify the domination of one group by another. Yet where there is oppression, resistance exists. For those struggling to be recognized in the full dignity of humanity, a Christ who is Cuban provides an alternative. But who exactly is this

Cuban Christ? Until now, we have been exploring the historical development of the cultural Christ of Cuba. We are now ready to turn our attention toward a present-day quest. In the second part of this book, we begin to search for the Cuban Christ of today. A Christ I will call "the *ajiaco* Christ," able to tie together all the diverse ways of understanding Christ from the underside of Cuban history.

II

A Present–Day Quest

The Ajiaco Christ

José ran quickly to his makeshift home. Although a newlywed, he had been married long enough to know his wife, María, would be asleep by now, along with their newborn son. "*Despierta mi amor,* wake up my love," José told his wife as he gently shook her. "I just heard from a messenger that *la milicia,* the militia, will be coming for us. I fear for our lives. *Apúrate,* hurry up, wrap up our baby boy, we leave tonight for a safe land where this brutal dictatorship cannot touch us." They had time neither to pack any belongings nor to say goodbye to friends and family. José took his small family into *el exilio,* the Exile. They would arrive at a foreign country with only the clothes on their backs. For them, safety and opportunity lay south of the border.

Over two thousand years ago this family arrived in Egypt as political refugees, fleeing the regime of Herod. Over forty years ago my father came home to his wife, my mother, with similar news. Because of his involvement with the Batista regime, he was now a fugitive of the newly installed Castro government. They gathered me, their six-month-old son, and headed north. Like Jesus, I too was a political refugee, a victim of circumstances beyond my comprehension or control. The historical Christ knows the Exilic Cuban pain of being a foreigner in an alien land. Seeing Jesus as a refugee is more than simply locating my story in the biblical narrative. Rather, the story of Jesus becomes my story, as I expand the interpretational flow from my social location as an Exilic Cuban to the biblical text (De La Torre 1999b, 5).

Understanding the Cuban Christ becomes an act of faith, derived from two sources: the Cuban social existential location (reality) and the paradigm (ideal) derived by the community of faith, a model based on justice. The communal expression of faith avoids the Euroamerican pitfall of a utilitarian individuality that relegates religion to the private sphere and transforms the public Christ into a personal savior. Conversion ceases to be simply a call to a new religion founded by Jesus, but becomes a radically subversive Cuban lifestyle.

The quest for the Cuban Christ becomes fruitful when Cubans struggle with their dis-membered re-membrance as a people. Faith becomes a special form of consciousness containing specific consequences for the will. Satisfaction of intellectual needs (the modernity project) is not the ultimate goal. Rather, the longing of the heart to answer the unanswerable questions of the Cuban alienated existence (from God, from patria, and from the Cubans ninety miles away) becomes a religious quest for meaning.

This quest creates a sacred space where Cubans can grapple with their spiritual need to reconcile with their God and their psychological need to reconcile with their siblings on the other side of the Florida Straits. The construction of Cuban spirituality requires symbols that can generate a unifying dialogue among Cubans. In the previous chapters we examined cultural symbols by which we understood a Christ who is Cuban. Because all people depict ultimate reality in a visible form native to their own culture, a Euroamerican Christ, although appropriate for Euroamericans, is impotent for Cubans. What we then search for is the Christ who knows what it means to be Cuban.

Lilian Lazo, the Exilic Cuban painter, captures this concept of a Cuban Christ. She is best known as "Popa" for her television series in Cuba during the 1950s and on the New York Hispanic station during the 1960s. Her painting *Nativity* portrays a biracial Mary and child. The birth of Christ occurs beneath a *bohío*, the traditional Taíno thatched-roof dwelling hut, historically used as housing by Cuba's peasants, and presently used as a status symbol by Exilic Cubans who adorn their backyards with them in Miami. Tropical fruits common to Cuba are offered to the baby Jesus as Cuba's country life becomes transferred into the biblical narrative. The participants of this Christmas story are clothed in local peasant garb, juxtaposing twentieth-century Cuban reality with the birth of Christ.

Exilic Cuban Lourdes Gomez-Franca also situates Christ within the Cuban space. In her painting *El Cristo Cubano* (the Cuban Christ) she depicts a crucified Christ within the Cuban countryside (figure 2). The ever-present hot Cuban sun looms over the work, while Cuban palm trees punctuate the landscape. Both Lazo and Gomez-Franca connect the deity with their homeland. "Paradise Lost" becomes a fitting setting for a Christ to whom Exilic Cubans pray for their return to the promise land.

Fig. 2. Lourdes Gomez-Franca, *El Cristo Cubano,* courtesy of Pablo D. Cano.

Throughout this book, our quest for a Christ who is indigenous to the Cuban culture has revealed multiple manifestations of how Christ has been presented throughout Cuban history. We explored the dichotomy between the Christ of the conquistadors and the Christ of those they conquered; the Christ of the Spaniards and the Christ of Varela and Martí; the Christ of the Cuban dominant culture and the Christ of los humildes; the Christ of the revolution and the Christ of el exilio. Yet, with so many ways of understanding the Cuban Christ, is it possible to reconcile these diverse views? With so many different groups, perspectives, and interests, how do Cubans transcend their fragmentation as a people to create a genuine sense of cultural integrity? Can Cubans become more than what Jorge Mañach terms a *patria sin nación* (a nation without nationhood) (1944a, 64)? Is it possible to come together as a people and see a synthesized Cuban Christ that can serve as a common symbol for all Cubans, black and white, rich and poor, male and female, Resident and Exilic?

The consolidation of these vastly different expressions of the Cuban Christ can be found in what I will call an *ajiaco* Christ. What do I mean by the term *ajiaco*? Fernando Ortiz, Cuba's famed cultural interpreter, was the first to use this term as a metaphor for the Cuban experience. Specifically, ajiaco is a Cuban consommé made from a variety of roots. I still recall that as a child, whenever my mother made an ajiaco, she would comment on its hearty qualities by stating, "*Hice un ajiaco que levanta los muertos* (I made an ajiaco that can raise the dead)." Ajiaco, the collection of our indigenous roots, becomes a life-giving substance, something that can raise the dead (in life). These roots symbolize the diverse ethnic backgrounds of Cubans and how they came together to form our cubanidad, our Cuban community.

Ortiz used this term within the context of a Cuba composed of immigrants who, unlike those who came to the United States, reached the island on the way to someplace else. For him, ajiaco was a renewable Cuban stew where the Amerindians contributed the maíz, papa, malanga, boniato, yuca, and ají. The Spaniards added calabaza and nabo, while the Chinese added Oriental spices. Africans, contributing ñame and with their culinary foretaste, urged a meaning from this froth beyond mere clever cooking. Ortiz did not use "ajiaco" to mean that Cuban culture has achieved complete integration; rather, Cuba remains "a mestizaje [mixture] of kitchens, a mestizaje of races, a mestizaje of cultures, a dense broth of civilization that bubbles on the stove of the Caribbean" (1940, 165–69). Furthermore,

Ortiz recognizes that Cuban culture is not a finished product. Like the ajiaco, our culture is a "vital concept of constant fluidity" (1939, 4).

Ajiaco symbolizes our cubanidad's attempt to find harmony within our diverse roots, to create Martí's idealized state of a secularized vision of Christian love that is anti-imperialistic, antimilitant, antiracist, moral, and radical. Cubanidad is more than just a Cuban community. For Ortiz, cubanidad is a "condition of the soul, a complexity of sentiments, ideas and attitudes . . . a heterogeneous conglomerate of diverse races and cultures, which agitate, tremble, and disintegrate in the same social effervescence" (1939, 3–5). Unlike the Euroamerican melting pot paradigm, maintaining that all immigrants who arrive on these shores are somehow placed into a pot where they "melt down" into a new culture that nevertheless remains Eurocentric in nature, an ajiaco retains the unique flavors of its diverse roots while enriching the other elements. Some "ingredients" may dissolve completely while other "ingredients" remain more distinct, yet all provide flavor to the simmering stew, a stew that, by its very nature, is always in a state of flux. For example, although the Taíno left few visible traces of their existence, they continue to influence Cuban culture, popular memory, and imagination. Runaway slave communities incorporated the cultural influences of the Amerindian's dwindling population, reintroducing them to the overall Cuban culture.

While none of the inhabitants representing the "ingredients" of this ajiaco originated from the island, all repopulated the space called Cuba as displaced people. While not belonging, they made a conscious decision to be rooted to this particular land. For this reason, ajiaco is and should be unapologetically the Cubans' authentic space from where they approach Christ and the wider world (De La Torre 1997, 59–61). It is a space that collapses the dichotomy existing between those who have historically been called the oppressors and those whom they have oppressed. No longer is the binary relationship between "us" and "not us" acceptable. Cubanidad, the elusive ideal social order, becomes reality with the demise of hierarchical social structures that depend on dominant/subordinate relationships (the Exilic model), and the prevention of a uniform social structure that reduces everyone to a given norm (the Resident model). Rather, an ajiaco Christ honors and celebrates the diverse elements of the stew, which come together in harmony to establish a new creation.

Although Ortiz's language helps us understand a diverse Cuban Christ, we still lack a means by which to visualize this Christ. After all, Ortiz, as most scholars quoted throughout this book, is part of a dominant patriarchal Cuban culture. How do we include the voices of the disenfranchised in this discourse? For this reason we turn to visual art, specifically that depicting Jesus, to aid in comprehending how cubanidad—believers and non-believers, powerful and marginalized alike—see a Christ indigenous to the Cuban culture. José Martí undertook a similar project in his January 28, 1887, article, titled "The Munkácsy Christ," which was published in *La Nación*, a Buenos Aires newspaper. In 1886, the Hungarian painter Michael Lieb, also known as Munkácsy (1844–1900), conducted a U.S. tour featuring his works. Martí attended the exhibition and was fascinated with one particular painting, *Christ Before Pilate*. He wrote how Munkácsy's depiction of Christ signified the desire of the Hungarian people for independence. Through Munkácsy's art, Martí constructs a theological perspective for liberation that is linked to the national character of a politically oppressed people. I propose that Martí's methodology can be replicated through the use of identifiable Cuban art that developed mostly after his death.

Through the art of Cubans, we may glimpse how the Cuban culture at large "sees" the divine and themselves. Juan Marinello, the Cuban poet, essayist, and intellectual, found in the development of national art the potential for liberation. He argued that to insure a universalization of Cuban themes the Cuban artist must learn to view the indigenous with foreign eyes and the foreign with Cuban eyes. He wrote, "As long as Cuba did not offer the world a significant culture of originality and strength she would remain half free. Only art could achieve our total liberation" (1925, 304). Through Cuban art we may gain insight into national consciousness and the domain of the spiritual. By turning our attention to art, I do not begin a discourse of religion in art, but rather, art that is religion, where theological signs, symbols, and iconography merge with popular culture to create a postmodern hermeneutical reading.

Unfortunately, the examination of art to inform a Cuban Christology is somewhat problematic. Present-day politics prevent Cubans from exploring all aspects of their ajiaco via art. Due to the estrangement existing between the Exilic Cubans of Miami and the Resident Cubans of La Habana, it becomes impossible for either community to consider solely the artistic merits of a work, apart from the ideological filter by which it must first past. For Resident Cubans, the art of *gusanos* (worms—a derogatory term used by Resident Cubans to describe Exilic Cubans) is the art of those who have sold out their talents to the "Miami Mafia," trading aesthetic value for monetary gain. For Exilic Cubans, the art of *comunistas* (communists) represents agents who have chosen to paint for Fidel.

The events surrounding the 1988 fund-raiser for the Cuban Museum of Arts and Culture, located in Miami, illustrate the consequences of political ideology upon artistic institutions. When the museum held its fund-raiser by auctioning off works of art by Resident Cubans, Miami exploded in protest. Daily demonstrations were held at the museum, one of the works of Manuel Mendive, a Resident Cuban, titled *El Pavo Real*, was bought and publicly burned in the presence of five hundred people. Additionally, two bombs were detonated, one in the museum, another under the car of a museum official, both causing extensive damage. The city government response? They moved to evict the museum from its premises, prompting the museum to sue the city for violating its First Amendment rights, a case the museum won. However, the legal and physical threats frightened away visitors and patrons, eventually forcing the museum to declare bankruptcy. El exilio inflicts scars upon the Cuban ethos that are meant not to heal, but to remind what awaits those who deviate from the Miami party line.

Cuban Art as a Way of Seeing Christ

Great works of art can inspire the soul. They can also impose upon the viewer what interests the artist, interests based upon the artist's worldview. Such interests exist transhistorically, as intentional signs, as symptoms regulated by something or by what someone else does. Still, the inherent social structures behind visual art are products of the same social location in which the artist finds him or herself, for artists do not exist in a social vacuum. They are shaped by the sociohistorical space they occupy, a space influencing their works. Their artistic creations serve as historical documents expressing the social life they know, including its hopes, its struggles, its disappointments, its joys, and its tragedies. Seeing their works allows us to hear the unheard, the forgotten, and the undocumented voices of los humildes. These voices, missing from the writings of Cubans because they are usually the voices of the illiterate, find expression in Cuban art. Upon the empty canvas, the artist transforms the canvas's empty space into ideas, ideas kept silent through the normative gaze of those with power and privilege.

Theoretically, artistic expressions concerning Cuba are aligned with recent studies in anthropology and other social sciences, especially when they concern issues of nationalism, collective cultural expression, and ideological formation (Moore 1997, 5). Because art opens a path toward transcendental knowledge, I maintain that through art, specifically art representing the vision of los humildes, we can construct a vision of the Cuban Christ, a vision that weaves the sacred together with the profane, the religious with the political, the forgotten with the normalized. Studying Cuban artistic representations of Christ provides information on the construction of both Cuban identity and Cuban sacredness, past and present. By looking toward Cuban art, we give voice to the unheard voices of the Cuban ajiaco, voices that come from, but are not limited to, Amerindians, Africans, and women. Hence, Cuban art becomes the unifying substance of the Cuban ajiaco's understanding of Christ, where the diverse if not contradictory expressions of Christ are transformed virtually and discursively into a Christ for all Cubans.

This quest for an indigenous Cuban Christ, through art, creates an alternative to understanding the deity, an alternative that stands against the institutionalized establishment of church dogma, a dogma that at times is used for the continuation of Cuba's structures of oppression. Looking at art to seek and discover "theological truth" about the nature of Christ is an approach not commonly used by Western theologians. Eurocentric institutions of higher learning have taught us that the "truth" of Christ can either be found through the "God-inspired or God-dictated" revelatory message of the Bible, or obtained intellectually through the systematic use of logic. While these approaches are preferred by academics, turning our attention to art as the expression of the *pueblo* (people) is equally valid for the body of believers. Yet I suggest that a third approach, while not the exclusive path toward understanding Christ, can be intuitively determined by accessing the depths of one's soul. Artists, regardless of their race, class, or gender, who force us to witness what is normally kept quiet, what is purposely marginalized, confront the observer with the observer's own spirituality. For the remainder of this book, I intend to demonstrate how art reveals and provides insight about, and affords an entry into, Cuban reality. I will consider several works by Cuban artists past and present, Resident and Exilic, for the purpose of depicting the mysteries of God, the construction of an ajiaco Christ, the search for a common intra-Cuban identity, the introduction of the voices of los humildes, the dilemma of intra-Cuban estrangements, and the possibility of intra-Cuban reconciliation.

A painting is capable of interrupting that complicity which unites artist and observer in the same relation, a relationship that negates the reality expressed in the painting. Knowledge, illustrated by the painting, is revealed in a way that does not proclaim what that truth is; this differs dramatically from a supposedly objective or scientific reading. Works of art are able to tackle serious issues without taking themselves completely seriously. This form of non-communicated truth allows for the emergence of the deepest reality and the best-hidden structures of power, veiled so as to allow the painter and observer to discern the artistic expression while closing their eyes to it. Art is more than escaping from reality into imaginary worlds. A painting reflects the inability to take reality seriously, because it cannot appropriate the present in the way the present presents itself (Bourdieu 1995, 32–34).[1]

Originally Cuban artists, like most artists from colonialized countries, attempted to assimilate to the dominant European culture (Spain). By imitating Spanish artists, Cubans sought to prove that they were as skilled as the "masters." During the early attempts to forge a national identity through art, artists portrayed the Cuban ethos as equal to Spain's cultural heritage. With time, Cuban art began to speak to Cubans, not Spaniards. Artists tried to awaken a revolutionary commitment to la lucha. The development of Cuban identity through culture fosters nationalism, or as Frantz Fanon states, "Every culture is first and foremost national" (1963, 216).

Art becomes a document that raises human consciousness by unmasking the false consciousness of utopias. A painting, as a sign, contains within it the meanings given to it by the particular culture from which it arises. Even though the meaning of the signs is created by the dominant culture, peripheral groups can resignify these signs and destabilize normative power structures. Consequently, the reality by which we measure a painting merely becomes the recognized referent of a shared illusion. Yet, this illusion becomes a self-contained whole subordinate to its own order and structure. Through the artist's rendition, the inner structure of the work not only surpasses the power structures of reality, but also transforms those structures by providing a vision, an illusion that challenges the prevailing normalized gaze and discourse. The success of the artist is in his or her ability to evoke the images of the dominant reality while subverting them. Consequently, our aim in contemplating artistic paintings is not to offer insight or feelings about the piece, nor is it to provide a critique on art. Rather, through paintings, we glimpse a reality so familiar that its rules and regulations are unquestionably followed. We accomplish this task by constructing systems of intelligible relations capable of making sense of data.

The cardinal issue modern Cuban artists wrestle with is the question of identity from the underside of Cuba's political, cultural, social, and religious history. Resident Cuban artist Arturo Cuenca best characterizes the aim of the artist, and the task of the observer in understanding it. He describes his purpose as the "universal theoretical generalization of aesthetics in the praxis of an individual work of art . . . achieving not an aesthetic that describes art, but one that proposes itself as a new code for anthropological communication" (Camnitzer 1994, 205). To hear the voice of los humildes through visual art, we must decipher this "new code." Such a code is communicated by abrogating the oppressive hold that language has over minds as a means of indoctrinating, normalizing, and domesticating. As Herbert Marcuse reminds us, to communicate a consciousness-raising revolutionary message, an equally nonconformist "language" is required, a "language" that subverts the use of traditional material. Such a language exists in the domain of art (1972, 79–80).

The Spanish Christ

We can begin the decoding of this subversive language with the Spaniard Diego Velázquez (1599?–1660), by seeking Christ through his masterpiece, *Cristo de San Plácido* (figure 3). Velázquez is considered to be one of Spain's greatest artists, revealing the predominance of passion over the will and intellect. By 1623, appointed as court painter by King Philip IV, he excelled within the aristocratic baroque style. His free brushstroke technique, along with his mastery of tone and values, merges figures with surrounding atmosphere, creating an effect of striking realism. The art he produced, specifically that depicting the crucifixion, becomes a path by which we seek the Christ whose roots are Spanish. Art as symbol contains the capacity to transcend the limitations of language by expressing ideas and concepts in nondiscursive forms. Through Velázquez's paintings, the artist peers into a mystery and invites us to consider concrete issues. Art has the ability to transcend a specific space and time in order to transform society. Not limited to interpreting reality, art is capable of reconstructing it.

Fig. 3. Diego Velázquez, *Cristo de San Plácido*, courtesy of Museo Nacional del Prado, Madrid.

Miguel Unamuno, the great philosopher of early twentieth-century Spain, attempts to reconstruct reality in his book-length poem *The Christ of Velázquez*. By anthropomorphizing the abstract God of the theologians, he humanizes the divine. He reconciles Descartes's bifurcation of human passion and reason by way of art. His poetry, as an outpouring of hopes, fears, and desires, is converted into ideas as products of passions for life, as a response to the inevitable: death. Death for him is a crucial concept in becoming human. Unamuno counters Descartes's "Cogito, ergo sum" ("I think, therefore I am") with "sum, ergo cogito" ("Since I am human, I am also capable of thinking"). For Unamuno, Descartes is guilty of reducing individual humans to insignificant postscripts of progress. Aristotle's political animal, Rousseau's social animal, the Manchester School's economic animal, or Linnaeus's homo sapiens transform humanity into an abstraction and therefore rob it of its reality. Terms such as these objectify the individual person, denying his or her particular, unique, and intrinsic value. As social, political, or economic animals, individuals can be manipulated to accomplish the needs of the community, or the goals of the state, or the required increase in production. Instead, Unamuno insists that the individual should be viewed as the subject and the supreme object of all theological thought, including the discourse of understanding Christ. The individual, as subject and object, like Velázquez's Christ, is a tangible creature who is born, suffers, and dies, the emphasis here being on death. This emphasis is contrary to the Eurocentric development of the concept of sin in its understanding of Christ. Spanish literature lacks the Eurocentric motif of wrestling with one's individual sins. No Spanish literature corresponding to *The Pilgrim's Progress* exists. It is not sin that is feared, but rather dying in vain.

The "irrationality" of the cross for Unamuno became the cornerstone rejected by modernity but desperately needed by modernity. So also the cross as depicted by Velázquez becomes a scandal. The philosopher's quest for the rational justification of suffering in human existence often concludes with despair and a sense of God's absence or impotence. Yet a Cuban Christ offers God within that suffering. For Unamuno, the bloody Christ repels, if not repulses, all who fail to understand the Christ and the cult of suffering attached to Christ (*Obras completas* 2:273–76). Surely the divine could redeem the world by a more civilized and less gory process. Here, Christ is presented to us as a bruised, blood-streaked victim of human hatred who struggles in anguish with death. He is presented as the Christ who suffered freely, not as a price demanded by God, nor as a model for future generations to emulate so that they can find some redemptive glory in the suffering. Christ's suffering is the consequence of a world that suffers, a suffering and violence that spills over into the divine.

The Spaniard philosopher José Ortega y Gasset, a contemporary of Unamuno, also saw reality and art in a close embrace, where all superior works become an expression of experience molded by passion and elevated to universal legitimacy. Art serves as the historical vanguard resisting societal manipulation by providing a space where any major alteration in philosophy can first appear. Velázquez's masterpiece treats an insoluble situation by presenting a particular point of space and time as an expression of the entire world and the tragic problem of human life. Velázquez's Christ is not a synthesis of a series of movements. Rather, it is a single arrested instant in the existence of Christ, a distinct moment capturing a Christ who is always dying but never dies, self-negating but never empty. He paints time by giving eternity to that very instant. Art portrays existence as it is: condemned to be, to pass, and to decay, concrete and never completed (1972, 100, 105–6). Velázquez finds hope in the experience of death, giving immortality to the moment when the dying Christ refuses to die so that we can live. Liberation is achieved through the "failure" of Jesus' ministry as depicted in Christ's struggle upon the cross. This Christ who liberates us reconciles us to himself and to each other (De La Torre 1997, 73–74).

The vision of the crucified Christ seen through the eyes of Spaniards like Ortega and Unamuno offers a theological foundation capable of decentering the reigning Eurocentrism. Although Euroamerican theologies can provide some insight and direction about an ajiaco Christ, they ultimately fall short of understanding the Cuban location because it is not their location. Even Unamuno, Ortega, and Velázquez may express exclusively the Spanish side of the Cuban heritage. For an ajiaco Christ to be relevant, to capture the essence of cubanidad, we must now turn our attention to how Cuban artists depict this Christ.

Early Cuban Renditions of Christ

During the early Europeanization of Cuba, the *criollo* elite and the mercantile urban middle class were the only ones wealthy enough to patronize the arts. Aspiring to a cosmopolitan lifestyle, they created a demand for portraits of themselves, as well as for religious art. Due to the criollo's desire to imitate the European center's artistic vision, early Cuban artists modeled themselves upon European artists, and as such were classified as provincial artists. For example, *The Holy Trinity*, painted by Cuban master José Nicholás de Escalera (1734–1804), has been dismissed as an imitation of the Spanish master Bartolomé Murillo (Poupeye 1998, 29–30).

For centuries Cuba simply echoed the art of the cultural centers, making the Eurocentric norm an essential part of Cuba's art tradition, even though tension existed (and still does) between the resentment of artistic dependency and the desire to define a collective identity. The 1920s and 1930s witnessed the rise of global nationalism, as both new and old nations attempted to carve out for themselves a space within the changing world order. Among colonized nations, anti-imperialist hopes soared. Chronologically, Cuba was the second nation, after Mexico, to abandon Eurocentric academicism and to develop an artistic style in which, according to Cuban art critic Jose Sicre, Cuban artists learned never to say "Sir" to anyone (1987, 9). Throughout the Caribbean, anticolonialist sentiments found expression in national art movements, the best known being the Cuban "vanguardia," the first Caribbean School to gain the attention of Europe and North America. Influenced by Fernando Ortiz's concepts of nationalism as rooted in the ethnic makeup of Cubans (Amerindian, Spaniard, African, and Asian), these painters attempted to define Cuban consciousness through their works. In 1944 the Museum of Modern Art in New York City held a major exhibition of modern Cuban art.[2] Such initiatives were partly motivated by an effort in the United States to exhibit and acquire Latin American art as part of Roosevelt's overall Good Neighbor Policy.

The start of modernism in Cuba occurred when the vanguardia painters exhibited their works in the 1927 exhibit called *Exposición de Arte Nuevo*, sponsored by the Revista de Avance. Their works defined a distinct break with academic art, which was prevalent in the San Alejandro School, definer of Cuban art since its founding in 1818. The vanguardia synthesized modernist European styles, specifically primitivism and "négrophilie," while also employing regional symbols and themes. It is significant that these first modernist, or vanguardia, painters all traveled to European cities early in their careers. It was in Paris during the 1920s that they came in contact with cubism, constructivism, dadaism, expressionism, fauvism, and surrealism.

The vanguardia painters included Eduardo Abela (1891–1965), Jorge Arche (1905–1956), Carlos Enríquez (1900–1957), Arístides Fernández (1904–1934), Victor Manuel García (1897–1969), Antonio Gattorno (1904–1980), Wifredo Lam (1902–1982), Amelia Peláez del Casal (1895–1968),

Marcelo Pogolotti (1902–1988), Fidelio Ponce de León (1895–1949), and Domingo Ravenet (1905–1969). They, like Cuba, were born during the turn of the century, reaching maturity simultaneously with Cuba, linking artist and nation in their individual and collective struggle to define identity. While cultural interpreters like Fernando Ortiz attempted to define cubanidad as a condition of the soul whose elements consist of the dynamic mixture of Amerindian, Spaniard, and African heritages, resulting in a sense of national pride and a patriotic duty toward political and economic reform (1939, 3), these artists attempted to represent visually this concept through images based on reality and illusion. They, along with the intelligentsia, believed that art contributed to the construction of cubanidad. Art was for them a means of advancing the cause of liberation, for if a cultural identity could be created, the island's political, economic, and social conditions would be advanced. Hence, it is no surprise that by the mid-1920s they positioned themselves against La Academia Nacional de Bellas Artes de San Alejandro, which they considered to be antiquated, rigid, and greedy for the limited state resources for art. Even though San Alejandro continued to be Cuba's main art school, by the start of the twentieth century it was hopelessly conservative and out of touch with modern art currents that began with postimpressionism (Martínez 1992, 13). Although the vanguardia rejected academic art, they did not reject tradition.

Those who went to Europe returned by the 1930s to La Habana and visibly contributed to the city's cultural life. They did not attempt to imitate these new forms; rather, they adapted international trends to define Cuban identity. African art was then the current fashion in Paris. Nostalgia for the homeland encouraged these artists to develop and valorize one of Cuba's most significant national identity themes, afrocubanismo.[3] Alejo Carpentier, a leading vanguardia writer, commented on the development of this theme by claiming, "The Afrocuban [theme] is, for today's Cuba, modern!" (Martínez 1996, 43–46). Yet it must be remembered that the vanguardia artists were mostly middle-class whites conversing with their own kind. Hence their depictions of Cuba were not inclusive, but represented the avant-garde segment of the middle class. Three exceptions are Lam (who was not white), and Ponce and García (who were not middle class), and through their art we continue our quest for the ajiaco Christ.

Wifredo Lam, one of Cuba's most celebrated artists, serves as our first guide. In his attempt to forge cubanidad, he incorporates what Cubans consider sacred. Lam, a protégé of Picasso and the first Caribbean painter acknowledged by the West as an important figure in modern art, elucidates why we turn to aesthetics to introduce the voices of los humildes into the discourse of creating an ajiaco Christ. He was the first painter in the history of Western art to give us a vision of the Americas from an African perspective, using symbols engendered by the sacred and profane customs of Cuba's African roots. Until then, if Cuba's blacks ever appeared in any scenes created by Cuban artists, they were generally depicted in a derogatory fashion, parodying slave mannerisms with exaggerated *bembas* (lips) and *narizes mala* (bad noses). Afro-Cuban women usually looked sensual, while Afro-Cuban men appeared grotesque, something to fear. A Cuban of Afro-Sino descent, Lam did not journey far to discover and uncover his roots, specifically his Santería roots. Lam used art to converse with the sociopolitical structures of oppression, describing his work as "an act of decolonization."

Strongly influenced by Picasso's cubism, Lam synthesized cubism and surrealism with Afro-Cuban images, permitting him to develop a mythical view of Cuba. He was able, according to Julia Herzberg, "to subvert traditional subjects by redefining the empirical world in terms of the spiritual world" (1996, 150). His masterpiece *The Jungle*, which ranks with Picasso's *Guernica* as one of the century's most haunting images, may be the first manifesto of the Two-Third World (figure 4). The scissors (symbolic of Oggún, patron of blacksmiths) in the hand of the fourth figure on the right signifies the ritual of cutting herbs for medicinal purposes. The amalgamation of human, plant, and animal forms creates a rhythmic movement or dance that brings honor to the spiritual aspects found throughout nature and suggests the phenomenon of spiritual possession. His exposure to these African motifs present in the Caribbean coincided with the region's consciousness-raising movement known as negritude, and with the poetry of its leading exponent, Aimé Césaire (whom Lam met in Martinique in 1941).

Lam succeeded in introducing an anticolonial agenda into Picasso's primitivism. He considered his work to be a means designed to de-center normative racism. His use of sugar cane and tobacco leaves in his work reminds the observer of Ortiz's allegorical study of Cuban culture, *Cuban Counterpoint of Tobacco and Sugar*. In 1976 Lam described his work as follows: "La Habana was a land of pleasure, of sugary music, rumbas, mambos, and so forth. The Negroes were considered picturesque . . . I refused to paint chá-chá-chá. I wanted with all my heart to paint the drama of the plastic art of the blacks. In this way I could act as a Trojan horse that would spew forth hallucinating figures with the power to surprise, to dis-

Fig. 4. Wifredo Lam, *The Jungle*, courtesy of the Museum of Modern Art, New York.

turb the dreams of the exploiters" (Mosquera 1996, 232–35; Poupeye 1998, 9, 51, 62).

Lam's paintings show that knowledge comes through imagination, through art, and not always or only through logical discourse or rational exposition. His art demonstrates emotions and passions of the intentions and the knowledge of everyday life. This quality of Lam's art places it among the most powerful "stories" of the plight of los humildes. Through art, Lam shows how knowledge is achieved through imagination. Our task is to analyze paintings for the purpose of reconstructing the religious-social "reality" of the artist, and by so doing, find the Cuban Christ.

Among the most original of these first avant-garde painters was Fidelio Ponce de León. Ponce liked painting personal interpretations of Christ in an expressionistic manner. He never left Cuba, living a bohemian life characterized by poverty and alcoholism; he eventually died of tuberculosis. An admirer of El Greco, Modigliani, Murillo, and Harmensz Rembrandt, he developed an unmistakable melodramatic style presenting languid and sickly colorless figures. Ponce's iconography rested on Christian mystical themes, a subject matter ignored by his contemporaries.[4] Unlike other vanguardia painters, Ponce shared none of their interest in defining a Cuban sense of place or optimism. Instead, using a colorless palette, he offered powerful, detached, humanistic images that reveal the pessimism and tragedy of the human condition. Even when painting children at play in the countryside, he treated the scene with a ghostly sadness and despair. They look emaciated, reduced to "play" on a spartan canvas.

In an attempt to transcend his own human existence racked with tragedy and insecurity, he mystically depicted three forsaken Christs through tense chiaroscuro, compressed in an impoverished space emerging from a desolated and misty backdrop. These figures have few facial features; their thin and gloomy appearance gives the whole painting a ghost-like quality. Images of Christ bear expressionless faces and somber demeanor. His alienated Christ does not seem to reassure, for Christ appears insecure. Ponce moved away from traditional portrayals of Christian subjects associated with emotions of hope and transcendence, and instead presented an image that emotes anguish and desolation. In his work *The Faces of Christ*, Ponce successfully captured the dismal realities of los humildes, reflection of his own human condition, his particular fear of death, and the influence of Cuba's brand of Catholicism. Only the impasto lines, appearing as rays of light radiating from the top of the head and the eyes, hint at promise.

Fig. 5. Fidelio Ponce de León, *The Faces of Christ,* courtesy of the Ramón and Nercys Cernuda Collection.

From the solitary barrenness of these Christs appear rays of light, minute rays of hope for the human condition (Martínez 1996, 47–48) (figure 5).

A third vanguardia painter, Victor Manuel García, was influenced by Paul Gauguin and Paul Cézanne, and along with Antonio Gattorno introduced the ideas and styles of these French postimpressionist masters to Cuban art. A primitivist interpretation of Jesus can be noted in Victor Manuel's *Christ,* where he simplifies reality (figure 6). He is more concerned with revealing the character of Christ than with his status. Christ is not seated on a throne in full regalia with a crown or halo upon his head; rather, Christ appears like un humilde, one of the common folk. We do not look toward heaven for Christ, for he is among the disenfranchised. Even though Victor Manuel lived in poverty, the privation of life is ignored in his works as rural life is romanticized in his countryside renditions. Yet in his *Christ* is present a reminder of the cross that Jesus (along with all los humildes) must carry. In the midst of a placid and tranquil portrait to which the painter and viewer can escape, crucifixion is present. The horror of the cross invades the rustic and timeless world that Victor Manuel usually created.

Since the vanguardia painters, Cuban art has continued to reflect the island's political turmoil as succeeding generations of artists wrestle with the issue of national identity. By 1938 a new group of artists had emerged, known as the "second generation," which included Cundo Bermúdez, Mario Carreño, Alfredo Lozano, Mariano Rodriguez, Luis Martínez-Pedro, and René Portocarrero. Like the vanguardia painters before them, they shared an interest in exploring Cuban identity by adapting international styles. Often, however, this identity was portrayed as predominately white. Portocarrero is a case in point. In his *Virgin and Child,* portraying La Virgen de la Caridad del Cobre, Cuba's patron saint, he ignores the fact that she is of dark complexion and paints her as a white blonde with blue eyes (figure 7). He distorts Cuban identity by whitewashing la virgen and erasing her African roots. Cubans are to be seen as a white people; to suggest otherwise borders on heresy. Hence, Portocarrero not only reflects racial views normalized by the dominant Cuban culture, but the work itself perpetrates the continuing attempt of de-Africanizing Cuban culture.

By the 1950s, another group developed, known as Los Once (The Eleven). They made a modest impact with the introduction of geometric abstract expressionism. Artists characterized by a radical and polarized view, they rebelled against the canons of the nationalist schools, seeking instead a universal expression within formalist modernism influenced by

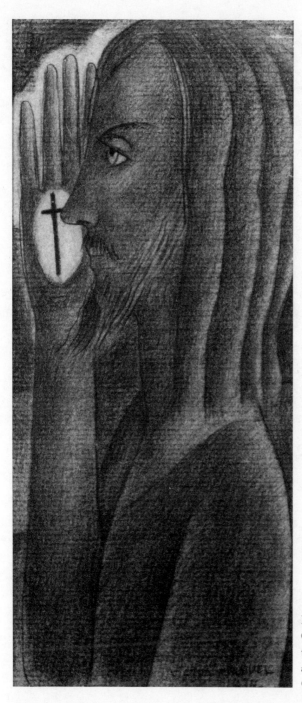

Fig. 6. Victor Manuel García, *Christ*, courtesy of the Ramón and Nercys Cernuda Collection.

Fig. 7. René Portocarrero, *Virgin and Child*, courtesy of the Ramón and Nercys Cernuda Collection.

Afrocubanismo. For Los Once, the first contemporary avant-garde group, art was for art's sake.

The Resident Christ of the Revolution

The search for national identity and self-determination continued with the coming of the 1959 revolution. At that time Cubans turned to their long tradition of producing powerful political posters as a way of expressing a new national consciousness. These posters were inexpensive to manufacture and reached a literate audience. Art posters were placed into the service of the revolution to promote a socialist worldview and to advance the morals of the "new" Cuban. Issues ranged from advocating proper communist morality to mobilizing the country for nationwide campaigns. At times, poster art revealed Cuban spirituality, specifically how Resident Cubans see and understand Christ. This was the case with the 1969 poster of Alfredo Rostgaard, *Cristo guerrillero* (*The Guerrilla Christ*) (figure 8).

Rostgaard's poster reveals a Hispanic-looking Christ compatible with the revolution. In this poster, Christ appears with a halo around his head and a rifle swung over his shoulder. The artist was inspired by the Colombian priest Camilo Torres, an early advocate of liberation theology. Torres believed that if Jesus were alive today, he would be a *guerrillero*, a guerrilla rebel. Faithful to his understanding of Christ, he left the security of church buildings to minister to those in the jungles who were battling the Colombian dictatorship of his time. Shortly after joining the armed struggle, he was killed. Rostgaard's poster, produced shortly after Torres's death, commemorates the revolutionary priest's version of Christ and advocates the Christ of the revolution.

Although Exilic Cubans view the revolution as satanic, several Resident Cubans see God's hand moving through Castro. Resident Cuban artist José A. Toirac provides an excellent example of the merging of Christ with heroes of the revolution (figure 9). In his work *Hechos en Manila* (*Made in Manila*), Toirac attempts to show the correlation between the life and death of Christ and Ernesto "Che" Guevara (1928–1967). El Che, as he is known in Cuba, reached mythical proportions both in Cuba and Latin America. Argentinian by birth, he was trained as a doctor but waged guerrilla warfare against rightist dictatorships. Before meeting Castro in Mexico, he joined the forces that attempted to depose Juan Peron in Argentina and joined the government of Jacobo Arbenz in Guatemala against the

Fig. 8. Alfredo Rostgaard, *Cristo guerrillero,* courtesy of the International Institute of Social History, Amsterdam.

U.S.-sponsored overthrow. Afterward, Guevara joined Castro's revolutionary cadre. He traveled with Castro to Cuba, where he fought in Castro's army, even helping to shape its strategy.

With the success of the revolution, Guevara became the new Cuban government's minister of industry (1961–65). But his passion remained in fighting rightist dictatorships of Latin America. In 1965 he left Cuba to lead Cuban-style revolutions in South America. He eventually reappeared in Bolivia, where in 1967 his group was decimated by Bolivian forces near Santa Cruz (Holy Cross). El Che was captured and executed.

Since his death, Che has come to represent the ideal Cuban citizen. Resident Cubans are to model their life on Che in the way Christians are called to model their life on Christ. José Toirac captures the correlation of Che and Christ's death in his art. He uses a body bag as the tablecloth for the Last Supper, foreshadowing the death of Christ (Che?) on whose body believers eat (communion). On the cloth appear sketches of the plants and animals that Che wrote about in his diary as he recorded what he captured and ate during his revolutionary days in Bolivia. Toirac points out the biblical theme of sacrificial death. These animals gave their life to sustain the lives of El Che and his followers (Toirac 2000). Next to the figure is the date, which corresponds with Che's diary entry indicating the animal captured and eaten. Thirteen plates, as if for Jesus and his twelve disciples, are neatly stacked. On the plates is the image of Che Guevara, the photo taken after his execution as proof that he had been captured. In the photo he has a countenance similar to that of Christ. In effect, Che becomes the Christ of the Americas, a view not limited to Cuba. In the mural by José Antonio Burciaga titled *Last Supper of Chicano Heros,* which appears in the dining hall of Casa Zapata (the Chicano-theme student residence at Stanford University), Che takes the position of Christ.

The head of El Che on the plate also alludes to the biblical story of John the Baptist's head being served on a platter. The first martyr for the cause of Christ, John the Baptist is murdered by Herod, the tetrarch, as payment for his stepdaughter's entertaining him and his guests with a dance. For Toirac, John the Baptist and Jesus had to die so that someone else could live. So too does it become necessary for Che Guevara to become the sacrificial lamb for the sins of the world, a sacrifice capable of bringing new life and hope to the Cuban people.

Fig. 9. José A. Toirac, *Hechos en Manila*, courtesy of the Arizona State University Art Museum, Tempe.

The Christ of the Exilio

Exilic Cubans have also developed their own understanding of the function of Christ. During the recent Elián crisis in Miami, posters of Christ were used to mobilize the Exilic Cuban community in their campaign against the Castro government. Elián was the small boy rescued off the Florida coast who became the epicenter of a political custody battle between Exilic and Resident Cubans during the first half of 2000. During the predawn hours of April 22, Elián was forcefully removed by federal agents from his Miami home and returned to his biological father, who was waiting for him in Washington, D.C. His forceful removal occurred on Holy Saturday. On Easter morning, the day after the raid, pulpits throughout South Florida prayed for Elián, his Miami family, and the community at large. That evening, during the mass at Our Lady of Charity shrine, the congregation, carrying prints of Jesus Christ on the cross with his blood dripping down over the island of Cuba, heard Reverend Francisco Santana proclaim, "Elián is staying and Fidel is leaving." When Elián's Miami family stood before the congregation, the parishioners waved miniature Cuban flags as they burst into the Cuban national anthem. Like their Resident Cuban counterparts, the poster of a Christ whose blood drips upon Cuba merges the Exilic Cuban political worldview with religious fervor. According to Reverend Santana, the poster answers the question most asked by the Exilic Cuban community: Will a bloodbath ensue in a post-Castro Cuba? The artist captures the sentiments of Reverend Santana, who said, "The only blood needed to be shed in Cuba is the blood of Christ which brings forgiveness and redemption" (Santana 2000). The blood of Christ not only symbolizes the means by which Cuba will be "liberated" from Castro, but also the sacrifice of many Christlike figures who shed their blood combating Castro's government.

Some of those Christlike figures can be found among the more than 40,000 *balseros* (rafters) who, seeking economic and political freedom, braved the Florida Straits and, in several cases, tragically perished at sea. These balseros, as in the case of Elián's mother, Elizabeth Brotons, risk their lives in the hopes of a better existence for themselves and their children. Those who do succumb to the sea are elevated by the Exilic Cuban community in Miami as imitators of Christ, where through them others might be saved. This sentiment is captured in the portrait *Cuban Martyr*, where one of these balsero is seen crucified over the raging sea (figure 10). The caption under the balsero Christ-figure states, "dedicated to those who rest in the liberation of the sea." The Christian martyrs of the twenty-first century

Fig. 10. Fernando Chirife and Liberator Brothers, *Cuban Martyr*, courtesy of the artist.

are seen and perceived by the Miami community as being these Resident Cubans who risk everything to become Exilic Cubans. Yet, this way of seeing is not limited to Cubans in Miami. This mix-media portrait was designed by a Paraguayan, Fernando Chirife, and two Argentine brothers, Pablo and Gabriel Liberato, who were responsible for making the computer image a reality. Presently, they are selling this image on t-shirts through the internet. While the artists are not Cubans, they claim to identify with the ultimate sacrifice of the balseros because they too endured a totalitarian regime in their countries during the 1970s (Liberato 2001). The Exilic Cuban Christ ceases to be a symbol for just Cubans in Miami, but also becomes a symbol of hope for all who overcome immeasurable obstacles in search of liberation.

A Macho Christ

During the 1980s a new generation of Resident artists known as the "Six New Painters" (José Bedia, Juan Francisco Elso Padilla, José Manuel Fors, Gustavo Pérez Monzón, Ricardo Rodríguez Brey, and Rubén Torres Llorca) participated in an exhibit called *Volumen I*. This new generation shared an interest in experimentation, beginning a process of increasingly radical ruptures with Cuban traditional art. They assumed a condition of the diaspora, dealing with themes of migration and expressing what was being said by everyone behind closed doors. On the other side of the Florida Straits, among Exilic Cubans, an art style emerged known as the "external Cuban community," a product of a forced political exodus where the artists, displaced from their native culture, sought a different space defined by a different time. These artists represented what was distant and what was previous, a mythological rendition of lost land and lost time. In the 1990s both Resident and Exilic artists continued to operate within the social realm, searching for the testimonies of the disenfranchised while simultaneously mystifying the island. They engaged in the postmodern enterprise of reclaiming forgotten, repressed, and lost memory, history, and identity.

For example, the art of Rubén Torres Llorca, now living in exile and one of the "Six New Painters" of the 1980s, reflects Cuba's repressed African and Amerindian traditions. He is critical of the style used by Picasso, specifically Picasso's fascination with African art, that is, arbitrarily incorporating non-Western objects into Western art works. As a self-proclaimed contemporary medicine man, Torres Llorca creates a space between magic and psychology in which he intervenes, shamanlike, in his art to channel magic in solving personal problems. His first "magical" work, *Adivinanza* (*Conundrum*), exemplifies Torres Llorca style. Its iconography derives from a typical Cuban altarpiece created with both handmade and found objects (figure 11).

In this work, Torres Llorca forces us to deal with Christ's and Cuba's machismo. His Amerindian Christ, unashamed in exposing his masculinity, becomes a fetish figure and a powerful talisman against evil. It proclaims the artist's triumph over his personal enemies, represented by the two heads (one in the dog's mouth, the other on top of the sword). Incantations common to Santería are displayed by the scissors, which represent how his enemies are made impotent by their upside-down placement in a clay jar filled with the soil from his yard in Cuba. The message on the altar states, "Moral: The King Who Knows Will Not Die Like the King Who Does Not Know Will Die." This motto warns that vigilance and awareness safeguard against harm.

Torres Llorca taps into the Latin American idiom *"Dios dice, 'Ayúdate que yo te ayudaré'"* ("God says, 'Help yourself and then I'll help you'"). He reveals a religiosity not dependent on a "pie in the sky" eschatology. Divine solutions to human problems exist now, in the present, for the vigilant and for those who possess the knowledge that defeats death. In this work, Torres Llorca captures the religious attitudes of los humildes. Hope for surviving the present condition rests on a commitment to participate in the divine's activity in history rather than simply waiting for it to happen. Yet the depiction of the decapitated, vanquished enemies creates a certain anxiety. Anyone looking at the altar finds it difficult to escape the macho rendition of divine justice and the call for the individual to help bring about that justice.

On the other hand, Tomas Sanchez, a recent Cuban refugee, depicts Christ as the victim of physical abuse. Sanchez usually concentrated on Cuban landscapes and emphasized the native flora and fauna. He used the wealth of symbols from the scenery to express a uniquely purified Cuban experience where human figures appear passive and sensual. His works basically provide the viewer with a mythical space to which they can escape. Yet Sanchez's *Christ* is nude and exposed, hanging from a cross (figure 12). The spectator is forced to deal simultaneously with the death passion and sexuality of Christ. Cubans who also find themselves naked before the aggression of colonialism and imperialism find a Christ who understands their exposure and emasculation. This portrayal of a frontal

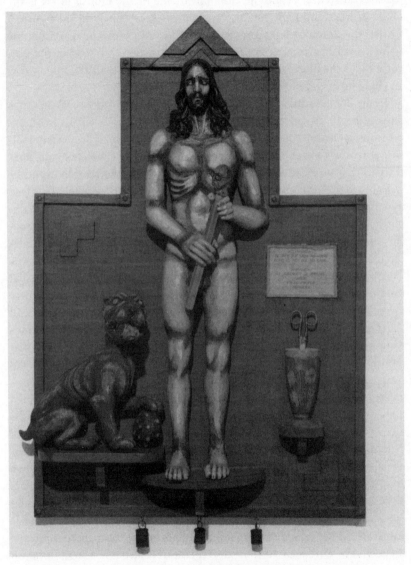

Fig. 11. Rubén Torres Llorca, *Adivinanza,* courtesy of the artist.

nude Christ attempts to elucidate the union of opposites that serve as the bases of existence. While the common theme of the erotica in art is the union of male and female, it also encompasses, especially in the figure of Christ, the union of light and darkness, life and death, the deity and the human. Sanchez creates an ambiguous scene where the God of the universe takes the place of los humildes by hanging exposed and vulnerable, an object to be gazed upon.

Ironically, Sanchez explains that when he first did the work in Cuba during the 1970s, political pressure forced him to depict Christ in an expressionist fashion. Government authorities would have rejected any realistic portrayals. An expressionist technique allowed the viewer to interpret the painting satirically. But by appearing to belittle the passion event, he was able to present his work to a larger audience (Sanchez 2000). In effect, by emphasizing what Cubans find detestable, that is, the humiliation, domestication, and conquest of a man rather than a celebration of his machismo, Sanchez provided a very realistic Christ with whom los humildes can identify.

A further irony occurred when Sanchez's works were first exhibited at the Cuban Museum of Arts and Culture in 1993. The Miami community exploded because he was a Resident Cuban. The museum was accused of collaborating with the enemy for highlighting "communist" art. Demands were made not to feature the works of Resident Cuban artists. Yet a few months later, while in Mexico, Sanchez sought political asylum. Unable to secure authorization from the Cuban government to establish an art foundation, he left the island. Immediately, the Miami community accepted him as one of their own. The works that were deemed tainted a few months earlier became sanctified.

Exilic Cuban artist Carlos Macía's *Trinity* also presents a nude resurrected Christ, but his work reveals the Eurocentric aspects of the Cuban ethos (figure 13). His rendition of Christ rests on his Spanish roots, roots he rediscovered while he was a seminarian at the Convento de Franciscanos in Spain preparing for the priesthood. He looks to the Spain of his ancestors for his religious foundation and his neoclassical approach to art, suggestive of European mythological themes. He also relies on his location within the United States to reveal a habitus shaped by his existence in exile during his formative teenage years. He forces the observer to come to terms with Christ's manhood, for the Cuban focus of machismo finds expression in the victorious, risen Christ who unashamedly presents his frontal nudity, along with the nude backside of God. The observers find

Fig. 12. Tomas Sanchez, *Christ*, courtesy of the artist.

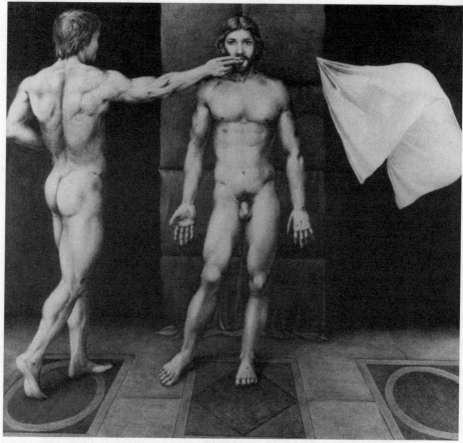

Fig. 13. Carlos Macía, *Trinity*, courtesy of the Milton Martinez, Jr., Collection.

themselves worshiping a Trinity that glorifies and celebrates God's masculinity.

The Female Cuban Christ

To counter these overly masculine versions of Christ, Cuban artists also present a feminine Christ. Carlito Suarez, a Resident Cuban artist known simply as Carlito, provides us with a stunning rendition of Christ as a woman. If Christ is symbolically understood as the "least of the community," then depicting Christ as a woman becomes a theological comment on gender oppression. A female Christ does not negate the historical fact that the person Jesus, who roamed in Judea two thousand years ago, was male; rather, it recognizes that Jesus can be found among the most marginalized of society. In Carlito's work *Crucifixion*, Jesus' body is a large-breasted woman whose skin is cast in iron, but the iron mask is breaking away (figure 14). According to the artist, this female Christ represents Cuba, who like Christ, is crucified (Suarez 2000). The shedding of the iron body cast symbolizes the hope of a society dominated by oppression (external and internal) but now attempting to free itself. Also, it refers to the oppression of machismo of Cuban patriarchal structures. Regardless of Cuba's history of repression, Christ, for the artist, continues to reside in the minds of Cubans, as symbolized by the portrait of Christ representing the female figure's head. Christ is not solely found in the minds of Cubans, but also in the hands. By locating the mouth where the right hand belongs the artist symbolizes that theology is done, rather than simply spoken. Theology is praxis, literally transforming what is said into what can be done through one's hands. As such, theology is doing (the purpose of hands), not solely the articulation of pious words. The other hand is nailed to the cross. The dripping blood atones for the sins of humans. On the ground where this blood falls, a new plant springs forth, signifying the new ideas being born on the island as a result of the saving act of Christ. The feet of Christ represent the estrangement of the Cubans in general, Cuban Christians in particular. One foot is in the water, identifying the exiled Christian church. The other foot is cast in a bricked pyramid, holding the resident Christian church in place. To the right of the female Christ is a square located in the water and displaying an apple. This represents the prohibition of immigration. Why an apple? Could it be that the apple is a Genesis (3:1–7) reference to the forbidden fruit of the "tree of knowledge of good and evil" located in Garden of Eden? The biblical account tells us that if humans eat of this tree "they would surely die." Yet the fruit is "pleasing to the eye." Likewise, the lure of el exilio with its glitter of economic success may appear pleasing, yet its taste may bring death to the Cuban soul. Exile is the forbidden fruit Resident Cubans long to eat.

Exilic Cuban Natalia Raphael also depicts a feminine Christ by placing a tortured female body on the cross in her work *Crucifixion II* (figure 15). Originally, she did not intend to make a crucifixion or a religious icon. Instead, she was attempting to find a metaphor to convey the inner conflict of what a woman should be, a woman striving to reconcile with the pain and loss of her homeland. Longing to walk once again in her grand-

Fig. 14. Carlito, *Crucifixion*, courtesy of the artist and Art Cubana, <www.art
cubana.com>.

mother's garden in Matanzas, she returned to Cuba as an adult only to discover the systematic whitewashing of Cuban history and culture by those living in el exilio. Her attempt to reconnect with her land inspired her to work with soil, dirt, and mud. She formed a female body modeled after her own body, to carry the consequences of the sins that caused the artist's loss. The individual, social, and mystical bodies become separate signs signifying each other. Like the Trinity, they are three separate identities, yet one inseparable unit. Raphael's tortured body becomes Christ's tortured body. The body is headless so as not to identify it solely with her or with any one person. Also, the body lacks arms, which represents the fragmentation of her identity and that of all Exilic Cubans. In short, Christ identifies with all women like her (Raphael 2000).

Woman artists like Raphael project their feminine bodies as metaphors for the struggles, hardships, and oppression experienced due to sociopolitical sexism found within the Cuban ethos. Raphael's body as Christ's body is reminiscent of Exilic Cuban artist Ana Mendieta (1948–1985), who more than any other Caribbean artist sought identification with Cuban soil in her quest for personal identity as a Cuban. In 1981 she created *Rupestrian Sculptures* in Cuba, the first Exilic Cuban artist to receive permission from Cuban authorities to conduct her work on the island. *Rupestrian Sculptures* are a series of carvings made in the walls of caves first inhabited by Amerindians, in the Jaruco forest, twenty miles from La Habana. The carvings appear as smaller-than-life-size female bodies taking vaginal forms in keeping with the artist's metaphor of earth as womb.

Each individual carving is named after a female figure from Taíno mythology. One such carving is titled *Guacar*, with the by-line *Our Menstruation* (figure 16). Using the earth as canvas, these carvings allude to the cycle of life and the transience of human experience. To create these works, Mendieta used her own body or a symbolic silhouette outline, in ritualistic performances and interventions upon the cavern walls. She explained her work, antecedents to Yves Klien body paintings or Ralph Ortiz's destructionism, as follows:

> I have been carrying on a dialogue between the landscape and the female body (based on my own silhouette). I believe this has been a direct result of my having been torn from my homeland during my adolescence. I am overwhelmed by the feeling of having been cast from the womb. My art is the way I reestablish the bonds that unite me to the universe. It is a return to the maternal source. Through my

Fig. 15. Natalia Raphael, *Crucifixion II,* courtesy of the artist.

earth/body sculptures I become one with the earth. (Poupeye 1998, 154–56)

Besides the use of a female body to represent Christ, artists like Raphael further provide us with an example of a common theme running through Latin American art by presenting a realistic crucifixion, capturing the event's essential horror, cruelty, and torture. Absent are all of the adornments common among traditional Eurocentric depictions of the Passion. Raphael, like Tomas Sanchez, refuses to let the observer's eye find a pleasant neutral space within the canvas on which to rest. Raphael presents a tortured female body, void of head and arms. The body bears the brunt of the pain, unable to comprehend the affliction, for it is headless, nor can the body do anything about it, for it has no hands. This female Christ can only submit, docilely, to its oppression like the domesticated humildes. Like Velázquez before them, Sanchez and Raphael are able to grasp the complexity of the human condition through the representation of this violent figure on the cross. They illustrate how philosophical reflections on evil and theodicy are interrupted by death, specifically the unjust death of the crucified.

Such depictions of the Cuban Christ portray the ultimate tragic victim who dies as do the innumerable oppressed victims of God's crucified people: Amerindians, Africans, and Asians. Jesus did not seek death; rather, it was imposed on him by the religious and political leaders. Nor did Jesus simply resign himself to his plight; instead, he freely chose to accompany los humildes, whose deaths are always required to protect the privilege of those who have power over them. With los humildes we can include those who suffered under Batista's regime[5] or el paredón,[6] all seemingly abandoned by God, as if God turned God's back to them. But God manifests God's presence, not as a transcendent power standing triumphantly over earthly injustice, but as the self-denying Christ who surrenders his life in the struggle against the political injustices of his day. Through Christ's unjust death, he is made the King of Life, drawing all to him as he is "lifted up" (John 12:32). Yet his agony does not end with the cross but continues to exist within the daily afflictions of all who suffer. Christ's crucifixion extended his reconciling power, first demonstrated to a particular oppressed group of his time, to embrace all oppressed groups of all times. Today's hope for immortality is found in the divine's self-negation, manifested as a love praxis, a praxis always leading toward justice, by reconciling Cubans to God and to one another.

Fig. 16. Ana Mendieta, *Guacar—Our Menstruation* from the Rupestrian Series, courtesy of the Estate of Ana Mendieta and Galerie Lelong, New York.

While the cross becomes a sacred common space, it remains important to avoid romanticizing it. If Jesus only suffers, then he cannot liberate. The cross moves beyond the cult of suffering toward redemptive solidarity with the oppressed. The solidarity forged in the shadows of the cross requires more than just establishing fellowship in suffering. Beyond Christ's suffering lies the realization of his salvation, liberation, and reconciliation.

The cross benefits not only humanity but God as well. At the cross, God learned firsthand about the nature of the human condition and the consequences of oppression. God discovered what total abandonment means, for Christ was betrayed by his friend, deserted by his followers, convicted by the elite in his Father's name, and condemned by the community that praised his entrance into Jerusalem a few days earlier. The cross becomes a place that allows the divine to become one with los humildes, the crucified people of God abandoned by those with wealth and power.

The Black Cuban Christ

The theme of Christ as one of los humildes is also illustrated in the paintings of the Exilic Cuban artist Alejandro Anreus. Anreus confronts the white Cuban perception that Jesus can only be seen as a white man. In his work *Cristo Negro* (*Black Christ*), he challenges Cuban white supremacy, especially the racism in Miami (figure 17). He dedicates this work to Nelson Mandela, inspired by the reception Mandela received when visiting Dade County. During the summer of 1990, a hero's welcome was being planned for Mandela's Miami visit. But prior to arriving, Mandela acknowledged, during an ABC television interview, his friendship with Fidel Castro. This "friendship" developed when Mandela languished in a South Africa prison due to his opposition to apartheid. Mandela had basically been forgotten by the world when Castro offered support and encouragement to Mandela. Although Cubans in Miami may perceive such a gesture as politically motivated due to Cuba's active involvement in African affairs during the '70s and '80s, still, a forgotten Mandela welcomed the support.

When Mandela expressed his appreciation for Fidel Castro, the Miami community rose up in arms. The Miami commission withdrew its official welcome, even though he had never accepted any local government invitation to speak; his visit was motivated by an invitation to address a union convention. The Cuban community, in charge of the political structures of the county, went out of their way to oppose Mandela's visit. When the African American community objected to Mandela's treatment by declar-

Fig. 17. Alejandro Anreus, *Cristo Negro,* courtesy of the artist and the Collection of M. Socarra and R. Jimenez.

ing a boycott of their own city and asking outside convention planers not to choose Miami, the Exilic Cuban political power structure charged that the African American community was insensitive to Exilic Cubans. This was not the first, nor last, racial conflict to ignite Miami. The needs and interests of the dominant Exilic Cuban power structure in maintaining fever-pitch hostility toward Castro outweigh the needs and interests of Miami's black community, even to the point of enforcing censorship and violating their basic civil rights.

Alejandro Anreus wrestles with such injustices by contrasting what he calls the legitimate authority of Mandela with the illegitimate authority of white Exilic Cubans who continue to maintain structural racism. The former's authority is legitimized because of the personal suffering endured for the cause of justice. The latter lacks moral authority because it disrespected an icon of the African American community of Miami, highlighting the unimportance and invisibility of African Americans in Miami's political affairs. A black Christ challenges this injustice. To force Exilic Cubans to consider a black Savior, a Christ who like the black community is unimportant and invisible to those white Cubans who have obtained privilege and power, is to challenge the entire Miami ethos.

But isn't a black Christ unacceptable to the mind of most white Cubans? After all, are not all Cuban churches, both in Miami and La Habana, adorned with portraits, sculptures, and stained-glass windows depicting a white Christ? Anreus responds with a question. "And why not a black Christ? As Cubans we forget that we are a mestizo people, while perpetuating a myth that we Cubans are a white nation. Shouldn't we see Christ through the lens of our own culture?" Anreus has no difficulty in presenting a Christ that represents the Cuban ajiaco ethos. He asserts that just as the Virgin Mary has appeared to the people in the skin color of the culture, so too Christ appears to a people through the ethos of that group (Anreus 2000).

The Asian Cuban Christ

If Christ can be portrayed as Amerindian, female, or black to represent these disenfranchised elements of the Cuban ajiaco, then he can also be Asian. Chinese workers were brought to Cuba to work and live in the same conditions as African slaves during the mid-1800s. They too toiled under Cuba's sun to enrich the dominant Cuban culture, facing discrimination and death. Esterio Segura, a Resident Cuban, highlights the Asian ele-

Fig. 18. Esterio Segura, *Paseo de carnaval*, courtesy of the Arizona State University Art Museum, Tempe.

ments of the Cuban ajiaco in his sculpture *Paseo de carnaval* (*Carnival Promenade*) (figure 18). But the Asian element Segura emphasizes merges with both Spanish and African roots. Upon an Asian decorated tank sits the Buddha, flanked by palm trees and an Asian-looking Virgen de la Caridad/Ochún. Segura's kitsch imagery is rooted in popular culture, synthesizing Buddha with Marx, the father of socialist ideas. For Segura, it is Marx who brings prosperity to Cuba.

The Cuban Christ with AIDS

Another segment within the Cuban population that has experienced oppression and marginality are homosexuals, specifically those who have contracted the AIDS virus. Can the theme of Christ's solidarity with victims be extended to include those who struggle with AIDS? Exile Cuban Humberto Dionisio, in his untitled 1986 work, raises this question (figure 19). While not a religious man, aspects of Santería appear integrated in his work, in the same way that Santería is present in all Cubans regardless of their acceptance or rejection of this most Cuban-based religious expression. Dionisio, who succumbed to AIDS in the 1980s, turned to religious themes as his life was coming to an end. This work, according to those who knew him, was a tribute to all of his friends who died of AIDS. At the base of the cross are these victims, rising toward heaven. On the cross is a crucified baby, the end of the innocence that came to the gay community with the outbreak of AIDS. The spoons adorning the sides of the cross are a reference to the drug culture, specifically cocaine, which was prevalent in Miami during the 1980s with the depiction of Cocaine Cowboys in the media. If Christ is reflected in what is despised and victimized by society, then the gay community, held in contempt due to Cuban machismo and ravaged by the AIDS epidemic, becomes a people where solidarity with Christ can be found.

The Cuban Christ of the Poor

As the ajiaco Christ of the Cuban culture takes form, Alejandro Anreus helps crystallize the economic significance of the Cuban Christ in his portrait titled *Los Nombres de Cristo* (*The Names of Christ*) (figure 20). He dedicated this work to Leonardo Boff, the Brazilian liberation theologian. Anreus attempts to visualize what Boff wrote in his book *Jesus Christ Liberator*. Anreus, like Boff, questions an understanding of Christ designed to

Fig. 19. Humberto Dionisio, untitled, courtesy of the Smithsonian American Art Museum, gift of Jim Kitchens in honor of Michael Ford.

justify the economic privilege of those with power over los humildes. He does this by pasting the nativity scene as captured by one of Spain's last and greatest inheritors of the sixteenth-century international Mannerist style of art, El Greco. Below El Greco's masterpiece, Anreus lists different phrases by which Jesus can be known. Some of the phrases are traditional, like "Messiah"; others create discomfort, like "Subverter" or "Revolutionary"; still others appear to be disrespectful, like the "Jewish Screwer." Terms like "Subverter" and "Revolutionary" give a political edge to the gospel. They reveal a Christ who sides with los humildes, a Christ whose teachings become revolutionary because they subvert the constructed legitimacy of those who profit at the expense of those they oppress. The more derogatory term, the "Jewish Screwer," while offensive, is accurate in terms of both the Cuban ethos and Christ's mission. Anreus reminds us that Jesus' mission "screwed" with those who have established themselves as the political and religious leaders of the people and from that position "screwed" those whom they were supposed to represent and protect—the poor. In effect, Jesus "screwed up" their plans.

By calling Christ these names, Anreus also unmasks the dichotomy between the Christ of religious institutions and the Christ as understood by los humildes. Surrounding the portrait of El Greco is the phrase "There is no Christmas without passion." Anreus rebels against the consumerism that presently defines our Christmas holidays (Anreus 2000). By bringing the focus of the season to the crucifixion, the reason for Christ's birth in the first place, Anreus heralds a Christ who came as liberator to fulfill the words of the first sermon Christ ever preached:

> The Spirit of the Lord is upon me, he has anointed me to preach the Good News to the poor. He has sent me to heal the brokenhearted, to preach liberation to the captives, and recovery of sight to the blind; to set free the oppressed, and to announce the year when the Lord will save his people. (Luke 4:18–19)

Behind the Cuban Christ

While Velázquez and Ponce reveal a Christ who, like los humildes, suffers the wages of the oppressor's sins, Torres Llorca and Macía remind us that the defeat of the cross must be understood in light of the success of the resurrection. They balance the bloody victim with the macho power of a Christ capable of defeating his detractors. While these artists grapple with

Fig. 20. Alejandro Anreus, *Los Nombres de Cristo,* courtesy of the artist and the Collection of R. Blanco and K. Edwards.

Christianity via Cubanism, they represent a minority voice. In a post-utopian atmosphere, it is not surprising that themes of the crucifixion are either ignored or seldom represented in constructing Cuban identity. Yet the major thesis of this book has been that Christ can be understood through Cuban cultural symbols. For this reason, we turn our attention to those few postutopian depictions of the cross painted by Cubans.

Exilic Cuban artist Consuelo Castañeda and Resident Cuban artist Lazaro Saavedra, of the Grupo Puré (Pure Group), illustrate what Cuban art critic Gerardo Mosquera termed the "post-utopian" vision, a term used to describe the late-twentieth-century mood in Cuban art. Cuban art reflects a self-consciousness created within a postmodernist framework, where political and religious dogmas are challenged through subversive humor (Poupeye 1998, 183–85). It takes advantage of both inclusiveness and postmodern plurality to provide a political or social edge. In Castañeda's *Perugino-Barbara Kruger*, the viewer is presented with a crucified Christ deemed unnecessary. The artist protests the tendency of Cubans to deify their national heros, be they Martí, Castro, El Che, or more recently the Miami miracle child Elián. No more Christs are needed. With the fall of the Berlin Wall and the end of utopias, hesitancy exists in seeking new "universal truths." As the caption on the crucifix states, "We no longer need another hero."

Saavedra's sharp critical edge is apparent in his portrait of a very Cuban-looking Christ in his work titled *Sagrado Corazon* (*Bleeding Heart*) (figure 21). The figure is pointing toward his chest, where he reveals the Cuban flag in the shape of a heart. From his mouth appears a voice bubble of the kind popularized in comic strips. However, instead of words, the hammer and sickle, symbol of communism, appears. Over Christ's head appears a thought bubble, also popularized by cartoons. Within this bubble is the flag of the United States. Through such graphic and conceptual art, Saavedra employs popular humor to explore the social and historical identity of Resident Cubans. In their hearts they may be Cubans, even though they speak with the ideals of the Soviet Union while dreaming of the lures of the United States. Cubans are unable to find shalom, that is, peace, wholeness, health, and completion. They are neither one with Christ nor with themselves. This is evidenced not only by the estrangement that exists between Miami and La Habana, but also by the alienation existing within each Cuban. Saavedra humorously captures the Cuban's dysfunctionality. He reveals the anguish and pain caused by the fracturing

Fig. 21. Lazaro Saavedra, *Sagrado Corazon*, courtesy of Edge Art Inc.

of a people, a pain that this quest for a Cuban Christ has attempted to express, elucidate, and exorcize.

Are Cubans, both Resident and Exilic, interested in searching for a Cuban Christ? Resident Cuban Tomas Sanchez, who depicted the naked Christ on the cross, did another work of Christ in 1975. The work is untitled so as not to offend the Cuban governmental officials. Even so, the work was not allowed to be exhibited for ten years. When the Cuban government began to allow the public display of religious themes and expressions in the mid-1980s, Sanchez's untitled work became public. The painting shows a crucifixion scene from the perspective of someone behind the cross. Both viewer and Christ gaze at the same thing. Before the cross is a Cuban village whose inhabitants go about their daily activities, unaware of the crucifixion at the margin of their town. Sanchez explains that his work challenges the little importance Cubans give to the crucified Christ (Sanchez 2000).

Exilic Cuban Thomas Fundora's controversial painting also places the viewer behind Christ. *The Back of Christ* (figure 22) points toward a simple yet subversive path in the Cuban search for Christ. Originally this 1962 painting was an act of rebellion toward a Christ who allowed el exilio to occur. With time, the artist concluded that true followers cannot see Christ from the front if he is leading; hence the painting evangelizes Cubans to follow. When the painting was displayed at the Spanish Pavilion during the 1964 World's Fair in New York City, it sparked controversy among Exilic Cubans, who immediately saw a political message. To them, Christ has turned his back on Cuba. In retaliation, three men broke into Fundora's studio and crushed his hands, preventing him from painting for nine years.

Recently, *The Back of Christ* has become the object of renewed interest. Replicas of the original have appeared in many churches both on the island and in el exilio. In 1998 it was displayed in the San Pedro Church in Cotorro, a working-class suburb of La Habana, and in the San Lazaro Church in Hialeah, a working-class suburb of Miami. On both sides of the Florida Straits, this painting symbolizes this book's search for a common sacred space where estranged Cubans gather. And what is the message this Cuban Christ proclaims? Follow me to the cross, the place of self-denial, the place where all must die to their power and privilege.

Unashamedly, the quest for the Cuban Christ has led to a Cuban well in which Cubans have merely seen their own reflection, only to proclaim they have found Christ. All cultures find their definition of Christ within

Fig. 22. Thomas Fundora, *The Back of Christ,* courtesy of the artist.

their own ethos. The quest for the Cuban Christ is no different. Hence, it requires a search through the indigenous cultural symbols of the Cuban people. Still, the Bible occupies a peripheral space in Cuban culture. In seeking Christ in Cuban art we discover images of who Cubans are and who Christ is. Also, through Cuban art, we can hear the voice of los humildes introduced to the overall discourse. Cuban art introduces Cubans to a Christ who relates to and informs their social location. Such a Christ is relevant because such a Christ is found among los humildes. This Cuban Christ is indeed an ajiaco, a mixture of heterogeneity. Yet cubanidad's spirituality can still define the incongruous identity, so that all Cubans can come together as one within their own unique Cuban space.

Notes

Chapter 1. The Conquistador Christ

1. The reader should be aware that all scriptural quotes are the translation of the author from the original Hebrew and/or Greek text.

2. Cuba's role as a satellite of the U.S.S.R. was not based on the Soviet Union's interest in political or economic hegemony. Instead, its interest was in securing a geographical foothold within the domain of the United States.

3. Las Casas's accounts of the barbarism led to the construction of the Black Legend. For Euroamericans, the Black Legend justified the superiority of Protestantism over Catholicism, diverting attention from the mistreatment and systematic genocide of the indigenous population of North America. Las Casas's "Brevísima Relación de la Destrucción de las Indias," known to Euroamerican readers as "Tears of the Indians," was translated for moral leverage during the political struggle for imperial dominance in the so-called New World. The not so hidden agenda of the translators was to document the inherent cruelty of the Spaniards and the moral failings of Catholicism. English-speaking nations were able to justify centuries of hostility toward Spain through these translations. As late as 1898, Las Casas's writings were reprinted in New York City to incite North Americans against the Spaniards during the Spanish-American War and the U.S. conquest of Spain's remaining colonies, including Cuba. Regardless of how the Black Legend was constructed for Euroamerican consumption, it cannot be denied that within one lifetime an entire culture birthed upon the islands of the Caribbean was exterminated. Surviving Taínos were assimilated within the dominant Spanish culture.

4. It would be an error to assume that only Las Casas was lifting his voice against the barbaric treatment of the indigenous population of the Americas. Contemporaries included Luis Beltran, Diego Medellín, Antonio San Miguel, Antonio de Valdivieso, Juan del Valle, Antonio de Vieyra, and Francisco de Vitoria. We concentrate on Las Casas because for a time he settled in Cuba.

5. Varela was not the only faculty member responsible for forging a nationalistic image. With him was José Agustín Caballero and José de la Luz y Caballero. All three

men, appealing to Christian principles, made a "preferential option for the poor" by defending the rights of those oppressed by the colonial powers through the process of raising Cuban consciousness. While all three men deserve extensive study, we will concentrate only on Varela because of the premier place he holds in Cuban memory.

Chapter 2. The Martí Christ

1. Then Secretary of State John Quincy Adams wrote in a letter to Hugh Nelson, minister in Madrid: April 23, 1823:

These Islands [Cuba and Puerto Rico], from their local positions, are a natural appendage to the North American continent; and one of them, Cuba, almost in sight of our shores, from a multitude of considerations has become an object of transcendent importance to the political and commercial interest of our Union. . . . It is scarcely possible to resist the conviction that the annexation of Cuba to our federal republic will be indispensable to the continuance and integrity of the Union itself . . . There are laws of political as well as of physical gravitation; and if an apple severed by the tempest from its native tree cannot choose but fall to the ground, Cuba, forcibly disjointed from its own unnatural connection with Spain, and incapable of self-support, can gravitate only toward the North American Union, which by the same law of nature cannot cast her off its bosom (1917, 372–73).

Thomas Jefferson wrote in a letter to President James Monroe: October 24, 1823:

I candidly confess, that I have ever looked on Cuba as the most interesting addition which could ever be made to our system of States. The control which, with Florida Point, this island would give us over the Gulf of Mexico, and the countries and isthmus bordering on it, as well as all those waters flow into it, would fill up the measure of our political well-being (1944, 708–10).

2. These three arbitrary stages of interpreting Martí's symbolic importance differ from those of Valdespino, who neatly divides Martí's literary significance into three distinctive phases: Martí's beatification (Martí as mythical figure), Martí's humanization (Martí as a human being), and Martí's falsification (Martí as a propaganda tool) (Valdespino 1968, 307). My proposed stages also criticize Kirk's assertion that only two forms of interpreting Martí exist: a traditional view (Martí as an idealized, reverential, and semi-mystical figure) and a "correct" post-1959 interpretation (Martí as a revolutionary). I disagree with Kirk's assertion that the Resident Cuban interpretation is entirely correct. While I agree that the post-1959 interpretation recaptures some of the radicalness of Martí's thought, both Resident and Exilic Cubans have ignored the liberation motif of Martí's writings by overly emphasizing independence. It appears Kirk appropriates Martí's symbolic value only for Resident Cubans, excluding Exilic Cubans, thus creating deeper divisions between both communities (Kirk 1983). My proposed stages closely resemble Kapcia's historical analysis of Martí's influence on Cuban life. While agreeing with his conclusion that Martí's influence on Cuban radicalism prior to 1959 was nonexistent, I question his

inference that only in 1959 with the Castro revolution was Martí's influence "un-equivocally felt" (Kapcia 1986, 63–64). For this reason I insist that while the adulteration stage demythologized Martí, it failed to prevent the manipulation of his works to justify political policies.

3. The Haymarket Riot occurred in Chicago on May 4, 1886. On the previous day police broke up a demonstration organized by striking workers. Police battled with laborers protesting at the McCormick Reaper Company for hiring nonunion workers while laborers struck for an eight-hour work day. During the police action, one person was killed. A rally was called for the next day at Haymarket Square to protest police brutality. As the police attempted to disperse the protestors, a bomb exploded within police ranks, inciting a riot. Eleven people were killed. Although the bomber was never identified, eight leaders of the protest (suspected of being anarchists) were convicted as accessories to murder. Four were hanged, one committed suicide, and three were jailed (receiving a gubernatorial pardon in 1893).

Chapter 3. The Black Cuban Christ

1. Although slaves imported African culture into Hispanic Cuba, it must be re-membered that African roots first touched Hispanic culture in A.D. 711 with the Moorish invasion of Spain by both East and North Africans.

2. Cuban racism was manifested in two distinct forms during the early twentieth century. The most influential view was based on a Darwinian racial evolution that advocated the inferiority of Cubans who were not "pure" descendants of the evolved white Spaniards. The second, advocated by intellectuals like José Martí and Fernando Ortiz, maintained that blacks had the potential of being equal to whites, but were "stuck" in an earlier stage of cultural development. The solution required assimilation to the "superior" white culture through a process of de-Africanization. In fact, Fernando Ortiz's early studies of African culture contained the ulterior motive of identifying the traditions of Afro-Cubans so that such customs could be effectively eradicated. Ironically, toward the end of his intellectual career, Ortiz's views concerning the Afro-Cuban culture changed, as he fought against racism and sought to validate aspects of Afro-Cubanismo by establishing the Society of Afrocuban Studies.

3. *Mambises,* from the African word *mambi,* is the offspring of an ape and a vulture, a derogatory term given to revolutionaries (regardless of skin color) by the Spaniards. Yet this slur became a name of honor. Today in Miami, one of the most ultraconservative radio stations, owned and operated by whites, is called Radio Mambí.

4. Ironically, while Santería resists the dominant culture, it simultaneously creates its own forms of oppression. As the following two examples show, the *babalawo* can take advantage of his position, which holds considerable power and prestige. First, as black slaves practiced their beliefs under Catholic eyes, a system of domination within the domination of the blacks began to develop. Among the subjugated

blacks, Santería created a space generating intimidation of group members by the power holders, whose position was assured because of the overall system of white supremacy. The babalawo as power-broker served as a priest, a doctor, and a counselor to the oppressed slaves. He possessed the esoteric knowledge of the preternatural and medicinal uses of herbs. Through his prophylactic brew, a panacea for physical or spiritual disorders could be developed, capable of casting or destroying spells. In short, the babalawo becomes the most important and powerful figure within the dominated group due to the sociopolitical vacuum created by slavery.

Second, Santería as practiced by some in the United States has infused its religious practices with capitalist paradigms of profit making. Originally, the babalawo traded a product for his services (a chicken for a necklace, or a pig for an initiation). Several santeros/as with whom I have had a relationship continue this practice by charging the monetary equivalent for these items. Thus, *elekes* (beaded necklaces and bracelets worn by those initiated into Santería) can cost less than $25 or an initiation a few hundred dollars. However, there are those who have charged up to $1,000 per necklace or as much as $30,000 for an initiation. These actions create a new form of religious economic oppression reflecting North American mores. Within the present Exilic Cuban community, Santería has ceased being confined to the disenfranchised. Many present-day santeras/os drive Mercedes and Cadillacs and live in some of Miami's most exclusive neighborhoods.

Chapter 4. The Female Cuban Christ

1. The name of the island was later changed to Fernandina and still later to Santiago and to Ave María. None of these Spanish names took hold. Cuba, derived from the Taíno word for the island, Cubanacan, endured.

2. The Latin legal concept known as *patria postestad* maintained the authority of the male as the head of the family. It was instituted in Spain during the mid-1200s and became law in Cuba (as well as the rest of Latin America) in 1680. This concept was reinforced by the 1809 Napoleonic Code and the 1886 Spanish Civil Code (Stoner 1991, 202).

3. It must be recognized that Santería maintains a patriarchal ecclesiastic hierarchy. Women can serve as santeras delegated to a subservient role within the faith community. They can never serve as *babalawos*. On January 22, 1985, a North American Jew, Patri Dhaifa, was initiated as a babalawo. This created an uproar within the New York Santería community that ended with her ostracization (Gonzalez-Wippler 1989, 110–20). The censorship of Ms. Dhaifa was justified by a legend concerning Orunla. Orunla was recognized by all the orishas as being the greatest diviner (through the sixteen cowrie shells). One day he formed a blissful union with Yemayá. While he was away, Yemayá discovered the secrets of Orunla's divination abilities and went into business for herself. She quickly became a greater diviner than Orunla. When he returned and discovered the violation of his trust, he ended the relationship and devised a new oracle that only his priests, the babalawos,

can read. Only men can be babalawos, insuring that women would never get access to its mysteries. Consequently, the so-called deceit of women justified the prohibition against their holding positions as religious powerbrokers.

4. According to one of the legends, Yemayá is presented as Ochún's older sister. In another, Yemayá is presented as Ochún's mother. Both agree that Yemayá is the maternal orisha of the oceans.

Chapter 5. Three Christs for the Twentieth Century

1. Liborio is a folkloric personification of the Cuban people in the same way Uncle Sam symbolizes the United States.

2. Specifically, according the Resident Cuban Sergio Arce Martínez, past president of the Christian Conference for Peace in Latin America and the Caribbean, theology in revolution is: (1) A contextual theology whose objective is to provide a response of faith and hope to the diverse situations lived in the process of the country's revolution. (2) A theology for and by the people. (3) A new theology in conversation with the Castro version of Marxism. (4) Theology that must pastorally commit to serve the Cuban people who are the force that makes history. (5) Theology that must break with its past role of supporting exploitation and stand with the revolution for liberation. (6) Theology that is less concerned with an abstract God, and instead seeks a biblical God in the here and now, living within Cuba's particular history. (7) Contextual theology that rejects capitalism as anti-Christian and makes a committed pastoral option to the revolution. (8) Theology with universal significance as commonalities are found with liberation theology, black theology, and feminist theology.

3. The flight of capital from Latin America to the economic and political security of the United States left an economic space for Exilic Cubans to manage said funds, leading to the creation and growth of banks. Once secured in banking positions they provided "character loans" to their compatriots to encourage business. It mattered little if the borrower had any standing with Euroamerican banks, had little collateral, or spoke English. Loans (usually from $10,000 to $35,000) were provided based on the reputation of the borrower in Cuba. This policy was discontinued in 1973 because the new refugees, who were not from the more elite first wave, were unknown to the lenders. This practice contributed to the development of an economic enclave (Portes and Stepick 1993, 132–35).

4. For the first time in U.S. history, this country became an asylum for a large group of refugees by assuming the financial burden of resettling them. Total aid of approximately $2 billion was disbursed through the Cuban Refugee Program. This amount does not include the millions spent by church and voluntary agencies who were never fully reimbursed. Over a twelve-year period, aid consisted of direct cash assistance, guaranteed health care, food subsidies, retraining and retooling programs, college loans, English-language instruction, and financial assistance for establishing small businesses. Even though most assistance was contingent on re-

settlement to another part of the United States, Miami's economic base, which at the time was undergoing a recession, helped transform South Florida. These programs became the prototype for future social programs like Aid to Families with Dependent Children (AFDC). Furthermore, loans granted by the U.S. Small Business Administration to Miami businesses from 1968 (when the agency began keeping racial/ethnic statistics) to 1979 show that Hispanics received 46.9 percent (or $47,677,660) of available funds, Euroamericans received 46.6 percent (or $47,361,773), and African-Americans received 6.3 percent (or $6,458,240) (Pedraza-Bailey 1985, 4–34; Pérez-Stable and Uriarte 1993, 155; Porter and Dunn 1980, 194–97).

Chapter 6. The Ajiaco Christ

1. The methodology I employ is based on Bourdieu's process for evaluating art. Specifically, he states:

First, one must analyze the position of the [artistic] field within the field of power, and its evolution in time. Second, one must analyze the internal structure of the [artistic] field, a universe obeying its own laws of functioning and transforming, meaning the structure of objective relations between positions occupied by individuals and groups placed in a situation of competition for legitimacy. And finally, the analysis involves the genesis of habitus of occupants of these positions, that is, the systems of dispositions which, being the product of a social trajectory and of a position within the [artistic] field, find in this position a more or less favorable opportunity to be realized (the construction of the field is the logical preamble for the construction of the social trajectory as a series of positions successively occupied in this field). (1995, 214)

2. An earlier exhibition took place at the Riverside Museum in New York in 1939. Ironically, only after the Museum of Modern Art of New York, one of the world's greatest art centers, bestowed its stamp of approval upon Cuban artists did their compatriots begin purchasing works by fellow Cubans. Until then, the republican white elitists displayed the aesthetics of the nouveau riche, totally devoted to art related to the U.S. consumer system. Those with financial means were not inclined to collect any type of Cuban art, either academic or modern.

3. Afrocubanismo in visual art was inspired by the paintings of Wifredo Lam, Eduardo Abela, and Jaime Valls. Yet afrocubanismo was not limited to visual art. Poetry was influenced by the works of Emilio Ballagas, José Tallet, and Nicoláa Guillén; novels by Alejo Carpentier; musical theater by Ernesto Lecuona, Rodrigo Prats, and Gonzalo Roig; and symphonic compositions by Alejandro García Caturla, Amadeo Roldán, and Gilberto Valdés (Moore 1997, 2).

4. Even though a biblical motif seldom appears in Cuban art, still it expresses the spirituality of the people. The strong visual accentuation of Cuba's popular Santería religion has thematically influenced Cuban art ever since Lam, who as an "insider" discovered it to be a fertile source for emphasizing the ideological significance of the

Afro-Cuban culture. Although a detailed examination of the emblematic images and objects of Santería as manifested in Cuban art would prove profitable, it is for now beyond the scope of this work.

5. A Batistiano who served as a corporal in Batista's secret police told me of the physical torture and death that were inflicted on those who opposed the regime. A specific technique used in interrogations, or simply to teach the prisoner "a lesson," was a beating conducted with tough rubber clubs. The rubber clubs were effective for they left no bruises or other physical marks on the victim.

6. "To the wall," the postrevolution rally cry that initiated purge trials in a Roman-circus-type atmosphere, always ended with the execution or long imprisonment of counter-revolutionaries, even when those on trial were found not guilty, as in the case of forty charged pilots on March 2, 1959.

Bibliography

ACU (Agrupación Católica Universitaria). 1954. *Encuesta Nacional sobre el Sentimiento Religioso del Pueblo de Cuba.* Havana: Buró de Información y Propaganda de la ACU.

Adams, John Quincy. 1917. "Letter to Hugh Nelson, Minister in Madrid: April 23, 1823." *Writings of John Quincy Adams.* Vol. 7. Ed. Worthington Chauncey Ford. New York: Macmillan.

Alegría, Ricardo E. 1978. *Apuntes en torno a la mitología de los indios taínos de las antillas mayores y sus orígenes suramericanos.* Barcelona: Centro de estudios avanzados de puerto rico y el caribe.

Anreus, Alejandro. 2000. Interview by Miguel De La Torre. June 2, Elizabeth, N.J.

Arce, Reinerio. 1996. *Religión poesía del mundo venidero: Implicaciones thelógicas en la obra de José Martí.* Ecuador: Ediciones CLAI.

———. 1971. "Theological Education: A Challenge and an Opportunity." In *Religion in Cuba Today.* Ed. Alice Hageman and Philip E. Weaton. New York: Association Press.

Arce Martínez, Sergio. 1971. "Is a Theology of the Revolution Possible?" In *Religion in Cuba Today.* Ed. Alice Hageman and Philip E. Weaton. New York: Association Press.

Arredondo, Alberto. 1939. *El negro en Cuba.* Havana: Editorial Alfa.

Barinaga y Ponce de León, Graziela. 1931. *El feminismo y el hogar.* Havana: n.p.

Batista, Israel. 1987–88. "The Bible and Christian Theological Education." *The Journal of the Interdenominational Theological Center* 15 (Fall-Spring): 102–17.

Behar, Ruth, ed. 1995. Introduction to *Bridges to Cuba.* Ann Arbor: University of Michigan Press.

Benjamin, Medea, Joseph Collins, and Michael Scott. 1984. *No Free Lunch: Food and Revolution in Cuba Today.* San Francisco: Food First Books.

Boff, Clodovis. 1990. *Feet-on-the-ground Theology: A Brazilian Journey.* Trans. Phillip Berryman. Maryknoll, N.Y.: Orbis Books.

Boff, Leonardo. 1987. *The Maternal Face of God: The Feminine and Its Religious Expression.* Trans. Robert R. Barr and John Diercksmeier. Maryknoll, N.Y.: Orbis Books.

————. 1978. *Jesus Christ Liberator: A Critical Christology for Our Time.* Trans. Patrick Hughes. New York: Orbis Books.

Boff, Leonardo, and Clodovis Boff. 1987. *Introducing Liberation Theology.* Maryknoll, N.Y.: Orbis Books.

Boloña, Concepción. 1905. *En pro de la mujer cubana.* Havana: Imprenta La Prueba.

Bourdieu, Pierre. 1995. *The Rules of Art: Genesis and Structure of the Literary Field.* Trans. Susan Emanuel. Stanford, Calif.: Stanford University Press.

Brandon, George. 1997. *Santería from Africa to the New World: The Dead Sell Memories.* Indianapolis: Indiana University Press.

Brubaker, Rogers. 1985. "Rethinking Classical Theory: The Sociological Vision of Pierre Bourdieu." *Theory and Society* 14:745–75.

Bulmer-Thomas, Victor. 1994. *The Economic History of Latin America Since Independence.* Cambridge, England: Cambridge University Press.

Büntig, Aldo J. 1971. "The Church in Cuba: Toward a New Frontier." In *Religion in Cuba Today.* Ed. Alice Hageman and Philip E. Weaton. New York: Association Press.

Caballero, Armando O. 1982. *La mujer en el 95.* Havana: Editorial Gente Neuva.

Camnitzer, Luis. 1994. *New Art of Cuba.* Austin: University of Texas Press.

Casal, Lourdes. 1989. "Race Relations in Contemporary Cuba." In *The Cuban Reader: The Making of a Revolutionary Society.* Ed. Philip Brenner, William M. LeoGrande, Donna Rich, and Daniel Siegel. New York: Grove Press.

Castro, Fidel. 1987. *Fidel and Religion: Castro Talks on Revolution and Religion with Frei Betto.* Trans. The Cuban Center for Translation and Interpretation. New York: Simon and Schuster.

————. 1971. "On Counterrevolutionary Activities of Priests." In *Religion in Cuba Today.* Ed. Alice Hageman and Philip E. Weaton. New York: Association Press.

CELAM. 1968. *La iglesia en la Actual transformacion de america latina a la luz del concilio.* 2 Conclusiones, 3rd ed. Bogotá: Secretariado general del CELAM.

Cepeda, Rafael. 1992. *Lo etico-cristiano en la obra de José Martí.* Matanzas: Centro de Informacion y Estudio.

Cepeda, Rafael, Elizabeth Carrillo, Rhode González, and Carlos E. Ham. 1996. "Changing Protestanism in a Changing Cuba." In *In the Power of the Spirit: The Pentecostal Challenge to Historical Churches in Latin America.* Ed. Bejamin F. Gutiérrez and Dennis A. Smith. Louisville, Ky.: Presbyterian Church, U.S.A.

Cole, George Douglas Howard. 1960. *A History of Socialist Thought: The Second International 1889–1914.* Vol. 3, part 2. London: Macmillan.

Columbus, Christopher. 1960. *The Journal of Christopher Columbus.* Trans. Cecil Jane. New York: Clarkson N. Potter.

Crahan, Margaret E. 1989. "Freedom of Worship in Revolutionary Cuba." In *The Cuba Reader: The Making of a Revolutionary Society.* Ed. Philip Brenner, William M. LeoGrande, Donna Rich, and Daniel Siegal. New York: Grove Press.

Daly, Mary. 1975. *The Church and the Second Sex.* New York: Harper and Row.

de Caturla, Brú. 1945. *La mujer en la independencia de America*. Havana: Jesus Montero.

de la Cruz. 1980. *Movimiento femenino cubano*. Havana: Departamento de Orientación Revolucionaria del Comité del Partido Comunista de Cuba.

De La Torre, Miguel A. 2001. "Ochún: [N]either the [M]Other of All Cubans, [N]or the Bleached Virgin." *Journal of the American Academy of Religion* 69, no. 4 (December): 837–61.

———. 2000. "Miami and the Babylonian Captivity." In *Sacred Text, Secular Times: The Hebrew Bible in the Modern World*. Ed. Leonard Jay Greenspoon and Bryan F. Le Beau. Bronx, N.Y.: Fordham University Press.

———. 1999a. "Masking Hispanic Racism: A Cuban Case Study." *Journal of Hispanic/Latino Theology* 6, no. 4 (May): 57–74.

———. 1999b. "The Quest for the Historical Hispanic Christ." *Perspectives: A Journal of Reformed Thought* 14, no. 10 (December): 5–8.

———. 1997. "Toward Cuban Reconciliation: An Ajiaco Philosophical Foundation." *Koinonia: The Princeton Theological Seminary Graduate Forum* 9, nos. 1 and 2 (Spring and Fall): 58–78.

De La Torre, Miguel A., and Edwin Aponte. 2001. *Introducing Latino/a Theology*. Maryknoll, N.Y.: Orbis Books.

Derrida, Jacques. 1972. *La Dissémination*. Paris: Éditions du Seuil.

Dewart, Leslie. 1963. *Christianity and Revolution: The Lesson of Cuba*. New York: Herder and Herder.

Didion, Joan. 1987. *Miami*. New York: Simon and Schuster.

Donghi, Tulio Halperín. 1993. *The Contemporary History of Latin America*. Ed. and trans. John Charles Chasteen. Durham, N.C.: Duke University Press.

Eliade, Mircea. 1963. *Patterns in Comparative Religion*. Trans. Rosemary Sheed. New York: Meridian Books.

Espín, Orlando. 1999. "An Exploration into the Theology of Grace and Sin." In *From the Heart of Our People*. Ed. Orlando O. Espín and Miguel H. Díaz. Maryknoll, N.Y.: Orbis Books.

———. 1994. "Popular Religion as an Epistemology of Suffering." *Journal of Hispanic/Latino Theology* 2, no. 2 (November): 55–78.

Fanon, Frantz. 1963. *The Wretched of the Earth*. Trans. Constance Farrington. New York: Grove Press.

Fedarko, Kevin. 1998. "Open for Business." In *Developing World 97/98*. Ed. Robert J. Griffiths. Guilford, Conn.: Dushkin Publishing Group/Brown and Benchmark Publishers.

Ferm, Deane William. 1992. *Third World Liberation Theologies: An Introductory Survey*. Maryknoll, N.Y.: Orbis Books.

Fernández de Oviedo y Valdés, Gonzalo. 1959. *Historia general y natural de las Indias*. Vol. 2. Ed. Juan Pérez de Tudela. Madrid: Biblioteca de Autores Españoles.

Foner, Philip S., ed. 1975. Introduction to *Inside the Monster: Writings on the United*

States and American Imperialism. Trans. Elinor Randall, Luis A. Baralt, Juan de Onis, and Roslyn Held Foner. New York: Monthly Review Press.

Franqui, Carlos. 1984. *Family Portrait with Fidel: A Memoir.* Trans. Alfred MacAdam. New York: Random House.

Freire, Paulo. 1995. "Conscientizing as a Way of Liberating." In *Liberation Theology: A Documentary History.* Ed. and trans. Alfred T. Hennelly. Maryknoll, N.Y.: Orbis Books.

———. 1994. *Pedagogy of the Oppressed.* Trans. Myra Bergman Ramos. New York: Continuum.

García, María Cristina. 1996. *Havana USA: Cuban Exiles and Cuban Americans in South Florida, 1959–1994.* Berkeley: University of California Press.

González, Justo. 1996. *Santa Biblia: The Bible through Hispanic Eyes.* Nashville: Abingdon Press.

González, Manuel Pedro. 1953. *José Martí: Epic Chronicler of the United States in the Eighties.* Chapel Hill: University of North Carolina Press.

González, Manuel Pedro, and Ivan A. Schulman. 1961. *José Martí, esquema ideológico.* Mexico City: Publicaciones de la Editorial Cultura.

González-Wippler. 1992. *Powers of the Orishas: Santería and the Worship of Saints.* New York: Original Publications.

———. 1989. *Santería: The Religion.* New York: Harmony Books.

Gray, Richard Butler. 1962. *José Martí: Cuban Patriot.* Gainesville: University of Florida Press.

Gutiérrez, Gustavo. 1993a. *A Theology of Liberation: History, Politics, and Salvation.* Rev. ed. Trans. Caridad Inda and John Eagleson. Maryknoll, N.Y.: Orbis Books.

———. 1993b. Foreword to *Bartolomé de Las Casas. Witness.* Ed. and trans. George Sanderlin. Maryknoll, N.Y.: Orbis Books.

———. 1993c. *Las Casas: In Search of the Poor of Jesus Christ.* Trans. Robert Barr. Maryknoll, N.Y.: Orbis Books.

———. 1991a. *The God of Life.* Trans. Matthew J. O'Connell. Maryknoll, N.Y.: Orbis Books.

———. 1991b. *The Truth Shall Make You Free: Confrontations.* Trans. Matthew J. O'Connell. Maryknoll, N.Y.: Orbis Books.

———. 1984. *The Power of the Poor in History.* Trans. Robert R. Barr. Maryknoll, N.Y.: Orbis Books.

Hageman, Alice. 1971. Introduction to *Religion in Cuba Today.* Ed. Alice Hageman and Philip E. Weaton. New York: Association Press.

Helg, Aline. 1995. *Our Rightful Share: The Afro-Cuban Struggle for Equality, 1886–1912.* Chapel Hill: University of North Carolina Press.

Helps, Arthur. 1900. *The Spanish Conquest in America.* London: John Lane.

Herzberg, Julia P. 1996. "Rereading Lam." In *Santería Aesthetics: In Contemporary Latin American Art.* Ed. Arturo Lindsay. Washington, D.C.: Smithsonian Institution Press.

Hewitt, Nancy A. 1995. "Engendering Independence: Las Patriotas of Tampa and the Social Vision of José Martí." In *José Martí in the United States: The Florida Experience.* Ed. Louis A. Pérez, Jr. Tempe: Arizona State University Center for Latino American Studies.

Huberman, Leo, and Paul M. Sweezy. 1989. "The Revolutionary Heritage." In *The Cuba Reader: The Making of a Revolutionary Society.* Ed. Philip Brenner et al. New York: Grove Press.

Ibarra, Jorge. 1972. "José Martí y el Partido Revolucionario Cubano." *Ideología mambisa.* Havana: Instituto Cubano del Libro.

———. 1967. *Historia de Cuba.* Havana: Dirección Política de las F.A.R.

Jefferson, Thomas. 1944. "Letter to President James Monroe: October 24, 1823." In *The Life and Selected Writings of Thomas Jefferson.* Ed. Adrienne Kock and William Peden. New York: Random House.

Jenks, Leland H. 1928. *Our Cuban Colony: A Study in Sugar.* New York: Vanguard Press.

Jeremias, Joachim. 1969. *Jerusalem in the Time of Jesus: An Investigation into Economic and Social Conditions during the New Testament Period.* Philadelphia: Fortress Press.

John Paul II, Pope. Speech at University of Havana, January 23, 1998. Vatican archives. <http:www.vatican.va/holy_father/john_paul_ii/travels/documents/hf_ip-ii_spe_23011998_lahavana-culture_en.html>.

Johnson, Elizabeth A. 1998. *She Who Is: The Mystery of God in Feminist Theological Discourse.* New York: Crossroad Publishing.

Kapcia, Antoni. 1986. "Cuban Populism and the Birth of the Myth of Martí." In *José Martí: Revolutionary Democrat.* Ed. Christopher Abel and Nissa Torrents. London: Athlone Press.

Kirk, John M. 1988. *Between God and the Party: Religion and Politics in Revolutionary Cuba.* Tampa: University Presses of Florida.

———. 1983. *José Martí: Mentor of the Cuban Nation.* Tampa: University Presses of Florida.

Las Casas, Bartolomé. 1971. *History of the Indies.* Ed. and trans. Andree Collard. New York: Harper and Row.

Liberato, Pablo. 2001. Interview by Miguel A. De La Torre. December 2. Miami.

Lodge, Henry Cabot. 1925. *Selections from the Correspondence of Theodore Roosevelt and Henry Cabot Lodge.* Vol. 2. New York: Charles Scribner's Sons.

Lovén, Sven. 1935. *Origins of the Tainan Culture, West Indies.* Trans. Göteborg, Sweden: Flanders Bokryckeri Akfiebolag.

Lumsden, Ian. 1996. *Machos, Maricones and Gays: Cuba and Homosexuality.* Philadelphia: Temple University Press.

Mañach, Jorge. 1944a. *Historia y estilo.* Havana: Minerva.

———. 1944b. *Martí El Apóstol.* Buenos Aires: Espasa-Calpe Argentina.

Marcuse, Herbert. 1972. *Counterrevolution and Revolt.* Boston: Beacon Press.

Marinello, Juan. 1925. "Nuestro arte y las circunstancias nacionales." *Cuba Contemporanea* 37 (April): 304.

Martí, José. 1999. *Reader: Writings on the Americas.* Ed. Deborah Shnookal and Mirta Muñiz. Chicago: Ocean Press.

———. 1977. *Our America by José Martí: Writings on Latin America and the Struggle for Cuban Independence.* Ed. Philip S. Foner. Trans. Elinor Randall, Juan de Onís, and Roslyn Held Foner. New York: The Monthly Review Press.

———. 1975. *Inside the Monster: Writings on the United States and American Imperialism.* Ed. Philip S. Foner. Trans. Elinor Randall, Luis A. Baralt, Juan de Onís, and Roslyn Held Foner. New York: The Monthly Review Press.

———. 1959. *Biblioteca Popular Martiana.* No. 4. Havana: Editorial Lex.

———. 1936–53. *Obras Completas.* 74 vols. Havana: Editorial Nacional de Cuba.

Martínez, Juan A. 1996. "Una introducción a la pinura cubana moderna, 1927–1950." *Cuba siglo XX: Modernidad y sincretismo.* New York: Worldwide Books.

———. 1994. *Cuban Art and National Identity: The Vanguardia Painters, 1927–1950.* Gainesville: University Press of Florida.

———. 1992. *Cuban Art and National Identity: The Vanguardia Painters, 1920s-1940s.* Ph.D. diss., Florida State University.

Martinez-Alier, Verena. 1974. *Marriage, Class and Color in Nineteenth Century Cuba: A Study of Racial Attitudes and Sexual Values in a Slave Society.* London: Cambridge University Press.

Martínez Bello, Antonio. 1940. *Ideas sociales y económicas de José Martí.* Havana: La Verónica.

Masó y Vazquez, Calixto C. 1998. *Historia de Cuba: la lucha de un pueblo por cumplir su destino histórico y su vocación de libertad.* Miami: Ediciones Universal.

Mason, Peter. 1990. *Deconstructing America: Representations of the Others.* New York: Routledge.

Maza, Manuel P. 1982. *The Cuban Catholic Church: True Struggles and False Dilemmas.* Masters thesis, Georgetown University, Washington, D.C.

McClintock, Anne. 1995. *Imperial Leather: Race, Gender and Sexuality in the Colonial Contest.* New York: Routledge.

Mesa-Lago, Camelo. 1989. "Revolutionary Economic Policies in Cuba." In *The Cuba Reader: The Making of a Revolutionary Society.* Ed. Philip Brenner et al. New York: Grove Press.

Mesters, Carlos. 1995. "The Use of the Bible in Christian Communities of the Common People." In *Liberation Theology: A Documentary History.* Ed. and trans. Alfred T. Hennelly. Maryknoll, N.Y.: Orbis Books.

Montaner, Carlos Alberto. 1971. *El pensamiento de Martí.* Madrid: Plaza Mayor Ediciones.

Montejo, Esteban. 1968. *The Autobiography of a Runaway Slave.* Ed. Miguel Barnet. Trans. Jocasta Innes. New York: Pantheon Books.

Moore, Carlos. 1988. *Castro, the Blacks, and Africa*. Los Angeles: Center for Afro-American Studies, University of California.

Moore, Robin. 1997. *Nationalizing Blackness: Afrocubanismo and Artistic Revolution in Havana, 1920–1940*. Pittsburgh: University of Pittsburgh Press.

Mörner, Magnus. 1967. *Race Mixture in the History of Latin America*. Boston: Little, Brown.

Mosquera, Gerardo. 1996. "Hacia una postmodernidad 'otra': África en el arte cubano." *Cuba siglo XX: Modernidad y sincretismo*. New York: Worldwide Books.

Neill, Stephen. 1990. *A History of Christian Missions*. London: Penguin Books.

Newman, Philip C. 1965. *Cuba Before Castro: An Economic Appraisal*. New Delhi, India: Prentice Hall.

Origen, 1953. *Contra Celsum*. Trans. Henry Chadwick. London: Cambridge University Press.

Ortega y Gasset, José. 1972. *Velázquez, Goya and the Dehumanization of Art*. Trans. Alexis Brown. New York: W. W. Norton.

Ortiz, Fernando. 1975. *El engaño de las razas*. Havana: Editorial de Ciencias Sociales.

———. 1973. Los negros brujas: Apuntes para un estudio de etnologia criminal. Miami: New House.

———. 1963. *Contrapunto cubano del tabaco y el azúcar*. Havana: Dirección de Publicaciones Universidad Central de Las Villas.

———. 1942. "Martí y las razas." In *Vida y pensamiento de Martí*. Vol. 2. Ed. Emilio Roig de Leuchsenring. Havana: Municipio de la Habana.

———. 1940. *Los factores humanos de la cubanidad*. Havana: Revista Bimestre Cubana, XLV.

———. 1939. "La cubanidad y los negros." *Estudio Afrocubanos* 3:3–15.

Pagán, Luis N. Rivera. 1992. *A Violent Evangelism: The Political and Religious Conquest of the Americas*. Louisville, Ky.: Westminister/John Knox Press.

Pedraza-Bailey, Silvia. 1985. "Cuba's Exile: Portrait of a Refugee Migration." *International Migration Review* 19:4–34.

Pérez, Louis A., Jr. 1999. *On Becoming Cuban: Identity, Nationality, and Culture*. Chapel Hill: University of North Carolina Press.

———. 1995. *Essays on Cuban History: Historiography and Research*. Gainesville: University Press of Florida.

———. 1988. *Cuba: Between Reform and Revolution*. New York: Oxford University Press.

Pérez-Stable, Marifeli, and Miren Uriarte. 1993. "Cubans and the Changing Economy of Miami." In *Latinos in a Changing U.S. Economy: Comparative Perspectives on Growing Inequality*. Ed. Rebecca Morales and Frank Bonilla. Newbury Park, Calif.: Sage Publications.

Pichardo, L. Ernesto. 1984. *Oduduwa y Obatala*. Miami: St. Babalu Aye, Church of the Lukumi.

Porter, Bruce, and Marvin Dunn. 1980. *The Miami Riot of 1980: Crossing the Bounds*. Lexington, Ky.: Lexington Books.

Portes, Alejandro, and Juan M. Clark. 1987. "Mariel Refugees: Six Years Later." *Migration World* 15 (Fall): 14–18.

Portes, Alejandro, and Alex Stepick. 1993. *City on the Edge: The Transformation of Miami*. Berkeley: University of California Press.

Poupeye, Veerle. 1998. *Caribbean Art*. New York: Thames and Hudson.

Poyo, Gerald E. 1975. "The Cuban Exile Tradition in the United States: Patterns of Political Development in the Nineteenth and Twentieth Centuries." *Cuba: cultura e identidad nacional*. Havana: Ediciones Union.

Prío Socarrás, Carlos. 1946. "Martí, arquetipo de lo cubano." *Archivo José Martí* 6 (Jan/Dec): 380–91.

Quirk, Robert E. 1993. *Fidel Castro*. New York: W. W. Norton.

Ramos, Marcos Antonio. 1989. *Protestantism and Revolution in Cuba*. Coral Gables, Fla.: University of Miami.

———. 1986. *Panorama del Protestantismo en Cuba*. San José, Costa Rica: Editorial Caribe.

Ramos, Marcos Antonio, and Agustin A. Román. 1991. "The Cubans, Religion, and South Florida." In *Cuban Exiles in Florida: Their Presence and Contributions*. Ed. Antonio Jorge, Jaime Suchlicki, and Adolfo Leyva de Varona. Coral Gables, Fla.: University of Miami.

Raphael, Natalia, artist. 2000. Interview by Miguel A. De La Torre. March 24. Grafton, Mass.

Richard, Pablo. 1987. *Death of Christendoms, Birth of the Church: Historical Analysis and Theological Interpretation of the Church in Latin America*. Trans. Phillip Berryman. Maryknoll, N.Y.: Orbis Books.

Ripoll, Carlos. 1984. *José Martí, the United States, and the Marxist Interpretation of Cuban History*. New Brunswick, N.J.: Transaction Books.

Said, Edward W. 1994. *Culture and Imperialism*. New York: Vintage Books.

Sanchez, Tomas, artist. 2000. Interview by Miguel A. De La Torre. July 29. Miami.

Santana, Francisco, priest. 2000. Interview by Miguel A. De La Torre. September 7. Miami.

Sauer, Carl Ortwin. 1966. *The Early Spanish Main*. Berkeley: University of California Press.

Sayles, John. 1991. *Los Gusanos: A Novel*. New York: HarperCollins Publishers.

Schreiter, Robert J. 1996. *Constructing Local Theologies*. Maryknoll, N.Y.: Orbis Books.

Scott, James C. 1990. *Domination and the Arts of Resistance: Hidden Transcripts*. New Haven: Yale University Press.

Scott, Rebecca. 1985. *Slave Emancipation in Cuba: The Transition to Free Labor, 1860–1899*. Princeton, N.J.: Princeton University Press.

Sicre, Jose Gomez. 1987. *Art of Cuba in Exile*. Trans. Ralph E. Dimmick. Miami: Editora Munder.

Skidmore, Thomas E., and Peter H. Smith. 1984. *Modern Latin America*. New York: Oxford University Press.

Smith, Christian. 1991. *The Emergence of Liberation Theology: Radical Religion and Social Movement Theory*. Chicago: University of Chicago Press.

Sobrino, Jon. 1993. *Jesus the Liberator: A Historical-Theological Reading of Jesus of Nazareth*. Trans. P. Burns and F. McDonagh. Maryknoll, N.Y.: Orbis Books.

Stockwell, Eugene. 1985. "An Interview with Ofelia Ortega." *International Review of Mission* 74, no. 295 (July): 35–37.

Stoner, K. Lynn. 1991. *From the House to the Streets: The Cuban Woman's Movement for Legal Reform, 1898–1940*. Durham, N.C.: Duke University Press.

Suárez, Bernardo Ruiz. 1922. *The Color Question in the Two Americas*. New York: Hunt Publishing.

Suarez, Carlito, artist. 2000. Interview by Miguel A. De La Torre. January 3. Havana.

Szulc, Tad. 1986. *Fidel: A Critical Portrait*. New York: Avon Books.

Thomas, Hugh. 1971. *Cuba: The Pursuit of Freedom*. New York: Harper and Row.

Tillich, Paul. 1957. *Dynamics of Faith*. New York: Harper Colophon Books.

Todorov, Tzvetan. 1984. *The Conquest of America: The Question of the Other*. Trans. Richard Howard. New York: Harper and Row.

Toirac, José A., artist. 2000. Interview by Miguel A. De La Torre. June 29. Tempe, Ariz.

Unamuno, Miguel. 1966–68. *Obras completas*. Ed. Manuel García Blanco. Madrid: Escelicer.

———. 1967. *The Life of Don Quixote and Sancho*. Trans. Anthony Kerrigan. Princeton, N.J.: Princeton University Press.

Valdespino, Andrés. 1968. "Imagen de Martí en las letras cubanas." *Revista Cubana* 1 (July-December): 307–31.

Varela, Félix. 1974. "Estado Eclesiástico en la Isla de Cuba." *El Habanero, Félix Varela Morales*. Miami: Revista Ideal.

Verger, Pierre. 1966. "The Yoruba High God: A Review of the Source." *Odu: Journal of Yoruba and Related Studies* 2, no. 2: 19–40.

Vitier, Cintio. 1971. "Imagen de Martí." *Anuario martiano* 3:231–48.

Weber, Max. 1963. *The Sociology of Religion*. Boston: Beacon Press.

Williams, Eric. 1994. *Capitalism and Slavery*. Chapel Hill: University of North Carolina Press.

Zavala, Silvio. 1968. *New Viewpoints on the Spanish Colonization of America*. New York: Russell and Russell.

Index

Miguel A. De La Torre is assistant professor of religion at Hope College in Holland, Michigan. He specializes in theologies of liberation, specifically in their relation to race, class, and gender oppression. He is the coauthor of *Introducing Hispanic/Latino Theology* and author of *Reading the Bible from the Margins*. He is also the author of the following forthcoming books: *La Lucha for Cuba: Religion and Politics on the Streets of Miami; Santería: The Beliefs and Rituals of a Growing Religion in America;* and *Handbook of U.S. Theologies of Liberation.*